SOME EARLY SCOTS
in Maritime Canada

Volume I

Pictou, from the road to Halifax. Lithograph by William Eagar, 1840.

SOME EARLY SCOTS

in Maritime Canada

Volume I

Terrence M. Punch, CM, FIGRS

Genealogical Publishing Company

Published by Genealogical Publishing Company
3600 Clipper Mill Rd., Suite 260
Baltimore, Maryland, 21211-1953

Library of Congress Catalogue Card Number 2011921375
ISBN 978-0-8063-1876-9
Made in the United States of America

ACKNOWLEDGMENTS

The publishers for encouraging me to research and write a volume about the Scots.

The staff at Nova Scotia Archives and Records Management for ordering in reels of microfilm for my perusal and for their unfailingly cheerful help, and for permission to use the picture that appears as the frontispiece, and to Anjali Vohra for preparing it for this book.

The Public Archives of New Brunswick for their obliging and prompt lending of microfilm, enabling me to conduct much of my research in Halifax.

Carolyn Smedley, my sister, whose sharp eyes detected typos that lurked undetected by my more indulgent eyes. She also made me explain things that to me were perfectly obvious, but which for an intelligent reader required more explanation.

My wife, Pam, who is one of the handful of people who will have read this book from cover to cover. Her comments, suggestions and questions helped more than can be imagined. Her patience mattered even more. Thank you all.

A'chiad sgeul air fear an taighe;
sgeul gu la air an aoidh.

The host owes the first story;
The guest owes tales until day.

This volume is dedicated to those Scots - whether Gael, Norse, Norman,
Saxon or Flemish - who crossed the western sea to
Maritime Canada, bringing their stories with them.

CONTENTS

INTRODUCTION

Four centuries ago the clerks and officials about the court of the man called "the wisest fool in Christendom" – King James I of England, or VI of Scotland – pondered a name for a piece of the eastern seaboard of North America. Between New England and New France lay what form today the Maritime Provinces of Canada: New Brunswick, Nova Scotia and Prince Edward Island. Since James was of the House of Stuart, the dynasty which had ruled Scotland for over 200 years, the territory was dubbed New Scotland.

It seems unlikely that either James or his scribes appreciated the irony in the Latin version of the name, *Nova Scotia*. Old Scotland itself had become "Scotia" when Irish Gaels, or Scotii, settled in the western isles and peninsulas of what we call Scotland. The Romans, who failed to subdue Scotland, called its people by several names, but when Hadrian built his wall he would have been surprised to learn that the people he was keeping out were Scots. Strictly speaking, *Nova Scotia* more properly translates as New Ireland.

The southern peninsular mainland, together with the island of Cape Breton, now forms the Canadian province of Nova Scotia. St. John's Isle, later renamed Prince Edward Island, passed under French rule until 1763 and was constituted a British colony in 1767. In 1784, the northerly mainland portion was established as New Brunswick to accommodate the influx of Loyalists after the American Revolutionary War. The three provinces today form what we know as the Maritimes.

King James knew that his courtiers and others liked titles, so he formed an order of hereditary knighthoods known as Baronets of Nova Scotia. For a fee, including a pledge to settle loyal Protestants in the new colony, James peddled baronetcies to raise "siller" for his projects. The enduring legacy of this activity in the 1620s is the flag and shield of Nova Scotia: St. Andrew's Cross in blue against a silver background, bearing at the centre a golden shield housing a red lion rampant.

The titles sold fairly well but, apart from a couple of abortive attempts at settling Scots in the region, the colonizing part of the scheme proved unproductive. For more than a century after 1632, greater Nova Scotia was inhabited by French Acadians and native people, except for a small British garrison at Annapolis Royal after 1710. Not even the most ardent Scot could argue that the English name for the place bore any relationship at all to the people actually living there.

Only after 1770 did the area began to acquire Scots, mainly but not exclusively from the Highlands. The Glenaladale settlers in Prince Edward Island and the valiant band of Highlanders in the *Hector* (1773) proved to be harbingers of the greatest mass immigration the region would ever see. More numerous than the New England Planters and Loyalists who preceded them, and outnumbering the contemporary Irish immigration, the Scots put their stamp on Cape Breton Island, the eastern mainland of Nova Scotia, much of Prince Edward Island, and coastal regions of New Brunswick from Restigouche in the north to the shores of the Bay of Fundy to the south.

This book attempts to put names and places to a few of those thousands in the hope that some readers find an ancestor or a kinsman herein. Fáilte.

Terrence M. Punch, CM, FIGRS

Saint Andrew's Day, 2010

SHIRES OF SCOTLAND circa 1840

1 - Linlithgow/ West Lothian
2 - Edinburgh/ Mid Lothian
3 - Haddington/ East Lothian
4 - Kinross
5 - Clackmannan
6 - Fife
7 - Stirling
8 - Dumbarton
9 - Renfrew
10 - Berwick
11 - Peebles
12 - Selkirk
13 - Roxburgh
14 - Dumfries
15 - Kirkcudbright
16 - Wigtown
17 - Lanark
18 - Ayr
19 - Bute
20 - Argyll
21 - Perth
22 - Forfar/ Angus
23 - Kincardine/ Mearns
24 - Aberdeen
25 - Banff
26 - Moray/ Elgin
27 - Nairn
28 - Inverness
29 - Ross and Cromarty
30 - Sutherland
31 - Caithness
32 - Orkney
33 - Shetland (not shown)

T. M. Punch, figrs

Map 1

Note: The Local Government (Scotland) Act, 1996, combined several shires with small populations to form new local authorities. Ross and Cromarty, Caithness, Sutherland, and Inverness became Highland. The Hebrides portions of Inverness, Ross and Cromarty became Na h-Eileanan Siar [Western Isles]. Banff, Nairn and Moray are now Moray. Kincardine has been absorbed into Aberdeen, while Kinross was attached to Perth. Argyll and Bute were united. Grouped as "Scottish Borders" were Berwick, Peebles, Selkirk and Roxburgh. Dumfries, Kirkcudbright and Wigtown became Dumfries and Galloway. Readers should consult detailed maps to learn the configuration of the populous Lowland areas surrounding and running between Edinburgh and Glasgow, Scotland's two largest cities which, together with Dundee City and Aberdeen City, became urban local authorities themselves.

AN OCEAN BRIDGED: SCOTLAND TO THE MARITIMES

Scotland the Place (See Map 1)

Scotland occupies the northern part of Great Britain. It can be divided into three approximate areas, known from south to north, as the Borders, the Lowlands and the Highlands. Since the first two are inhabited by much the same mixture of Anglo-Saxons, Celts and Normans, and since their geography and history are interlaced so closely, we usually speak of Scotland as consisting of the Lowlands and the Highlands. The Lowlanders were more likely to dwell in urban settings, to work at a variety of trades and crafts, and to speak a form of English known as Broad Scots.

The Scottish Highlands include all the islands and the mainland north and west of a line drawn roughly from the northeast near Nairn and Moray Firth to the southwest as far as the north bank of the River Clyde, opposite Greenock. To be strictly accurate the line is not a straight one but runs more southerly at first to touch the River Dee before curving away westward towards the Clyde.

The Highlands embraced parts of Nairn and Morayshire, but principally was composed of the shires of Argyll, Bute, Caithness, Inverness, Ross & Cromarty, and Sutherland, together with the northern island groups of the Orkneys and the Shetlands. The area was, and still is, rugged. The isolation of some of the region, even on the main island of Scotland, was so complete that, as late as 1800 there was not one mile of road in all of Sutherlandshire, the home of over 23,000 people!

To demonstrate the sort of territory that made up the Highlands here are two passages from a topographical dictionary of Scotland 160 years ago, describing the several parishes and districts:

The parish of **ASSYNT** (Sutherlandshire): [The] DISTRICT IS . . . WILD AND MOUNTAINOUS. . . THE HILLS ARE VERY NUMEROUS, AND MOST OF THEM ABOUND WITH SPRINGS OF EXCELLENT WATER. THERE ARE SEVERAL FINE LAKES. . . ABOUNDING IN TROUT. . . THE PRINCIPAL PART OF THE PARISH IS EMPLOYED IN SHEEP-FARMING, TO WHICH MUCH ATTENTION IS PAID. THE LARGER NUMBERS OF THE POPULATION DWELL ALONG THE SHORES, AND AVAIL THEMSELVES OF THE ADVANTAGES OFFERED FOR FISHING, FROM WHICH, TOGETHER WITH THEIR SMALL ALLOTMENTS OF LAND, THEY DRAW THEIR SUBSISTENCE. GAME IS PLENTIFUL . . .

The parish of **CLYNE** (Sutherlandshire): IN THE WELL-CULTIVATED DISTRICT ALONG THE COAST THE SURFACE IS TAME, BUT IN OTHER PARTS. . . PRESENTS THE MOST PROMINENT AND CHARACTERISTIC FEATURES OF HIGHLAND SCENERY . . . ABOUT NINE MILES FROM THE COAST, THE GENERAL ASPECT OF THE SCENERY BECOMES BLEAK AND HEATHY, WITH EXTENSIVE TRACTS OF MOOR AND MOSS, INTERSECTED BY NUMEROUS RIVULETS, AND LOFTY RANGES OF HILLS. THE RIVER BRORA . . . IS CELEBRATED FOR SALMON OF A SUPERIOR SIZE AND FLAVOUR. . . THE PRINCIPAL PART OF THE PARISH CONSISTS OF HIGH AND IRRECLAIMABLE HILL-PASTURE, AND IS LAID OUT IN EXTENSIVE SHEEP-WALKS; THE SHEEP ARE PURE CHEVIOTS . . . AND THE TOTAL NUMBER KEPT IS 11,000 [THERE WERE 1,765 PEOPLE IN CLINE AT THE TIME, ABOUT 1 FOR EVERY 6 SHEEP]. THE LAND IN TILLAGE . . [INCLUDED] 300 ACRES OF SANDY LOAM, FORMING AN EXCELLENT TURNIP SOIL. [THE REST IS]. . . POOR SHARP GRAVEL.[1]

---

[1] Samuel Lewis, *A Topographical Dictionary of Scotland . . .*, 2nd ed., 1851 (reprinted for Clearfield Company, Inc., Baltimore, 2002), Vol. I, pp. 79, 214-5.

In such places did the Highlanders dwell. Possibly surprising is the fact that the Highlanders, at their greatest number, in 1841, amounted to little over 17% of the total population of Scotland. That proportion has declined steadily ever since, due to emigration overseas or to the Lowlands and England for employment. The 2001 census reported that Highland areas accounted for under 5% of Scotland's people. In absolute numbers, the Highland population in 1841 of 456,000 had shrunk to 250,000, a 45% drop in population in a bit over a century and a half. Were these Highlanders a restless people with scant chance at a livelihood, driven to leave home?

The Highland Scots

There was a time more than 2,000 years ago when the Celtic tribes dominated central Europe. They made beautiful jewelry and carvings. They were poetic and warlike. They followed strong leaders, even to their deaths. But they refused to recognize leadership beyond their local tribes and so they did not become a nation. And they had a pervasive discontent that caused the more determined of them to keep pushing, every generation, a little bit further into the wild unknown.

. . . They moved up the British island, ever northward, each generation seeing the more restless and aggressive push farther, breeding a new generation of even more restless and aggressive travellers. To the far north they moved, into what is now called Scotland. When it ended or became too bleak they found sea bridges into Ireland. At last, after hundreds or even thousands of years of insistent wandering, the most imaginative or curious among them found that they were caught in a cruel genetic joke, all their energies bottled up in wild, desolate places that only faced each other across the sea. So back and forth they went, across the sea bridges from Ireland to Scotland and then back again, waves of them that they now called 'clans' taking out their fury on each other, then uniting once in a while when the Romans or the English attempted to conquer them. The wildest, most contentious people on all the earth, trapped in a sea-bound bottleneck, their emotions spattering out in poetry and music and brawls, calling each other Scottish and Irish now, Catholic and Protestant then, Arsenal and Celtics, anything that might make a reason for another good, hard fight.[2]

These people in time became the British Empire's greatest export, settling all around the world. When Henry Stanley uttered the memorable words, "Dr. Livingstone, I presume?" he was in central Africa and the man he was addressing was a Scot. Like fellow-Scot, Mungo Park, Livingstone's attraction to far frontiers led him to Africa. When another Scot, the man they called *Tusitala*, died in Samoa, it was the end of a career that had carried that wanderer by canoe and donkey pack throughout Europe, and when he found that too tame, drove him to pioneer California. He took his bride to live in a mining camp there, then they returned to Scotland from which he soon sallied forth to spend the rest of his life in the south Pacific. His name was Robert Louis Stevenson[3].

---

[2] James Webb, *Born Fighting; How the Scots-Irish Shaped America* (New York: Broadway Books, 2004), pp. 4-5.

[3] Stevenson spoke of how all Scots shared a common bond. He wrote "The fact remains: in spite of the differences in blood and language the Lowlander feels himself the sentimental countryman of the Highlander. When they meet abroad, they fall upon each other's neck in spirit; even at home there is a kind of clannish intimacy in their talk."

'[F]or three centuries, what we now know as Canada has received a constant infusion of ideas and attitudes from Scotland. . . . individual Scots . . . have aggressively initiated growth and development and placed themselves in positions of power, controlling and influencing key institutions at critical points in the development of the Canadian Nation. The ubiquity . . . and range of their accomplishments are truly astonishing. . . . Opportunities for enterprising Scots presented themselves throughout the far-flung Empire – in India, Australia, New Zealand, South Africa and the thirteen American colonies."[4]*

If you read the history of the early fur trading companies of Canada, you discover that most of the factors (agents) of the Hudson's Bay Company were Scots, and the crews frequently Orkney men, known for their stamina and ability to wade bare-legged through icy waters. An early rival to the Bay Company was the Northwest Fur Company, headed by William McGillivray and Simon McTavish, both natives of Inverness-shire. Who is better proof of the Scots urging towards far places than that intrepid explorer of the north and west, Alexander Mackenzie from Stornoway on the Isle of Lewis?

Sir Sandford Fleming, thanks to whom the world has standard time zones, was born at Kirkcaldy, in Fifeshire. I live less than a mile from his summer estate on the North West Arm of Halifax. Alexander Graham Bell, a native of Edinburgh, did much of his inventive work, notably in the field of flight, at Baddeck, Nova Scotia. Rev. Thomas McCulloch, founder of Pictou Academy, is recognized as a pioneer of Canadian education. He came from Neilston, in Renfrewshire.

Perhaps no one said it any better than the British Prime Minister Disraeli, "It has been my lot to have found myself in many distant lands. I have never been in one without finding a Scotch-man, and I never found a Scotchman who was not at the head of the poll."

Two hundred years ago, at a time when the more well-heeled immigrants of the eighteenth century had already gone to America, and before the great exodus after 1815, this was written about the Highlanders: "The people . . . are a hardy and insular race, an amalgam of Norse and Gael, cut off from the outside world by its indifference to it. . . They raise goats and black cattle, potatoes and inferior oats, brew a rough beer and distill a raw whisky for their dreams. They break the earth with wooden ploughs, live in crude huts of sod and stone."

In 1801 there were about 300,000 Highlanders. They were scattered across the countryside, content with very little, enduring poor food, clothing and housing. Englishmen and Lowlanders who came there described the condition of the people with the same impatient contempt their grandsons were later to express toward Africans and Indians.

As it becomes relevant to the story of why people emigrated, let us look at the arguments pro and con improving the types of farming pursued in the Highlands. But first consider what Canadian historian J. M. Bumsted writes:

---

[4] Matthew Shaw, *Great Scots! How the Scots Created Canada* (Winnipeg: Heartland Associates, Inc., 2003), p.9.

"No one asked what the people wanted. Improvement was a moral obligation and scarcely a matter for debate. But suspicious of improvements that announced themselves in writs of eviction, the Highlanders may have decided to live as they had always lived, to do without roads, bridges, wheeled vehicles and the religions of their lairds, to wear the bonnet or cotton cap, neckcloth and coarse plaid, to operate illicit stills, to sing the Psalms in Gaelic, and to believe in the Evil Eye. Yet, the Highlanders had one virtue on which the nation greedily fastened. This was their courage and their belief that nowhere in the world was there a fighting-man equal to the Gael with a broadsword in his hand."

The position taken by various people in the debate about emigration that raged in Scotland 200 years ago reflected their status in the socio-economic pyramid in the Highlands. You can build a clan out of this if you are so inclined, but after Culloden that structure was largely in ruins, partly due to deliberate government policy, but also due to the self-inflicted wounds the clans received through their loyalty to the exiled House of Stuart. The rebellions of 1715 and 1745 fractured clans and families and pitted Highlander against Highlander.

The men at the top in the Highlands were few and far between. The great landowners were peers of the realm. Some were clan chieftains or came from the immediate families of former chieftains. If once there had been a belief that clan members collectively possessed the right to use the clan territories for their own and their family's support, eighteenth century legal opinion affirmed that a chieftain held title to his lands and was free to treat them and his dependents accordingly.

The landed proprietors let out most of their vast holdings to tacksmen, or wadsetters (mortgage holders), whose concern was getting their money back with interest. Tenants leased all or part of a farm from the tacksmen who pressed them for the rents as the means of recovering the money they had loaned to the landlord. Beneath the tenants was the numerous class of subtenants, who were essentially landless labourers, with little more than a tiny garden patch reserved for their own use beside the cabin in which their families lived. These poor people were known by various names. The upper level, known as crofters or pendiclers, held a small piece of land called a croft and enjoyed some rights to summer grazing for their animals. The poorest people were the cottars, or scallags, as they were called in the Hebrides. They were little more than servants and retainers for those above them in the social structure. They had a hut, but had to work for a master five of the six working days of the week.

This was in fact a semi-feudal system. The significant difference from the mediæval feudal system was that people did not belong to their lord. They were free to leave if they so desired. The trouble was that, prior to the industrialization of England and the Lowlands, there was nowhere to go and no will to leave the warm ties of home and kin. Sir James Barrie wrote in his novel, *Margaret Ogilvy*, "So much of what is great in Scotland has sprung from the closeness of the family ties."

Most Highlanders, like their cousins the Gaelic Irish, were imbued with pre-industrial cultural values and habits that left them ill-equipped to find a ready place in the developing world of machine and sprawling cities. They lived by a natural clock, not a time clock. They spoke Gaelic, whereas city and business spoke English. No surprise, then, that Highlanders preferred to settle where farm and forest prevailed. The Lowlanders were more suited to the bustle of town and commerce. Scots were Presbyterian and Catholic, ruled by a monarch officially Anglican. They were brave men and raw, but except when John Bull had a war to be fought, Sandy was not in demand.

The Emigration Debate

Many arguments were advanced from various quarters as to the advisability of mass emigration from Scotland. One of the considerations that most strongly inhibited emigration was the lengthy war between France and Britain which went on during most of the period between 1793 and 1815. The military wanted to keep handy the martial capabilities for which the Highlanders were noted, in particular for use as infantry soldiers.

Others claimed that since the Highlands needed to be modernized and improved, it would be prudent to hold onto a labour force that was already just where it could be most cheaply utilized. If the landlords were forcing more efficient methods of production on a reluctant and backward population, it was conferring a benefit on those same recalcitrant people.

In order to bring about improvements, people would necessarily have to be dislocated. A slight amount of emigration might be expected but, proponents of modernization claimed, only as a temporary measure. It could have been summed up as clearances if necessary, but not necessarily clearances. Despite much that has been claimed by some recent writers, large-scale evictions and clearances did not get underway until the second decade of the nineteenth century, beginning about 1812 or 13.

The behaviour of the common people has typically been seen as merely reaction to landlord initiative. Some accounts suggest that the people were passive victims of evil proprietors and their agents. In this version, the laird oppresses, the people suffer and are eventually forced against their will to abandon their birthplace and emigrate. Not only does the landlord exploit, but so do the emigration agents, the crews of the vessels taking them to America, and colonial land speculators in the colonies. They leave their glens to become indentured servants and paupers in North America and, even when some few succeed, they yearn for the native land from which they were heartlessly evicted and expelled. Much of this impression was fed by the Gael's own mythology which tended to emphasize suffering and a constant nostalgia for the auld sod. Seldom was the Highlander portrayed – even by himself – as capable of rationally considered actions and decisions. True, he may have been uneducated and he was undeniably very poor, but he was not commonly abused, and he was certainly not ignorant.[5]

Many Highland lairds tried to increase their rentals without resorting to clearance of their tenants, which is to say that they moved people off of land which could be used for economically more profitable (to the laird) purposes. Such landowners sought to locate more people in the same space by putting them on smaller but more efficiently-run holdings. In the western Highlands the rise of a new source of income, the processing of kelp (seaweed), encouraged this strategy.

Manufacturing kelp meant that alkaline ash was extracted from the seaweed, a product that could be used in the making of glass and soap. Kelp making was a labour intensive industry, but required no great skill or capital investment, and the raw material was readily available. The weed was cut or gathered, then dried, after which it was taken to a kiln where it was burnt with peat until it was a brittle substance reduced to 5% of its original weight. What made this an attractive proposition was that any family could earn money doing it, in the Highland economy a rare instance

[5] J. M. Bumsted, *The People's Clearance; Highland Emigration to British North America 1770 - 1815* (Winnipeg: The University of Manitoba Press, 1982), pp. xiii-xiv.

of production that was not for subsistence but to earn income. The selling price for the alkaline ash rose obligingly. In 1750 a ton of "made" kelp sold for £2. Thirty years later the same ton fetched £8, in 1800 £10, and by 1810 was being bought for £20 the ton.[6] With the money this earned people could buy more necessities and required smaller holdings to produce the rest of what they needed. Such at least was the theory. Of course, some realized that such funds could also be used to buy a passage out of Scotland, so that this hopeful development proved a double-edged sword. This circumstance argues convincingly against the notion that Highlanders always lacked choices about what they might do, or, given the opportunity to choose, could not or would not do so.

Before exploring the pressing reasons which encouraged emigration, there is one other point to note. It would be reasonable to expect that the leading people in the colonies of British North America would welcome immigration. Such was not the case. The colonies, particularly the smaller ones on the Atlantic coast, were underfunded and underdeveloped. They had not been able to assimilate the great numbers of Loyalists who arrived following the Revolutionary War. Any considerable influx of population seemed to pose more problems than it solved. None of the Maritime colonies had an efficient administration big enough to cope with a large scale immigration. The Highland Scots, like the Irish, were frequently regarded as the dregs of British society. The argument seemed to be that, if those people had any ambition or talent, they would not have had to emigrate.

Overpopulation

The underlying and probably inexorable cause of Scottish Highland emigration in the early nineteenth century is to be found in the concept of carrying capacity, that is, the ability of the resources in a given area to sustain a human population. When the number of people outstrips an area's ability to provide for it, any of several things could happen. At one time it was possible to sally forth with axes and picks to clear additional acres to feed the increasing population. Sometimes, disease, privation or war provided sufficient attrition in numbers to restore the balance between supply and need. In more recent centuries societies have tended to rely on improved technique or technology to increase the productivity of a place so that its people are fed, housed and clothed adequately. Another method is out-migration (i.e., moving within the country) or even emigration of some of the hungry mouths. In the case of the Scottish Highlands that is precisely what happened. The large-scale migration was driven far more by overpopulation than it was by anything else. If someone wishes to assign blame, he should single out the natural fecundity of the Highland folk themselves. They were simply growing in numbers to the point where they were on the verge of eating themselves out of house and home.

There is no better way of showing the extent of Scotland's demographic crisis than by citing some statistics. (See Table 1, next page.) Between 1755 and 1841 Scotland's population more than doubled from about one and a quarter million to over two and a half million souls. The Highland shires rose by 55% in the same period, despite the considerable emigration that had gone on in the interval. The extent of arable land increased so marginally in the same period that early statisticians considered the difference to be negligible and did not report it.

---

[6] Bumsted, pp. 41–42.

Table 1 - DEPOPULATION BY EMIGRATION, HIGHLANDS & WESTERN ISLES

1 - By Shires

	Argyll	Caithn	Invnss	Ross&C	Suthrld	Orkney	Zetland	Total	Change (as %)
1755	66,286	22,215	59,593	48,048	20,774	38,591		255,507	
1801	81,277	22,609	72,672	56,318	23,117	24,445	22,379	302,817	+ 47,310 (+ 18.52%)
1811	86,541	23,419	77,671	60,853	23,629	23,238	22,915	318,266	+ 15,449 (+ 5.10%)
1821	97,316	29,181	89,961	67,762	23,840	26,979	26,145	361,184	+ 42,918 (+ 13.49%)
1831	100,973	34,529	94,797	74,820	25,518	28,847	29,392	388,876	+ 27,692 (+ 7.67%)
1841	97,371	36,343	97,799	78,685	24,782	30,507	30,558	396,045	+ 7,169 (+ 1.84%)

Between 1755 and 1841, the Highland population _rose_ by 140,538 souls, or 55%)

	Argyll	Caithn	Invnss	Ross&C	Suthrld	Orkney	Zetland	Total	Change (as %)
1851	89,298	38,709	96,500	82,707	25,793	31,455	31,078	395,540	- 505 (- 0.13%)
1861	79,724	41,111	88,888	81,406	25,246	32,395	31,670	380,442	- 15,098 (- 3.82%)
1871	75,679	39,992	87,531	80,955	24,317	31,274	31,608	371,356	- 9,086 (- 2.39%)
1881	76,468	38,865	90,454	78,547	23,370	32,044	29,705	369,453	- 1,903 (- 0.51%)
1891	75,003	37,177	89,317	77,810	21,896	30,453	28,711	360,367	- 9,086 (- 2.46%)
1901	73,642	33,870	90,104	76,450	21,440	28,699	28,166	352,371	- 7,996 (- 2.22%)

Between 1841 and 1901, the Highland population _fell_ by 43,674 souls, or 11%)

	Argyll	Caithn	Invnss	Ross&C	Suthrld	Orkney	Zetland	Total	Change (as %)
1911	70,902	32,010	87,272	77,364	20,179	25,897	27,911	341,535	- 10,836 (- 3.08%)
1921	76,862	28,285	82,082	70,818	17,802	24,111	25,520	325,853	- 16,055 (- 4.70%)
1931	63,014	25,656	84,930	62,802	16,100	22,075	21,410	295,987	- 29,493 (- 9.06%)
1951	63,631	22,710	83,480	60,508	13,670	21,255	19,352	284,606	- 11,381 (- 3.85%)
1961	59,390	27,370	83,480	57,642	13,507	18,747	17,812	277,948	- 6,658 (- 2.34%)

Between 1901 and 1961, the Highland population _fell_ by 74,423 souls, or 21%). The overall _loss_ in Highland population from its high point in 1841 to 1961 was 118,097 souls, or nearly 30%.

2 - In the Isles

In the 1841 census, 133 islands off the coast of Scotland were reported as being inhabited, ranging from as few as six people on Auskerry in the Orkneys to 23,082 on the Isle of Skye. In total, 175,927 souls called the isles home. By 1961 the number of inhabited islands had fallen to 124, with just one person on Erraid, but 24,107 on Lewis and Harris. Overall, 101,001 people were residents of the isles of Scotland in 1961. In 2001, only 88 islands had people living on them, with, in all, 99,623 inhabitants. Of the 88 inhabited islands, 31 of them shared only 168 souls.

While most of the depopulated isles had only had one to three families in 1841, a few had housed communities, e.g., Boreray had 181 souls, and Pabbay, also in the western isles, had 338. Other islands did not become devoid of people, but suffered drastic out-migration of young people. The Isle of Skye fell from 23,082 to 9,232, a loss of 60% of its population. Some other examples would be the Isle of Mull: 10,064 down to 2,667; Islay, 13,602 to 3,457; Coll, 1,442 to 164. Only the main Shetland Island, Great Cumbrae, and Bernerey 'A' today have more residents than they had 170 years ago. It is easy to see why there is so much Scottish ancestry in Canada and the United States when you study the census demographics of the Highlands and isles.

From 1841 to 2001, the Scottish isles lost 76,304 residents, a drop of 43.4%, attributable almost entirely to sustained migration. Prior to 1871, most of that was emigration overseas. Later, the people were moving to employment opportunities in industrial and commercial centres within the British Isles, most notably Glasgow, Dundee, Edinburgh, Manchester and London.

Since the population of the Highlands and indeed of all of Scotland had remained fairly stable for the century before 1755, an explanation for this extraordinary population growth is required. There seem to have been three contributing factors. The first was the introduction of the potato as a major food crop. In 1743 the potato was first planted in Uist in the Hebrides and proved so successful that the new crop was being grown in all the isles within a generation and across the Highlands by the 1780s. Whereas crops of oats and barley fared badly in the overcast isles in many seasons, the potato grew regardless of the summer weather. The improvement in nutrition and the greater variation in diet this permitted prevented the hunger and famine that regularly had visited the poorer people, carrying off children in particularly large numbers. More surviving children meant more marriageable adults, with the predictable consequence of a larger population than otherwise would have been the case.

If on the one hand more people survived childhood, another development kept more of them alive longer. During the late 18th century vaccination for smallpox spread across the Highlands. One authority estimated that this measure reduced mortality rates by as much as 20% within twenty years.[7]

Finally, such developments as the kelp manufacture began to give the poorer class of people the opportunity to earn at least some income. Raising black cattle was traditional to the Highland way of life. The sale price of an animal doubled in the period 1763-1794, and would go even higher once the wartime need for naval and military stores made itself felt. While £4 for a ton of kelp may seem a small amount, it represented twice its price thirty years before. Funds remitted by emigrants or serving soldiers to their relatives at home were becoming yet another source of money. If, before 1815, it was mainly people of the tacksman and crofter element who emigrated, now the sub-tenants began to possess just enough means to pay for passage to British America.

The extent of the emigration comes into focus when it is stated numerically. The high season of migration into the Maritimes from Scotland was from 1810 to 1850. The Highland population grew by almost 25%, or 77,000 people, in those years, yet Nova Scotia received at least 30,000 Highland immigrants in that same period, Prince Edward Island and New Brunswick rather fewer than that. Other emigration went to Red River, Canada and the United States. It is not so surprising to read that such-and-such a Scottish surname is more numerous on this side of the Atlantic that it is in its homeland. The pressure of the population at home **pushed** people to emigrate. The empty lands and the forests of eastern British America **pulled** people here. The third major consideration in discussing a large-scale migration is the means by which it was done – the **how** of it.

The Timber Trade

If people wish to go from one place to another and an ocean intervenes, regular communication by vessels is imperative. Had the motivation merely been a few thousand Highlanders seeking passage, the expense would have kept shipowners from providing the means of emigration. As events turned out, soon after 1800 circumstances worked in favour of the intending emigrants from Scotland.

---

[7] T. C. Smout, *A History of the Scottish People, 1560 - 1830* (London: Fontana Press, 1969), pp. 253-4.

The Royal Navy required oak and pine for masts. There was extensive construction of new wharves, piers and warehouses throughout Great Britain. The long period of war between Britain and France (1793-1815) cut off Britain's customary sources of timber in the Baltic – Sweden, Poland, Russia. After 1801, British North America became the major and almost the only source of spars, deals and squared timber. In 1805, for instance, 50 vessels carried 300,000 cubic feet of timber from the port of Pictou to the British Isles.[8]

The problem facing the shipowners was the lack of westbound cargo to fill the holds. The traffic in manufactured British goods to the colonies was slight, and shippers faced the expense of buying ballast for the return voyage to the Gulf of St. Lawrence. In Scotland there were thousands of intending emigrants willing to pay modest fares to be taken to the very areas to which the timber ships were to sail. The two circumstances were, as they say, a good fit.

On their return to America the vessels could carry human cargoes, mostly Scots pushed out of their homes by poverty and lack of resources, drawn here by the opportunity of certain employment in felling trees, hauling logs to the shore, milling the wood and loading the vessels. Most of these Scots immigrants came in families and in groups drawn from a single glen or island, since Highlanders did not commonly emigrate as isolated individuals. The cultural and moral support of relations and neighbours meant much to their identity and in time contributed not a little to their success.

While many Highland Scots sailed from Fort William in Inverness-shire and from Ullapool in northern Scotland, substantial emigration flowed from the timber ports of Aberdeen, Dumfries and Greenock. Some of the human traffic was drawn from the Lowlands. Anyone researching ancestry in Scotland has to realize that people emigrated through ports which were most accessible from where they lived, whether overland or by small boats hopping from harbour to harbour among the isles or down the coast.

Number of Ships

Genealogists like to discover the name of the ship which brought their ancestors to North America. Usually this is accomplished by reference to a passenger list. In the case of Scots and Irish immigrants into Atlantic Canada before 1850 such lists are few. If there ever had been nominal lists they have since been lost, destroyed, or gone undetected for decades.

The next best thing where Nova Scotia and New Brunswick are concerned is to learn the names at least of vessels which carried people from Scotland or Ireland to these shores. Newspapers of the time published weekly "Shipping News" columns (see page 18), enabling researchers to learn at least the names, points of origin and arrival of immigrant ships.

The main ports where Scottish emigrants landed were Pictou, Halifax and Sydney, in Nova Scotia; Saint John, Saint Andrews, Miramichi, Shediac and Bathurst, in New Brunswick; Charlottetown, Prince Edward Island.

---

[8] A. Shortt and A. G. Doughty, eds., *Canada and its Provinces. A History of the Canadian People and Their Institutions* (Toronto: Publishers Association of Canada, 1913-17), Vol. XIII, pp. 254-5.

PORTS FROM WHICH SCOTS SAILED, 1767 - 1842

Map 2

I have been able to identify 315 vessels which brought or could have brought people from Scotland to New Brunswick before 1830. The single most important port of departure was Aberdeen which accounted for 175 of the crossings. Less frequent were ships originating in the Clyde (at Greenock and Glasgow), the Firth of Forth (Leith and Kirkcaldy) and Dumfries. A scattering of other ports contributed to the flow, places such as Dundee, Montrose and Wick, on the North Sea coast of Scotland, Fort William, Irvine and Ayr on the western side of Scotland. (Map 2)

Similarly, there were at least 298 ships that brought or might have brought Scots to Pictou, Nova Scotia before 1850. Aberdeen and the Clyde each accounted for 81 vessels. Other ports of note include, in order, Leith, Cromarty, Fort William, Saltcoats and Ayr, Tobermory, Stornoway, Dundee, Inverness, and Thurso. Again, a number of lesser ports are noted, such as Dumfries, Ullapool/Isle Martin, Peterhead, Wick and Banff. A few came from lesser islands such as Barra, Islay, and Canna.

When you trace the route taken by the Aberdeen departures, you discover that they sailed around the north of Scotland past the Orkneys and then down the North Channel through the western isles to collect passengers or emigrants. Similarly, and even more obviously, departures from the Clyde sailed directly past the isles of Bute and Arran in order to get to the open sea. Kintyre Peninsula and the isle of Islay were along the route taking vessels around the north coast of Ireland.

The destination of most of these vessels supports the view that these were timber ships returning to the Gulf of St. Lawrence to take on yet another cargo of wood for the British Isles. No less than 174 of those 315 vessels arrived at Miramichi, and a further 29 disembarked their passengers in the Bay of Chaleur, Richibucto or Shediac. In all, about two-thirds of the Scotland to New Brunswick shipping was destined for the timber producing regions along the Gulf of St. Lawrence. Over a hundred of the remainder went to Saint John or St. Andrews to discharge their passengers. Pictou, Nova Scotia, was on what we might term "the timber coast".

The impact of this pattern can be seen in early federal Canadian census returns. In 1881, for instance, the highest proportions of people of Scots extraction in New Brunswick were reported in Restigouche (41%) and Northumberland (34%) counties. In Nova Scotia, Pictou (83%), Antigonish (68%) and Inverness (75%) counties, all predominantly Scottish in origin, likewise face the Gulf of St. Lawrence. In one census district, New Lairg, Pictou County, all 535 residents were of Scottish origin.

On the Gulf shores the earliest timber operations were conducted near the coastline. By degrees the cutting crews moved inland, preferably up rivers such as the Richibucto, Kouchibouguac, Nepisiquit and Restigouche, but the king of them all was the Miramichi with its many branches stretching far into the interior of New Brunswick. The West, Middle and East rivers unite in Pictou Harbour, Nova Scotia. Between 1806 and 1811, the exports of timber from British America to Great Britain increased by 800%. By 1809, Britain was importing two-thirds of its wood from British North America, mainly Nova Scotia, New Brunswick and Gaspé.[9]

There was a serious economic slump in the immediate post-war period (after 1815). Due to the rapid industrialization of England and Lowland Scotland, the demand for timber continued into mid-century, when metal hulls and steam power transformed ship design and reduced the demand for wood. At the same time as the economy went into recession, there was large-scale unemployment in Britain caused in part by loss of wartime industry, but also by the massive reduction in strength of the armed forces which threw thousands of men back into a labour force that didn't need them. Emigration offered a way out of their dilemma to tens of thousands of Scots, so the traffic continued down to mid-century.

The Voyage

There are many tales about people crossing the Atlantic in steerage and there were some appallingly dreadful crossings, due either to weather or the discomforts caused by crowding, confinement, or shortages of food and drink. In truth, however, it was in the interests of merchants and their ship masters to see that the Scots arrived healthy and able to work in the timber trade.

A typical timber ship that brought Scots to the region was a brig, a vessel with two masts (fore and main), both square-rigged. A fore-and-aft sail was rigged to the mainmast. Two or four jibs (triangular sails) could be rigged forward from the masts to improve manoeuvrability and catch favourable breezes. The tonnage (tons of 2240 pounds) was the amount of crew, cargo, stores and passengers a ship could transport. On brigs known to have come to the Gulf of St. Lawrence, tonnages between 200 and 350 tons were the norm.

There were two decks inside the hull, where provisions, cargo, human beings, and nautical equipment were carried. The *Sprightly* was a brig of 300 tons sailing out of Aberdeen to New Brunswick between 1814 and the 1830s. Considered as a timber carrier the *Sprightly* could handle 120 tons of cargo. This meant that the *Sprightly* carried 240 loads of timber sized 50 cubic feet apiece. Such ships carried from 35 to 100 people on an ocean crossing. One deck was occupied by food, water, nautical equipment and crew. Passengers shared an area 18 feet by 66 feet in size, giving as much as 34 square feet apiece, or as little as 12 square feet, barely room to lay down comfortably! The arithmetic is confusing, but if we are to make sense out of the stories about the

---

[9] Lucille H. Campey, *After the Hector; The Scottish Pioneers of Nova Scotia and Cape Breton 1773 - 1852* (Toronto: Natural Heritage books, 2004), p. 87.

ocean crossings on immigrant ships, we have to set emotion aside and take that sort of clear-headed look at the ships.

Now, for a moment, consider the emigrants. They were not modern people used to comforts that many a laird 200 years ago would have envied. These Scots were a tough-bodied, strong people, used to privation. They combined within themselves the apparent paradox of depending on their group, yet being fiercely independent-minded. They were used to poverty and unhygienic conditions, to a boring diet and danger. Salt fish, hard tack and ale, standard fare for crewmen on those vessels, were no great hardship. Confinement in limited space and lack of employment were more annoying than were the other physical discomforts of a voyage.

Let's follow a composite account of a typical Scots emigrant of the early nineteenth century. James Maclean had a wife and four children, the eldest eleven years old. They had to arrange for a boat to take them from the Isle of Skye to Greenock, a port on the western mainland of Scotland. They owned few portable possessions, and could take with them only a Bible, their clothing, some favourite tools and household utensils. If James had a fiddle or a pipe, you may be sure he brought it with him. That would be about all. A few people set out with a trunk of belongings, but they were exceptional. Almost no one landed in Pictou or Chatham with much.

Once anyone decided to emigrate, he had made an irrevocable decision. Then he and his family had to brave hostility, sea sickness, rough conditions, a poor diet and perhaps abuse. Some left against the expressed opinions of landlords and agents. Unlike emigrants such as the Germans, many Scots did not have to bid farewell to family and friends, because they were emigrating too. Still, the wish to be amidst the familiar soon led the Scots to put names they knew from old Scotland on pieces of their new homeland. New Brunswick has its Argyle, Campbelltown, Dalhousie, Dumfries, Glen Livet, Kincardine and Loch Lomond. In Nova Scotia you can find Inverness, Moidart, Knoydart, Loch Broom, New Lairg and New Glasgow. Prince Edward Island is home to Kilmuir, Gairloch, Appin Road and New Annan.[10]

The notion of an ocean so vast that it took from six to ten weeks to cross in fair weather, and perhaps twice as long in foul, was beyond the experience of a people whose knowledge of water was the short distance between one and other of the western isles. It was an act of courage, faith, and perhaps desperation to set out at all. The factors driving you out, or the inducements drawing you forward must have been powerful.

The **push** factors included lack of opportunity, poverty, loss of traditional lands and livelihood, and personal misfortunes, but mainly overpopulation. The **pull** influences included the promise of owning land, almost certain employment, a new chance in life, better prospects for one's children, and so forth.

The ocean voyage contributed to the list of woes: crowding, a lack of privacy, no fresh food or water, uncertainty, fear of being drowned or wrecked, sometimes the cruelty of captain and crew, pilfering, sickness. When a ship sighted land at this end of the voyage, people must have felt a weight lifting from their shoulders. No doubt there were many who murmured *"Thank God"* [BUIÐhEAÐAS LE ÐIA = buay-kuss leh deeh]. At least when they came ashore, the dangers of drowning and being castaways ceased to haunt the people. A new set of challenges awaited them.

---

[10] Other examples are mentioned in Leonard M. Reid, *Sons of the Hector* (New Glasgow, 1973).

The two maps which follow are intended to assist readers in locating some of the more frequently mentioned places in the Highlands. Map 3 below shows the three northernmost shires: Caithness, Sutherland, Ross and Cromarty (often simply Ross-shire). Map 4 (page 16) shows Inverness.

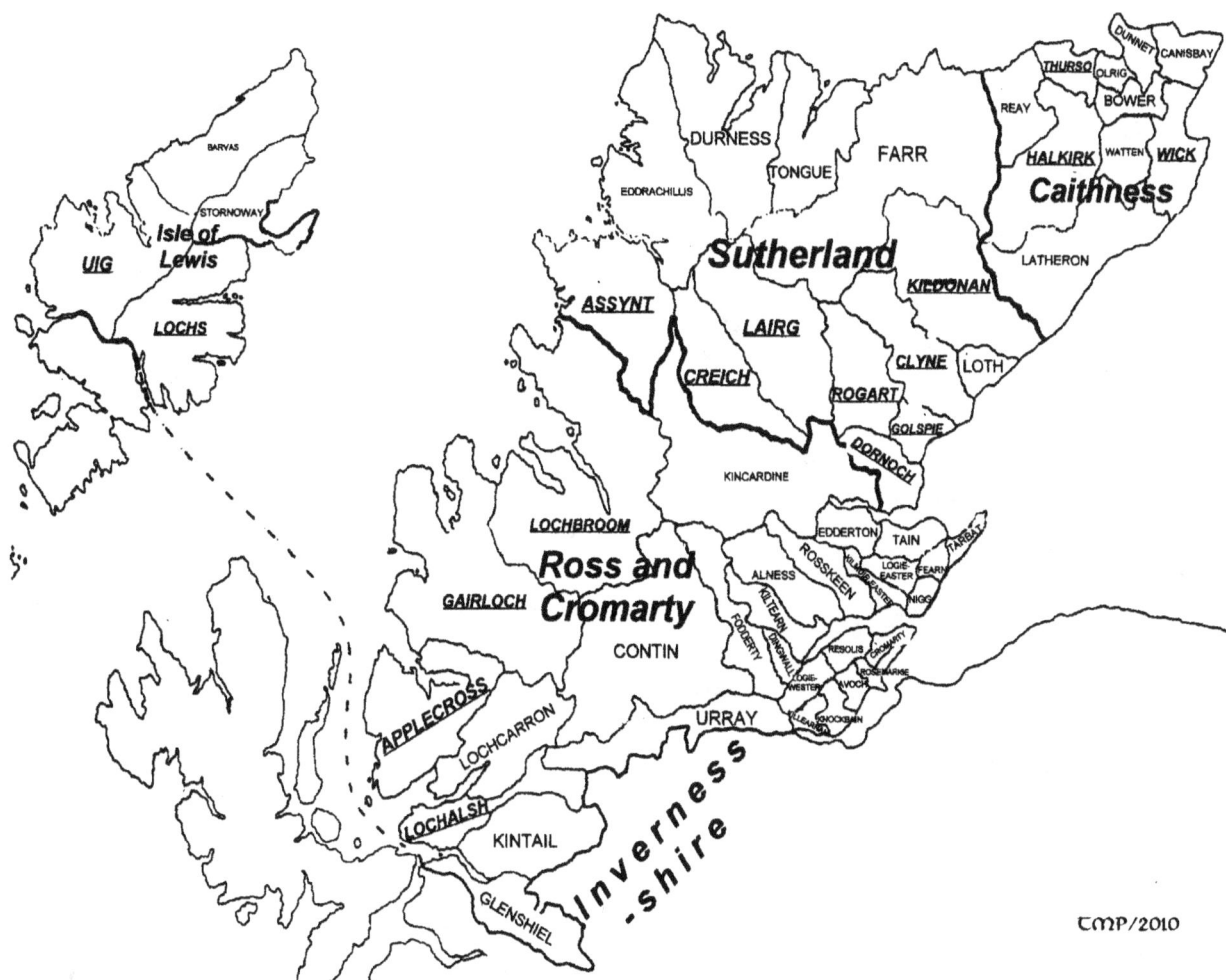

Map 3 - PARISHES IN CAITHNESS, SUTHERLANDSHIRE, ROSS AND CROMARTY

Substantial migration from particular parishes characterized the movement of Highland Scots to the Maritime Provinces. Those parishes have been indicated by italics and underlining on the map above. The old parochial (Church of Scotland) registers start at the dates below.

Caithness: Halkirk 1772, Thurso 1647, Wick 1701.

Sutherlandshire: Assynt 1798, Clyne 1782, Creich 1785, Dornoch 1730, Golspie 1739, Kildonan 1791, Lairg 1768, Rogart 1679.

Ross and Cromarty (also Ross-shire or Rothshire): Applecross 1797, Gairloch 1781, Lochalsh 1775, Lochbroom 1798, Lochs 1831, Uig 1824.

Inverness-
shire

Districts:
1 - Knoydart
2 - Morar/Arisaig
3 - Moidart
4 - Ardnamurchan
(in Argyllshire)

CMP/2010

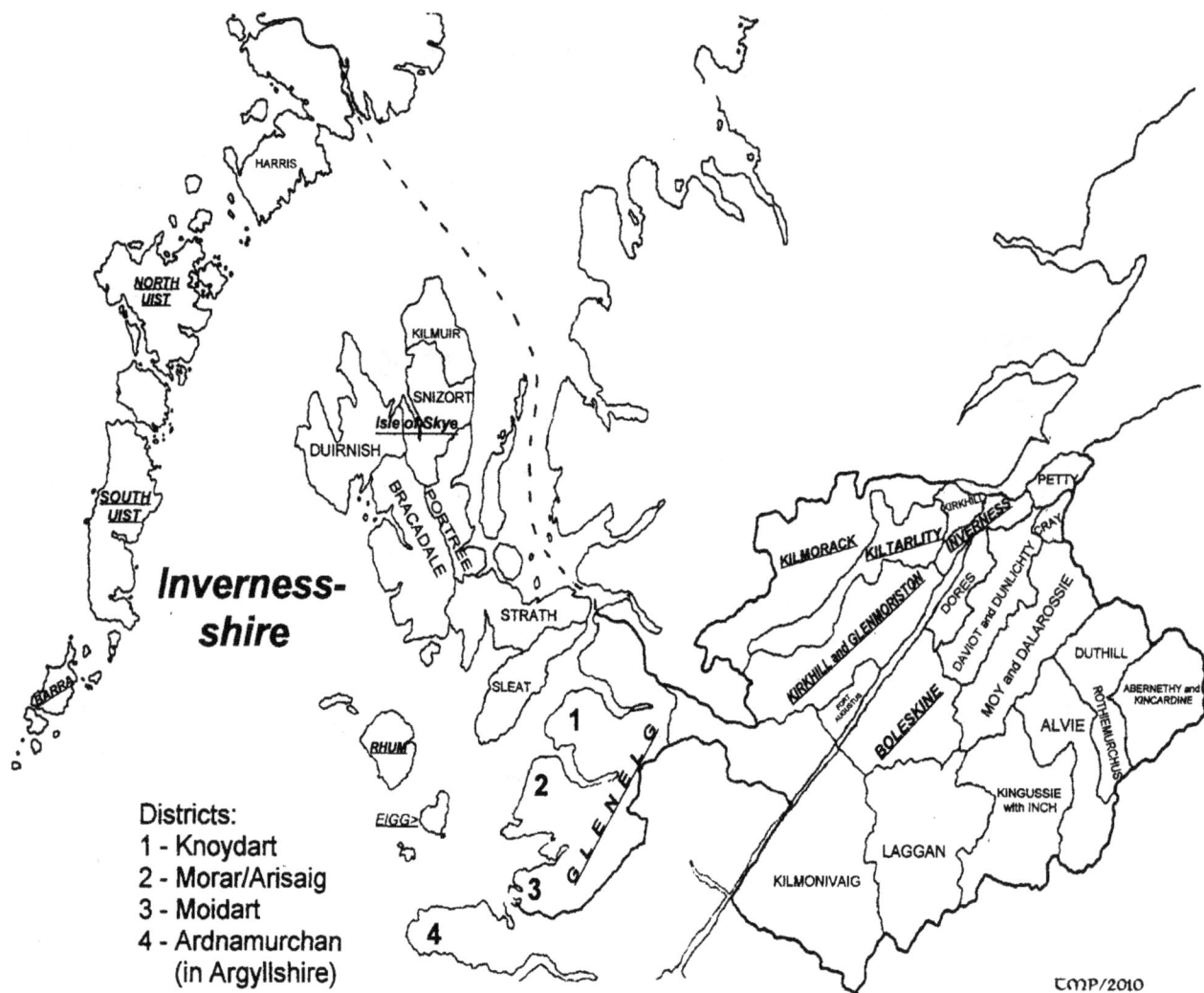

Map 4 - PARISHES IN INVERNESS-SHIRE

Substantial migration from particular parishes characterized the movement of Highland Scots to the Maritime Provinces. Those parishes have been indicated by italics and underlining on the map above. The old parochial (Church of Scotland) registers start at the dates below.

Inverness-shire: Isle of Barra 1704, Boleskine 1777, Eigg and Rhum 1855, Glenelg 1792 (contained the districts of Knoydart, Moidart, and Morar/Arisaig), Glenmoriston and Urquhart [or Kirkhill and Glenmoriston]1739, Kilmorack 1674, Kiltarlity 1714, North Uist 1821, South Uist 1839. On the Isle of Skye no parochial register predates 1800.

Argyllshire: Ardnamurchan 1777; also (not shown on map above) Campbeltown 1659, Isle of Coll 1776, Isle of Tiree 1766.

SELECT BIBLIOGRAPHY

Bumsted, J. M. *The People's Clearance; Highland Emigration to British North America 1770 - 1815*. Edinburgh: Edinburgh University Press, 1982.

Campbell, D., and R. A. MacLean. *Beyond the Atlantic Road: A Study of the Nova Scotia Scots*. Toronto: McClelland and Stewart, 1974.

Campey, Lucille H. *After the Hector; the Scottish Pioneers of Nova Scotia and Cape Breton 1773 - 1852*. Toronto: Natural Heritage Books, 2004.

Campey, Lucille H. *An Unstoppable Force; The Scottish Exodus to Canada*. Toronto: Natural Heritage Books, 2008.

Campey, Lucille H. *With Axe and Bible; The Scottish Pioneers of New Brunswick 1784 - 1874*. Natural Heritage Books, 2007.

Dunn, Charles W. *Highland Settlers: A Portrait of the Scottish Gael in Nova Scotia*. Toronto: University of Toronto Press, 1953.

Emmerson, Frank. *Scots (People of the Maritimes)*. Halifax: Nimbus Publishing Ltd., 1997.

Haliburton, Gordon. *"For Their God" – Education, Religion and the Scots in Nova Scotia*. Ethnic History Series, Vol. I. Halifax: International Education Centre, St. Mary's University, 1981.

Hornsby, Stephen, "Scottish emigration and Settlement in Early Nineteenth-Century Cape Breton," in *The Island; New Perspectives on Cape Breton History 1713 - 1990*, Kenneth Donovan, ed. Fredericton, NB: Acadiensis Press, 1990, pp. 49 - 70.

Lewis, Samuel. *A Topographical Dictionary of Scotland . . .*, 2nd. ed., London 1851. Reprinted, Baltimore: Clearfield Co., Inc., 2002, two volumes.

Logan, G. Murray. *Scottish Highlanders and the American Revolution*. Halifax: McCurdy Printing Co. Ltd., 1976.

MacDonald, James S. *Annals of the North British Society of Halifax, Nova Scotia, 1768 - 1893*. Halifax: John Bowes, 1894.

MacLean, R. A., "The Scots – Hector's Cargo", pp. 113-140, in Douglas F. Campbell, ed. *Banked Fires – The Ethnics of Nova Scotia*. Port Credit, ON: The Scribblers' Press, 1978.

Prebble, John. *The Highland Clearances*. London: History Book Club Ltd., 1966.

Reid, W. Stanford, ed. *The Scottish Tradition in Canada*. Toronto: McClelland and Stewart, 1976.

Shaw, Matthew. *Great Scots! How the Scots Created Canada*. Winnipeg: Heartland Associates, Inc., 2003.

Smout, T. C. *A History of the Scottish People, 1560 - 1830*. London: Fontana Press, 1969.

SHIPPING NEWS ITEMS

A "Shipping News" column
from *The Nova Scotian*,
19 May 1836.

Shipping Intelligence.

PORT OF HALIFAX.

ARRIVED.

Saturday—schr. Venus, Burk, P. E. Island—pork, beef, &c. to W. A. Black & Son, and others ; William, Deagle, do—pork, potatoes, oats, &c ; Packet, Graham, Antigonish—pork, oats, barley, &c. to W. A. Black & Son, and others ; brig Naiad, Brown, London, 45 days—dry goods, wheat, &c. to S. Cunard & Co. and others ; brig Adventure, Sibere, Jersey, 24 days—bread, vinegar, &c. to Creighton & Grassie.

Sunday—brig Broughton, Bell, Liverpool, 40 days—salt, dry goods, &c. to Fairbanks & McNab, and McNab & Cochran ; barque William, Shand, Boswell, Newcastle, 42 days—coal, glass, &c. to Fairbanks & McNab ; schr. Lively, P. E. Island—pork, oats, &c ; brig Ann, Able, Demerara, 24 days—rum and molasses, to J. Allison & Co ; schr. Sarah, Tooker, Yarmouth—passed an American brig from Kennebeck on shore at Cape Sable ; schr. Brothers, Bedique—produce ; schr. Mail Boat Margaret, Boole, Bermuda, 7 days ; brig Dalrymple, Dawson, Newcastle, 53 days—bound to St. Andrews ; on the 6th inst blowing heavy, lost foremast and main topmast.

Monday—mail boat Roseway, Boston, 4 days.

Tuesday—brig Nilus, Johnston, New York, 12 days—staves, bees-wax, &c. to J. Allison & Co. brigt. Royal William, Farrel, Jersey, 41 days—flour, bread, salt, &c. to Creighton & Grassie, and for Gaspe ; brig Reward, Lyle, Kingston, Jam. 23 days—pimento and logwood, to H. Lyle ; schr. Rising Sun, Sponagle, Boston 2½ days,—ballast ; brig Argus, Vautiere, Jersey, 43 days, 37 Plymouth Roads, flour, bread, salt, cordage, &c to Fairbanks & McNab, Creighton & Grassie, 13 passengers.

Wednesday—brig William, Boudrot, Fredericksburg, 14 days—flour, to J. H. Braine. schr. Jane, Wilson, Barrington, 2 days—ballast, to the Master.

Thursday—American brigt. William, Bears, Philadelphia, 12 days—flour, corn, meal, to J. Clark ; schr. Royal Adelaide, Ernst, Dominica, 20 days—sugar, hides to J. & M. Tobin.

CLEARED.

Monday—schr. Two Brothers, Burke, Boston—coals, by the master ; brig Tamar, Hatchard, Trinidad—dry fish, and flour, by Saltus & Wainwright ; Atlantic, Frith, B. W. Indies—dry and pickled fish, &c. by J. & M. Tobin. 10th, Atlantic, Johnston, B. W. Indies—assorted cargo, by J. L. Starr. 11th, schr. Abeona, Potter, Bermuda—assorted cargo, by Frith, Smith, & Co ; brig Grecian, Cann, B. W. Indies—lumber, &c. by D. & E. Starr & Co ; schr. Sarah, Campbell, P. E. Island—assorted cargo, by D. Ramsay & others ; Eight Sons, Jacobs, Labrador—assorted cargo, by

Acadian Recorder, 16 Oct 1819:

THE PASSENGERS IN THE SHIP *ECONOMY* OF ABERDEEN FROM TOBERMORRY TO PICTOU, DESIRE IN THIS PUBLIC MANNER TO EXPRESS THEIR GRATITUDE TO CAPTAIN JAMES FRASER, THE MASTER, FOR THE KIND TREATMENT THEY RECEIVED FROM HIM DURING THE PASSAGE, WHICH CONSISTED OF FIVE WEEKS. TWO HUNDRED AND EIGHTY-FIVE SOULS EMBARKED AT TOBERMORRY, AND WERE LANDED IN GOOD HEALTH AND SPIRITS, TOGETHER WITH FOUR CHILDREN BORN UPON THE PASSAGE. PICTOU, OCTOBER 4, 1819.

Acadian Recorder, 12 July 1828:

PORT OF SYDNEY, JUNE 26 . . . SHIP *UNIVERSE*, STORNOWAY, 464 PASSENGERS. BRIG *ANN*, STORNAWAY, 209 PASSENGERS. TWO OTHER VESSELS WERE TO LEAVE SCOTLAND WITH PASSENGERS FOR THE BRAS'DORE LAKE SHORTLY AFTER THE *UNIVERSE* SAILED ; SUCH WERE THE CROWDED STATE OF THE PASSENGERS IN THE *UNIVERSE*, THAT SIX FAMILIES WERE OBLIGED TO LIVE IN THE LONG BOAT DURING THE WHOLE VOYAGE.

NEWSPAPER MARRIAGES AND DEATHS OF SCOTS-BORN TO 1843

NOVA SCOTIA (all in Halifax)

Acadian = Acadian   (Friday)
AR = Acadian Recorder   (Saturday)
CP = Colonial Pearl   (Saturday)
FP = Free Press   (Tuesday)
HJ = Halifax Journal   (Monday)
HMP = Halifax Morning Post   (Tuesday-Thursday-Saturday)
HP = Halifax Pearl   (Saturday)
NS = The Nova Scotian   (Monday)
NSGWC = Nova-Scotia Gazette and the Weekly Chronicle (Tuesday)
NSRG = Nova Scotia Royal Gazette (Wednesday)
Times = The Times   (Tuesday)
WC = The Weekly Chronicle   (Friday)

NEW BRUNSWICK

CG = City Gazette   (Saint John; Wednesday)
GNS = Gleaner & Northumberland Schediasma   (Chatham; Saturday)
MCN = Morning Commercial News (Saint John; Monday-Wednesday-Friday)
MM = Miramichi Mercury   (Chatham; Saturday)
NBC = New Brunswick Courier   (Saint John; Saturday)
NBRG = New Brunswick Royal Gazette (Fredericton; Wednesda; Friday)
SJG = Saint John Gazette (Saint John; Monday)
STA = Saint Andrews Standard (Saint Andrews; Wednesday)
WO = Weekly Observer   (Saint John; Tuesday)

NEWFOUNDLAND

RGNA = The Royal Gazette and Newfoundland Advertiser   (St. John's; Tuesday)

Died 9 Dec 1786 on the new road between Liverpool and Shelburne, NS: William **WHITE** from Glasgow, Scotland - *NSGWC*, 2 Jan 1787.

Died 2 Oct 1798 at Saint John: David **BLAIR**, merchant, born 20 Mar 1733 at Inverness, Scotland - *SJG*, 2 Oct 1798.

Died 19 Aug 1800 at Saint John: John Alexander **CAMPBELL**, 38, native of North Britain, lately of Tobago - *NBRG*, 22 Aug 1800.

Died 1 Feb 1804 in Scotland: Thomas **PAGAN**, merchant, late of Saint John - *SJG*, 16 Apr 1804.

Drowned 10 June 1804, "in attempting to pass through Falls": David **LAWSON**, 26, blacksmith. He was a native of Fifeshire, Scotland, and resided in the Parish of Kingston, Kings County, New Brunswick - *SJG*, 18 June 1804.

Died in Dec 1804 at Fredericton: David **KENNEDY**, carpenter, native of Ayrshire, Scotland
- *NBRG*, 5 Dec 1804.

Died 17 Mar 1805 at Truro, NS: Rev. Daniel **COCK**, 87, senior pastor of the Truro Presbyterian Church, where he had served since 1772. [He was a native of Clydesdale, Scotland.] - *NSRG*, 28 Mar 1805.

NOTICE: SEEKING ROBERT **STEWART**, PRIVATE, 42ND REGT., DISCHARGED AT THE PEACE IN 1783. BORN IN GLENBUCKY, PERTHSHIRE, SCOTLAND, ELDEST SON OF DAVID AND ELIZABETH STEWART. CAME ABROAD WITH 42ND REGT. DURING AMERICAN WAR. SUPPOSED TO HAVE SETTLED IN NEW BRUNSWICK OR NOVA SCOTIA - *SJG*, 22 Dec 1806.

Died 4 Aug 1807 at Greenwich St., New York: David **WILLIAMSON**, native of North Britain
- *SJG*, 24 Aug 1807.

Died 2 Oct 1807 at Saint John: David **BEVRIDGE**, 56, native of Edinburgh, North Britain
- *SJG*, 5 Oct 1807.

WRECK OF SHIP *HIBERNIA* OF LEITH, SCOTLAND, BOUND FROM SAINT JOHN TO LIVERPOOL, 19 JAN 1810. PERISHED: JAMES **HARDY**, CAPT.; ALEXANDER **DOLLAS**, MATE; JOHN **WILKEY** AND JAMES **ELPS**, SEAMEN; WILLIAM **BROWN** AND PATRICK **HAVEN**, BOYS. SURVIVORS: HENRY **LUNDY**, BOATSWAIN; HENRY **McKENZIE**, JAMES **LYNDER** AND RICHARD **ROBERTS** - *NBRG*, 26 Feb 1810.

Died 28 Apr 1810 at Pictou, NS: Hector **MacLEAN**, Esq., 40, native of Kingerloch [Kingairloch, Parish of Lismore, Argyllshire], Scotland, leaving a widow and four children - *WC*, 4 May 1810.

Died in 1810 in Scotland: John **SANGSTER**, merchant, formerly of Saint John
- *NBRG*, 24 Sep 1810.

Died 23 Sep 1810 at Glasgow, Scotland: David, 16, son of Dr. David **BROWN** of Saint John
- *NBRG*, 4 Feb 1811.

Died 12 May 1812 at Maitland, NS: Rev. Alexander **DICK**[11] - *WC*, 5 June 1812.

Died 24 Dec 1812 at Saint John: Capt. Alexander **McDONALD**, 46, of Wigtown, Gal[lo]way, Scotland - *NBRG*, 28 Dec 1812.

Died 9 Mar 1814 at Cartfide, Greenock, Scotland: Colin **CAMPBELL**, Esq., 66, late Surveyor and Searcher of H.M. Customs of Saint John, NB - *CG*, 1 Aug 1814.

Died 22 May 1814, drowned at the mouth of the Columbia River: Donald **McTAVISH**, Esq.[12], a partner in the North West Company, and native of Strasberrick [Strath Errick], Scotland - *NSRG*, 20 Dec 1815. [Note how long it took news to travel east from the Pacific coast.]

Married 29 Oct 1814 by Rev. James Robson, Halifax: Edward **SMITH**, master in HM schooner *Pictou*, and Margaret **MILLNE**, both from Aberdeen, Scotland - *NSRG*, 2 Nov 1814.

---

[11] Native of Bridge of Earn, Dunbarny Parish, Perthshire - A. E. Betts, *Our Fathers in Faith*, p.31.

[12] **McTAVISH** was 42 when he drowned. His career was written up by Jean Morrison in the *Dictionary of Canadian Biography*, V, pp. 559-560.

Married 4 Feb 1815 by Rev. James Robson, Halifax: Capt. Andrew **TROOP**, Port Glasgow, Scotland, and Elizabeth **McKERLEY**, Halifax - *AR*, 11 Feb 1815.

Died 26 Apr 1815 at Sheet Harbour, NS: James **SUTHERLAND**, Esq., 78, a native of Caithness-shire, Scotland; joined the Army in 1758 - *WC*, 12 May 1815.

Died 13 June 1815 at New York: Helen, native of Aberdeen, Scotland, wife of George **IRONSIDE** - *WC*, 30 June 1815.

Died 14 Oct 1815 at Halifax: John Fergus **ORRICK**, 37, native of Scotland - *AR*, 28 Oct 1815.

Died 2 Jan 1816 at Halifax: Thomas **DONALDSON**, 59, native of Scotland, leaving a widow[13] and children. He had lived 20 years at Halifax - *AR*, 6 Jan 1816.

Married 18 Jan 1816 at Liverpool, NS: Neil **LEVINGSTON**, Scotland, and Martha, dau of Isaac **DEAN** of Liverpool, NS - *HJ*, 29 Jan 1816.

Died 19 Mar 1816 at East River, Pictou, NS: Jannet, 75, native of Scotland, wife of William **McKAY**, Esq., leaving six children, 50 grandchildren and three great-grandchildren. She had lived at Pictou for 43 years - *AR*, 23 Mar 1816.

Died 18 Apr 1816 at Halifax: Capt. **RITCHIE**, native of Scotland - *HJ*, 22 Apr 1816.

Died 5 May 1816 at Halifax: Peter **SMITH**, native of Galloway, Scotland[14], and for about 30 years a merchant at Halifax - *AR*, 11 May 1816.

Married "lately" at Glasgow, Scotland: James **EWING**, Esq., late of Halifax, and Miss **MIRRILEES** of Glasgow - *AR*, 31 Aug 1816.

Died 27 Aug 1816 at Halifax: Genet, wife of Thomas **HENCHER**, late from Scotland - *NSRG*, 28 Aug 1816.

Died 21 Sep 1816 on *Protector*: James **FULTON**, native of Paisley, Scotland - *RG*, 16 Oct 1816.

Died 25 Sep 1816 at Annapolis Royal, NS: William **GIRDWOOD**, native of Edinburgh, Scotland, and lately of Demerara - *WC*, 11 Oct 1816.

Died 31 Dec 1816 at Dartmouth, NS: James **MUNN**, carpenter, 65[15] - *AR*, 4 Jan 1817.

Married in January 1817 at Pictou: William **McKAY**, Esq., 86, and Miss **FRASER**, 25. "Fifty-two of his grandchildren were invited to the wedding" [He was born in Scotland] - *AR*, 8 Feb 1817.

Died 18 Mar 1817 at Musquash, NB: James **BLACK**, 32, carpenter, native of Rothsay, Isle of Bute, Scotland - *NBC*, 26 Apr 1817.

---

[13] Jane, 45, widow of Thomas **DONALDSON**, died 30 June 1820 at Birch Cove, near Halifax - *HJ*, 3 July 1820.

[14] The will of Peter "**SMYTHE**", merchant, dated 6 Feb 1816 and proved 9 May 1816 (Halifax Will Book III, *folio* 507) includes a bequest of £100 to his native Parish of Penningham [Wigtownshire], and mentions a half-brother, James **SMITH** of Wigtown, Scotland.

[15] **MUNN** was a native of Ayrshire, Scotland, and had lived in Nova Scotia since at least 1784.

Died 11 May 1817 at Halifax: Alexander **WILLIAMS**, 22, native of Aberdeen, Scotland
- *AR*, 17 May 1817.

Died 1 Aug 1817 at Liverpool, NS: James **EASTOR**, 24, native of Scotland - *AR*, 16 Aug 1817.

Died 31 Aug 1817 at the house of Isaac **SHAW**, Bedford Basin, NS: James **FERGUSON**, Jr.,
27, native of Aberdeen, Scotland - *AR*, 6 Sep 1817.

Died 22 Oct 1817 at Saint John: George **RIDPATH**, 37, native of Mid-Lothian, Scotland
- *NBC*, 25 Oct 1817.

Died 1 Dec 1817 at Aylesford, NS: Archibald **TURNER**, 40, native of Greenock, Scotland
- *AR*, 13 Dec 1817.

Married 28 Jan 1818 by Rev. Dr. John Inglis, Halifax: George **BATCHELOR** from Scotland and
Mary Ann, eldest dau of George **RAY**, King's Pilot at Halifax - *AR*, 31 Jan 1818.

Married 17 June 1818 by Dr. Gray, Halifax: Francis **DOBSON**, Selkirk, Scotland, and Euphemia
TURNBULL from near Selkirk - *AR*, 27 June 1818.

Married 26 June 1818 by Rev. Dr. Gray, Halifax: Capt. W[illiam] **THOMSON** and Susan
THOMSON, both from Dumfries, Scotland - *FP*, 30 June 1818.

Died 31 July 1818 at Saint John: Capt. Thomas **HUNTER**, 50, formerly of the Transport Service,
a native of Scotland - *CG*, 5 Aug 1818.

Married 21 Aug 1818 at Greenock, Scotland: John **ARCHIBALD** of the brig *Freetown* of Halifax
and Isabella **McCALL**, Greenock - *AR*, 14 Nov 1818.

Inquest 22 Sep 1818 at Saint John, on the body of John **FERGUSON**, mechanic, native of
Scotland, resident of Queens County, NB, the last 18 months. He left a wife and five
children. Accidental death - *CG*, 23 Sep 1818.

Married 8 Dec 1818 by Edward Mortimer, Esq., at Pictou, NS: James **DAWSON**, merchant, and
Mary, dau of the late William **RANKINE**, Esq., of Lone Ridge, Stirlingshire, Scotland
- *FP*, 22 Dec 1818.

Died 7 Jan 1819 at Halifax: William **SMITH**, [24], native of Banffshire, Scotland - *AR*, 9 Jan 1819.

Died 13 Jan 1819 at Halifax: Alexander **GODSMAN**, 66, native of Banffshire, Scotland
- *AR*, 16 Jan 1819.

Died 5 Feb 1819 in Cumberland County, NS, at the house of Nicholas **SIMMONS**: Robert **MARTIN**,
a pedlar from Ayrshire, Scotland - *HJ*, 15 Feb 1819.

Died 4 Mar 1819 at Halifax: Miss Anne **CUMING**[16], 85, "descended from a Scots family that
came here by way of the United States" - *AR*, 6 Mar 1819.

---

[16] Her headstone in the Old Burial Ground, Halifax, says that she was a daughter of Robert and
Elizabeth **CUMING** of Concord, MA.

Died 12 Mar 1819 at Saint John: Hon. William **PAGAN**, [75], native of Glasgow, Scotland. He was a merchant in New York and came with the Loyalists in 1783 to Saint John. He was the Member of the Legislature for Saint John[17] - *CG*, 24 Mar 1819.

Died 24 Mar 1819 at Edinburgh, Scotland: Margaret[18], dau of George **RENNY**, Esq., Falkirk, [Stirlingshire], Scotland - *AR*, 22 May 1819.

Died 14 Apr 1819 at Saint John: George, 19, son of the late James **McPHERSON**, Edinburgh, Scotland - *CG*, 21 Apr 1819.

Died 17 Apr 1819 at Kingston, Jamaica: Capt. Robert **KELLY** of the sloop *Betsey* of Halifax, 33, native of Scotland - *AR*, 26 June 1819.

Died 17 May 1819 at Antigonish, NS: Rev. James **MUNRO**, 79, minister of the Church of Scotland for 50 years. He wrote a treatise on Baptism. [He was born in Scotland] - *AR*, 29 May 1819.

Married 18 July 1819 by Rev. Dr. George Burns, Saint John: George **ROBSON**, late of the Royal American Artillery, and Isabella **STEWART** from Perthshire, Scotland - *NBC*, 24 July 1819.

Married 23 July 1819 by Rev. Dr. George Burns, Saint John: John **CARSON** and Isabella **PROUDFOOT**, both from Dumfries-shire, Scotland - *NBC*, 24 July 1819.

Married 27 July 1819 at Bowieshall, Stirlingshire, Scotland, by Rev. Patrick McFarlane: George **COATS**, merchant of Saint John, and Elizabeth, youngest dau of John **ESPLIN** of Bowieshall - *NBC*, 11 Sep 1819.

Died 11 Oct 1819 at Bécancour, near Three Rivers, Québec: John **CAMPBELL**, Esq., native of Argyllshire, Scotland, and former Lt-Col., 78th Regt. - *WC*, 26 Nov 1819.

Died 16 Oct 1819 at Port of Spain, Trinidad: Peter James **ROBERTSON**, Esq., captain on half pay from the 27th (Enniskillen) Regt. He had been a planter in Nova Scotia but at 16 returned to Scotland and enlisted in the Army. He was a younger brother of Hugh Robertson, Esq., of Caparo - *AR*, 18 Dec 1819.

Died 18 Oct 1819 near Fredericton: John **SMALL**, 87, native of Kilbride, near Glasgow, Scotland. He came to America in 1757 as a soldier in the 77th (Montgomery's) Regt., and was with General **WOLFE** in the Battle of the Plains of Abraham at Québec - *CG*, 3 Nov 1819.

---

[17] William **PAGAN**'s career is written up by David Macmillan and Roger Nason in the *Dictionary of Canadian Biography*, V, pp. 645-647. Pagan was unmarried and was the eldest son of William and Margaret (**MAXWELL**) Pagan.

[18] Margaret was a sister of Agnes **RENNY** who married John **YOUNG** (1773-1837), who settled in Nova Scotia in 1815 and was a member of the House of Assembly from 1824 until his death. He was nicknamed *Agricola* due to his *Letters of Agricola* (Halifax, 1822), advocating applying scientific methods to agriculture. A son, Sir William Young (1799 - 1887), was twice Premier of Nova Scotia. Another son, George Renny Young (1802-1853), was also a member of the Assembly, and in 1824 founded the *Novascotian* newspaper.

Married 26 Oct 1819 by Rev. Dr. George Burns, Saint John: John **McDOUGAL** from Argyllshire, Scotland, and Mary, widow of John **MASON**, Saint John - *CG*, 3 Nov 1819.

Married 8 Dec 1819 at Kingsclear, NB: Robert **JARDINE**[19], [Applegarth], Dumfries-shire, Scotland, and Gloranah, eldest dau of Benjamin **REED** - *NBRG*, 14 Dec 1819.

Died 13 Jan 1820 at Québec: Hon. William, 36, eldest son of William **SCOTT**, Esq., of Wooler, Roxburghshire, Scotland - *AR*, 19 Feb 1820.

Died 16 Jan 1820 at Halifax: John **SIMPSON**, 51, son of the late Rev. James Simpson, minister of the Parish of Eastwood, Renfrewshire[20], North Britain - *AR*, 22 Jan 1820,

Died 20 Feb 1820 at Pictou, NS: Capt. William **LOWDEN**, native of Dumfries, Scotland. He came to Nova Scotia 30 years before - *AR*, 18 Mar 1820.

Died 26 Feb 1820 at Pictou, NS: Elizabeth **MILLAGAN**, 73, native of the Stewartry of Kirkcudbright, Scotland - *AR*, 11 Mar 1820.

Died 25 Mar 1820 at Saint John: Elizabeth, widow of Arthur **DINGWALL** of Renneston, Aberdeenshire, Scotland, late merchant at Saint John[21] - *CG*, 29 Mar 1820.

Died 7 Apr 1820 at Haywood Hill, NS: Mark **LUMSDEN**, 67, native of Scotland - *AR*, 8 Apr 1820. [*HJ*, 10 Apr 1820, gives his name as Mark **LUNN**.]

Died 4 May 1820 at Halifax: John **BLACK**, 25, native of Glasgow - *AR*, 6 May 1820.

Inquest 13 May 1820 at Saint John, on the body of William **McALPINE**, 40, native of Irvine, [Ayrshire], Scotland, cook of the ship *Protector* of Saint John. Fell off the wharf while boarding ship and drowned - *CG*, 17 May 1820.

Married 14 May 1820 by Rev. Dr. George Burns, Saint John: David **MATHER** and Margaret **EASTON** of Forfar, Angus, Scotland - *CG*, 17 May 1820.

Married in November 1820 by Rev. Dripps at Shelburne, NS: William **LOUDETT**, Esq., native of Scotland, and Elizabeth, 2nd dau of late Capt. **McLEAN**, Shelburne - *AR*, 25 Nov 1820.

Died 10 Nov 1820 at Falkirk, Scotland: Mrs. William **YOUNG**[22], 79 - *AR*, 17 Mar 1821.

---

[19] Robert **JARDINE** died 10 Feb 1875 at Indiantown, Northumberland County, NB, age 76, leaving a widow, seven sons and three daughters - *Union Advocate*, 24 Feb 1875.

[20] The Parish of Eastwood is in Berwickshire, not Renfrewshire.

[21] Arthur **DINGWALL**, merchant, was drowned on 21 Dec 1814 in the shipwreck of the brig *Star*, en route from Saint John to Liverpool, England - *CG*, 9 May 1815.

[22] Mrs. **YOUNG** was the mother of John Young, who married George **RENNY**'s daughter.

Died 14 Nov 1820 at Port Glasgow, Scotland: George **RENNY**, Esq., late of Berkhill, Stirlingshire, Scotland - *AR*, 17 Nov 1820. [See note under Margaret Renny, 24 Mar 1819.]

Drowned 17 Nov 1820 "while passing through Falls": David **PRINGLE**, 23, shipwright from Dunbar, Scotland. Came to Saint John a few weeks ago. John **OWEN** was saved - *CG*, 22 Nov 1820.

Died 23 Dec 1820 at Halifax: Hugh **McLENNAN**, 44, native of Inverness, Scotland - *AR*, 23 Dec 1820.

Married 28 Dec 1820 at Saunders' Island, York County, NB: Thomas **FRASER** and Susannah **THOMSON**, "both late emigrants from North Britain" - *NBRG*, 9 Jan 1821.

Died 8 Jan 1821 at Lunenburg, NS, at the home of her brother-in-law, Rev. Roger **AITKIN**: Miss [Margaret], 72, eldest dau of the late Charles **CHEYNE**, Esq., merchant in Edinburgh, Scotland, and niece of Dr. George Cheyne of Esalmont, Aberdeenshire - *AR*, 20 Jan 1821.

Died 6 Feb 1821 at Carlton Village near Shelburne, NS: Gilbert **McKINNEE**, 69, Loyalist in 1783, native of Galloway, Scotland. He was a son of William McKinnee who was lost from the vessel *Countess Dalhousie* - *AR*, 24 Feb 1821.

Died 13 Mar 1821 at Halifax: Mrs. Jessey **GOODBRAND**, native of Aberdeen, Scotland, leaving two infant children - *FP*, 15 Mar 1821.

Drowned, 2 Apr 1821, at Saint John: Robert **NICOL**, mate of the brig *Victory*, a native of Scotland - *CG*, 4 Apr 1821.

Drowned, 9 Apr 1821, at Saint John: Finlay **McKENZIE**, 25, carpenter of ship *James*, native of Scotland. "It is said he has a mother living at Bay Chaleur" - *CG*, 11 Apr 1821.

Died 12 Apr 1821 at Spryfield, NS: George **McINTOSH**, Esq., 71, native of Scotland - *AR*, 13 Apr 1821.

Died 1 May 1821 at Saint John: John **MILLIGAN**, 47, architect from Dumfries, Scotland. He arrived here "last Autumn", and left a widow and four children, and an aged mother-in-law - *CG*, 2 May 1821.

Died 3 June 1821 at Halifax: John **McPHEE**, 79, cooper, native of Scotland - *HJ*, 11 June 1821.

Married 8 June 1821 by Rev. Robert Willis, Saint John: John **BROWN**, master of ship *Dunlop* of Greenock, Scotland, and Elizabeth, 3rd dau of Jahiel **PARTELOW**, Jr., Saint John - *NBC*, 9 June 1821.

Died 6 July 1821 at St. Margarets Bay, NS: John **UMLACH**, Sr., 89, native of Scotland - *AR*, 14 July 1821.

Died 26 Sep 1821 at Baltimore, MD: Christopher **KINNEAR**, 27, native of Dysert, Fifeshire, Scotland, and formerly of Halifax, NS - *FP*, 13 Nov 1821.

Died at Three Rivers, Québec [no date]: Allan **McDONELL**, Esq., 99, native of Glengarry, Inverness-shire, Scotland - *HJ*, 26 Nov 1821.

Died 23 Nov 1821 at St. Andrews, NB: Robert **PAGAN**, Esq., 71, native of Glasgow, Scotland, came to New Brunswick as a Loyalist from Penobscot in 1783, and was a member of the first House of Assembly in the province[23] - *CG*, 28 Nov 1821.

Died 21 Dec 1821 in the brig *Freetown*, three days out from Kingston, Jamaica, outbound: William **BROWN**, carpenter, from Stromness, Orkney Islands - *AR*, 9 Feb 1822.

Died 10 Jan 1822 at Edinburgh, Scotland: Andrew **SMITH**, Esq., late of Bridgetown, Barbados - *AR*, 27 Apr 1822.

Married 7 Mar 1822 by Rev. Dr. Burns, Saint John: William Walker **EMSLIE** from Aberdeenshire, Scotland, and Harriet Ann, dau of late William **KENNEDY**, Saint John - *CG*, 13 Mar 1822.

Married 11 Apr 1822 by Rev. John Sprott, Newport, NS: James **SPROTT**, Wigtownshire, Scotland, and Lemoira, youngest dau of Archibald **SMITH**, Kennetcook, NS - *AR*, 27 Apr 1822.

Died 14 Apr 1822 at Halifax: James **MONRO**, 38, native of Scotland - *FP*, 16 Apr 1822.

Married 22 June 1822 by Rev. Samuel Bacon, Chatham Head, Miramichi, NB: Alexander **FRASER**, Jr., merchant, and Katherine **FRASER** of Edinburgh, Scotland - *CG*, 18 July 1822.

Died 18 July 1822 at Truro, NS, from a fall from his horse "on the day he was to marry": James **BEATIE**, 23, a native of Dumfries-shire, Scotland. "He came to New Brunswick in 1820 and later joined his father at Truro" - *AR*, 27 July 1822.

Died 15 Sep 1822 at Shelburne, NS: James **LESLIE**, 74, native of Dunkeld, [Perthshire], Scotland - *AR*, 28 Sep 1822.

Died 29 Oct 1822 at Shubenacadie, NS: James **MILNE**, native of Scotland - *FP*, 7 Jan 1823.

Married 2 Nov 1822 by Bishop William Fraser at East River, Pictou, NS: Hugh **McLENNAN** of Antigonish, NS, and Isabella, only dau of Alexander **GRANT**, lately from Scotland - *AR*, 14 Dec 1822.

Died 25 Nov 1822 at Kingsclear, NB: James **BURRESS**, 115 [sic], native of Scotland. "We are informed in the Chevalier Prince Charles army at the Battle of Culloden in the year '45" - *CG*, 5 Dec 1822.

Died 2 Dec 1822 at Halifax: James **FRASER**, 77, native of Perthshire, Scotland - *FP*, 10 Dec 1822.

Died 25 Jan 1823 at Halifax: Thomas, 24, native of Scotland, eldest son of James **MOFFAT** - *AR*, 1 Feb 1823.

---

[23] Robert **PAGAN**'s career is written up by David Macmillan and Roger Nason in the *Dictionary of Canadian Biography*, VI, pp. 561-563. Pagan was born, 16 Nov 1750, the third son of William and Margaret (**MAXWELL**) Pagan. He married Mariam **POTE** (d. 11 Jan 1828, age 81), but had no children.

Died 10 Feb 1823 at Saint John: William **CAMPBELL**, Esq. 82, native of Argyllshire, Scotland, and a former mayor of Saint John for 20 years. He emigrated to [Worcester], Massachusetts, but after the evacuation [March 1776] he came with other Loyalists to Halifax, and removed to Saint John in 1786 - *CG*, 13 Feb 1823.

Died 6 Mar 1823 at Bridgetown, Barbados: Capt. Robert **IRVINE**, native of Scotland and late ship master of Saint John, NB, and a half pay officer from the Royal Navy - *CG*, 8 May 1823.

Died 15 Mar 1823 at Saint John: Peter, 21, only son of late Peter **DAVIDSON** of Aberdeen. He fell from the foreyard of the ship *Waterloo* - *CG*, 20 Mar 1823.

Died 10 Apr 1823 at Halifax: Alexander **DUNCAN**, 52, native of Scotland - *AR*, 12 Apr 1823.

Died 6 July 1823 at Saint John: Charles **McPHERSON**, 70, [grocer], native of Perthshire, Scotland. Left there 50 years ago, and sailed from England in a man-of-war for America, and settled at Kingsbridge, New York, in 1776. Came as a Loyalist to New Brunswick in 1783. He left a widow [Catherine **McLEOD**] and large family - *CG*, 10 July 1823.

Died 7 July 1823 at Nipisighit, Bay Chaleur, NB: Alexander, 21, native of Scotland, and brother of John **MILLER** of Nipisighit - *HJ*, 28 July 1823.

Inquest 16 July 1823 at Maugerville, NB, on the body of Alexander **SMITH**, joiner from Edinburgh, Scotland. He was drowned - *NBC*, 26 July 1823.

Died 22 July 1823 at Port Medway, NS: John **McVICAR**, 63, native of Scotland - *AR*, 23 Aug 1823.

Died 4 Sep 1823 at Summer-Hill, Aberdeenshire, Scotland: Hon. James **BLACK**, 60, Member of H. M. Council for Nova Scotia - *CG*, 23 Oct 1823.

Married 20 Sep 1823 by George Smith, Esq., at Pictou, NS: Adam **GORDON**, native of Aberdeen, and Agnes, eldest dau of J. **CARR**, late of Dumfries, Scotland - *HJ*, 22 Sep 1823.

Died in October 1823 at Stranraer, [Wigtownshire], Scotland: James **SPROTT**, father of [Rev] John and James Sprott of Nova Scotia - *AR*, 7 Feb 1824.

Died 12 Dec 1823 at Saint John: Andrew **WALKER**, 51, of Roxburghshire, Scotland, leaving an only daughter - *CG*, 18 Dec 1823.

Married 27 Jan 1824 by Rev. John Thomas Twining, [Anglican] Halifax: Alexander **GARDEN** and Henrietta **COUTTS**, both of Aberdeen, Scotland - *HJ*, 2 Feb 1824.

Died 28 Jan 1824 at Halifax: Alexander **ANDERSON**[24], 30, from Rotherson Spy, Scotland, leaving a widow and child - *AR*, 7 Feb 1824.

Died 7 Feb 1824 at Turnult, Scotland: Lt. Archibald **CAMPBELL**, 33, 59th Regt., native of St. Andrews, NB - *CG*, 6 May 1824.

---

[24] Alexander **ANDERSON** married 10 Nov 1818 at St. Matthew's Presbyterian Church, Halifax, Isabella **McLEAN** and had a daughter Agnes baptised at St. Matthew's on 25 Sep 1819.

Died 18 Feb 1824 at Gardner's Creek, NB: Agnes [**LITTLE**], 51, formerly of Dumfries-shire, Scotland, wife of Andrew **CUNNINGHAM** [from Dysart, Fifeshire] - *NBC*, 28 Feb 1824.

Died 1 Mar 1824 between Granville and Annapolis, NS: James M. **ERSKINE**, [41], native of Scotland, leaving a widow and three children - *AR*, 8 May 1824.

Died 26 Mar 1824 at Saint John: Daniel **McKAY**, 57, native of Scotland; served over 24 years with the Royal Military Artificers - *CG*, 1 Apr 1824.

Died 21 Apr 1824 at Nerepis, NB: Jane, 54, wife of Alexander **MATHER**, "natives of Meanshire [?], Scotland"[25]. She left a husband and family - *CG*, 29 Apr 1824.

Died 27 Apr 1824 at Truro, NS: William **ROSS**, native of Scotland - *AR*, 8 May 1824.

Died early 1824 at Annan, Dumfries-shire, Scotland: Sarah Elizabeth, wife of W. **JOHNSON**, Esq., Attorney-General of Prince Edward Island - *AR*, 1 May 1824.

Died 5 June 1824 at Bogton, Cathcart Parish, Glasgow, Scotland: Miss **PAGAN** of Bogton, 66, sister of late Hon. William Pagan of Saint John, NB - *CG*, 9 Sep 1824.

Died 21 June 1824 at L'Etang [Charlotte County], NB: Capt. Joseph **KIRK**, late of the ship *Nancy* of Dumfries, Scotland - *NBC*, 3 July 1824.

Died 26 Oct 1824 at Queensbury, NB: Alexander **ROSS**, 93, native of Scotland. He was at the Battle of Minden in the 20th Regt. of Foot, on 1 Aug 1759. He left a wife and five children - *NBRG*, 2 Nov 1824.

Married 30 Oct 1824 by Rev. John Martin, Halifax: James **THOMPSON** and Christian **SUTHERLAND**, both of Sutherlandshire, Scotland - *AR*, 6 Nov 1824.

Died 23 Nov 1824 at St. Mary's Parish, Nashwaak, NB: Francis **McDONALD**, 110, born in Halkirk Parish, Caithness-shire, Dec 1714 - *NBRG*, 30 Nov 1824; *AR*, 18 Dec 1824.

Died 26 Nov 1824 at Halifax: James **SINCLAIR**, 39, Quartermaster Sgt., 74th Regt., from Edinburgh, Scotland - *HJ*, 29 Nov 1824.

Died 1 Dec 1824, when he drowned crossing the river at Maugerville: George **BAINE**, 29, printer, native of Dumbarton, Scotland - *NBRG*, 7 Dec 1824.

Died 6 Dec 1824 at Saint John: Donald **CAMPBELL**, 40, native of Scotland - *NBC*, 11 Dec 1824.

Died 7 Dec 1824 at Halifax: John **DENNISON**, 43, native of Scotland - *NSRG*, 8 Dec 1824.

Died 18 Jan 1825 at East River, Pictou, NS: Margaret, 94, widow of John **ROBERTSON** of "Ballinlon", [Scotland] - *AR*, 5 Feb 1825.

---

[25] Probably Mearnshire, or The Mearns = Kincardineshire.

Died 23 Jan 1825 at Saint John: Peter **STEWART**, 32, steamboat engineer, native of Stirlingshire, Scotland - *NBC*, 29 Jan 1825.

Died 5 Mar 1825 at Saint John: Robert **MEEK**, 39, native of East Lothian, Scotland. He left a widow and six children - *NBC*, 5 Mar 1825.

Married 9 Mar 1825 by Rev. Dr. George Burns, Saint John: Alexander **MUIR** and Ann **BONE**, both natives of Ayrshire, Scotland - *NBC*, 12 Mar 1825.

Died 12 Mar 1825 at Saint John: William **HAMILTON**, baker, 40, native of Lanarkshire, Scotland - *NBC*, 19 Mar 1825. [He left a widow, Agnes.]

Died [5 Apr] 1825 at Edinburgh, Scotland while on his way to his birthplace, Aberdeen: Alexander **EDMOND**, merchant at Saint John - *NBC*, 21 May 1825.

Married 26 Apr 1825 by Rev. Martin, Halifax: James **FINLEY** and Elspeth **SHEARER**, both just arrived from Rothes, [Banffshire], Scotland - *AR*, 30 Apr 1825.

Died 5 May 1825, when he drowned after falling off Peter's Wharf, Saint John: William **LOCKHART**, a cooper, native of Scotland, leaving a wife and child - *NBC*, 7 May 1825.

Died 18 May 1825 at Morristown, Antigonish County, NS: John **BOYD**, 95, from the Highlands of Scotland, "emigrated here when 71" - *HJ*, 27 June 1825.

Married 5 June 1825 by Rev. John Thomas Twining, Halifax: James **ROSS** and Christiana Charlotte, 3rd dau of the late John **SMITH**, Esq., Aberdeen, Scotland - *AR*, 11 June 1825.

Died 23 July 1825 at Saint John: John **THOMSON**, Esq., 70, merchant, native of Stirlingshire, Scotland, leaving a widow [Mary]. He emigrated to New York "early in life", and came to NB as a Loyalist in 1782 [*sic*]. He was chamberlain of Saint John for 18 years, and an elder of the Scots Church of St. Andrew in Saint John - *CG*, 26 July 1825.

Died 12 Sep 1825 at Halifax: John **BROWN** from Glasgow, Scotland - *AR*, 17 Sep 1825.

Died 17 Sep 1825 at Saint John: John **ALLAN**, [apothecary], 39, native of Aberdeen, Scotland, leaving a widow [Maria Ann] and three children - *NBC*, 24 Sep 1825.

Married 30 Sep 1825 at Lancaster, NB: William **CLARKE** and Mary, dau of James **THOMSON** from Argyllshire, Scotland - *NBC*, 1 Oct 1825.

Married 31 Oct 1825 by Rev. John Martin, Halifax: John **STIRLING**, Halifax, and Nancy[26] **ROSE**, from Caithness, Scotland - *AR*, 5 Nov 1825.

---

[26] The register at St. Andrew's Presbyterian Church calls the bride Frances **ROSE**.

Married 6 Nov 1825 by Rev. John Carroll, Halifax: John **BURNES**, Scotland, and Charlotte, youngest dau of late Nathaniel **HATFIELD**[27] - *AR*, 12 Nov 1825.

Married 14 Nov 1825 by Rev. B. G. Gray, Saint John: John **JAMIESON** of Kilmarnock, Scotland, and Eleanor Agnes, 4th dau of the late John **COOK** of Halifax, NS[28] - *NBC*, 19 Nov 1825.

Died 17 Nov 1825 at Preston, NS: Alexander **McNEIL**, 83 [native of Scotland] - *AR*, 19 Nov 1825.

Died 23 Nov 1825 in Lanarkshire, Scotland: Mrs. Janet **THOMSON**, mother of Rev. J[ohn] **MARTIN**, Halifax - *AR*, 11 Feb 1826.

Died 23 Dec 1825 in Scotland: Mrs. **HANNAH**, youngest sister of Rev. J[ohn] **SPROTT**, Musquodoboit, NS - *AR*, 25 Mar 1826.

Married 28 Dec 1825 by Rev. Donald Allen Fraser, Pictou, NS: Rev. Kenneth John **McKENZIE** and Catharine McFarlane, youngest dau of late Hector **MacLEAN**, Esq., Kingairloch, Scotland - *AR*, 7 Jan 1826. [See Hector's obituary on page 20.]

Died in April 1826 at Annapolis, NS: James **STEVENSON**, 49, native of Aberdeenshire, Scotland - *AR*, 8 April 1826.

Married 1 Apr 1826 by Rev. James Somerville at Kingsclear, NB: Joseph **MURRAY** and Agness, eldest dau of John **CAMPBELL** of Scotland - *NBRG*, 4 Apr 1826.

Died 12 June 1826 at Halifax: Agnes, 70, native of Kirkcudbright, Scotland, widow of James **CLARK** - *AR*, 17 June 1826.

Died 10 Aug 1826 at St. David, NB: John **McDOUGALL**, 80, a former member of the 74th (Argyllshire) Highlanders[29] - *AR*, 9 Sep 1826.

Married 14 Aug 1826 in Edinburgh, Scotland: Rev. John **SPROTT** and Mrs. **McCLEARY**, 3rd dau of Mr. **NEILSON**, Kirkowen[30] - *AR*, 14 Oct 1826.

Died 16 Sep 1826 at Halifax: Rev. Archibald **GRAY**, DD, 62, [native of Forres, Morayshire, Scotland] - *AR*, 16 Sep 1826.

---

[27] St. Peter's Catholic Church register says that John was the son of David and Christiana (**DAVISON**) **BURNES** of Kirkcaldy, Scotland, and that Charlotte was the dau of Nathan and Mary (**MURPHY**) **HATFIELD** of Dartmouth, NS.

[28] Eleanor Agnes was baptised 23 Apr 1809 at St. Paul's Anglican Church, Halifax, the youngest child of John **COOK**, a sawyer, and his wife Sarah **PYSH**. John **JAMIESON** was a carpenter by trade.

[29] John **McDOUGALL** was born in Scotland and had been a piper in the 74th Regt. He and his wife Mary **McGREGOR** came to New Brunswick as Loyalists. They had been living in Maine.

[30] John **SPROTT** was born at Stoneykirk, Wigtownshire, 3 Feb 1780, and died in Nova Scotia, 15 Sep 1869. His third wife (marriage above) was Jane **NEILSON** of Wigtownshire - *cf.*, A. E. Betts, *Our Fathers in the Faith* (Halifax, 1983), p. 123.

Died 18 Sep 1826 at Halifax: Alexander **BROWN**, native of Greenock, Scotland
- *AR*, 23 Sep 1826.

Died 18 Sep 1826 at Halifax: John **STRANG**, Esq., native of the Orkney Isles - *AR*, 23 Sep 1826.

Died 13 Feb 1827 at Halifax: Thomas **SHAW**, 37, native of Dumbarton, Scotland
- *AR*, 17 Feb 1827.

Died 14 Feb 1827 at Miramichi, NB: Elspet, 81, widow of James **LOW** of Aberdon Seat [Aberdour, Fifeshire?] - *MM*, 20 Feb 1827.

Died 22 Feb 1827 at Saint John: William **JAFFREY**, 38, gardener, from Aberdeen, Scotland, leaving a widow [Hannah] and two children - *CG*, 1 Mar 1827.

Married 27 Feb 1827 by Rev. Benjamin G. Gray, Saint John: John **THOMSON** from Inverary, [Argyllshire], Scotland, and Margaret **CAMPBELL** from Caithness, Scotland - *CG*, 1 Mar 1827.

Married 28 Mar 1827 by Rev. Robert H. Crane, [Methodist] Wallace, NS: Elijah **TUTTLE** and Jane **GILMORE**, late of Scotland - *AR*, 7 Apr 1827.

Died 2 May 1827 at Halifax: James **ISLES**, 75, native of Perthshire, Scotland - *AR*, 5 May 1827.

Died 19 May 1827 at Halifax: John **SCOTT**, native of Aberdeenshire, Scotland - *AR*, 26 May 1827.

Died 20 May 1827 at Halifax: John **PATTERSON**, native of Galloway, Scotland
- *AR*, 26 May 1827.

Died 26 May 1827 at Halifax: John **McALPINE**[31], 78 - *Acadian*, 1 June 1827.

Married 7 June 1827 at Liverpool, Kent County, NB: Capt. Edward H. **FRANK** of the brig *Sarah* of North Shields and Miriam, 3rd dau of John **McDONALD**, Esq., of Cork-Cockle Moor, Dumfries-shire, Scotland - *NBC*, 23 June 1827.

Married 14 June 1827 by Rev. Benjamin Gerrish Gray, Saint John: Robert **McBETH** of Saint John and Ann E. C., 3rd dau of Robert **ALLAN**, Aberdeen, Scotland, master in the Royal Navy
- *CG*, 20 June 1827.

Married 16 July 1827 by Rev. Matthew Dripps, [Presbyterian], Shelburne, NS: John **MATHISON**, from Ross-shire, Scotland, and Mrs. Mary **BARBER** from Ireland - *AR*, 21 July 1827.

---

[31] If ever a brief death notice failed to do justice to its subject, this has to be it. John **McALPINE** was born in the Scottish Highlands, the son of Peter and Christian McAlpine. In 1773 he emigrated to the Lake Champlain area then disputed between New York and New Hampshire. Evicted by the "Green Mountain Boys", McAlpine was then caught up in the American Revolution. After several adventures, McAlpine briefly returned to Scotland where he published his *Genuine narratives and concise memoirs of . . . J. M'Alpine . .* (Greenock, 1780), in which he essentially invoked "a plague on both your houses" upon the British and the Americans. He had a stormy and variegated career in Nova Scotia over the next 45 years. His career is outlined by Terrence M. Punch in the *Dictionary of Canadian Biography*, VI, pp. 411-412.

Died 31 July 1827 at Lancaster, NB: James **ROBSON**, 47, native of Dumfries-shire, Scotland, leaving a wife and six children - *NBC*, 4 Aug 1827.

Died 3 Aug 1827 at Little Harbour, NS: D. **McDONALD**, 60, native of Scotland - *NBC*, 25 Aug 1827.

Married 6 Aug 1827 by Rev. Prof. Buist at St. Andrews, Fifeshire, Scotland: Rev. George **BURNS**, DD, minister of the Scots Church in Saint John, to Esther C. W., only surviving dau of the late Rev. James **STRUTHERS**, Edinburgh, and granddau of Robert **BRIGGS**, Esq., MD, University of St. Andrews - *NBC*, 15 Sep 1827.

Married 20 Aug 1827 at Edinburgh: Archibald Glen **KIDSTON**, Esq., and Janet Lindsay, dau of John **PEARSON**, Esq. - *AR*, 29 Sep 1827.

Died 4 Sep 1827 at Saint John: Archibald **WILLIAMSON**, 45, native of Cambleton [Campbeltown], Argyllshire, Scotland - *CG*, 5 Sep 1827. [He left a widow, Lucy.]

Died 17 Oct 1827 at Halifax: John **McKINLEA**, 55, native of Scotland[32] - *AR*, 20 Oct 1827.

Married in Nov 1827 by James Blackall at Caraquet, NB: William **GRAY**, Bathurst, NB, and Margaret **McDONALD** of Aberdon [Aberdeen, Scotland] - *MM*, 20 Nov 1827.

Died 16 Nov 1827 at Kingston, Jamaica: Alexander **McDOUGAL**, native of Dumbarton, Scotland, and mate in the brigantine *Elizabeth* of Halifax - *AR*, 21 Jan 1828.

Married in Nov 1827 by Rev. Dr. Somerville: John **ADAMSON**, MD, Halifax, and Ann Brady, eldest dau of John **MASON**, Esq., Claremont, York County, NB, native of the Highlands of Scotland - *NBC*, 1 Dec 1827.

Died 28 Dec 1827 when he drowned after being knocked overboard by one of the sheets [sails] near Partridge Island: Duncan **McGINNIS**, native of Scotland - *NBC*, 29 Dec 1827.

Died 30 Dec 1827 at Pictou, NS: William **RANKINE**, 44, merchant, native of Stirlingshire, Scotland - *AR*, 12 Jan 1828.

Died 2 Jan 1828 at Douglas, NS: Catherine **CHISHOLM**, 98, native of Inverness, Scotland - *AR*, 19 Jan 1828.

Died 9 Jan 1828 at Saint John: David **OGILVIE**, 33, stonecutter, native of Scotland[33] - *NBC*, 12 Jan 1828.

Died 29 Mar 1828 at Hampton, NB: James **SPENCE**, 66, native of Banffshire, Scotland; resident of NB since 1783 - *NBC*, 5 Apr 1828.

---

[32] Christiana, 45, wife of John **M'KINLEY**, died at Halifax 29 Aug 1827 - *AR*, 1 Sep 1827.

[33] The administration papers of his estate mention that his nearest relative was his widowed mother, Elizabeth **ALLAN**, residing at Brechin, Forfar, North Britain,

Died 7 Apr 1828 at Halifax: Alexander **JACKSON**, 69, native of Scotland - *AR*, 12 Apr 1828.

Died 12 May 1828 at Shelburne: Rev. Matthew **DRIPPS**[34], 60 - *AR*, 31 May 1828.

Married 17 May 1828 by Rev. Dr. Robert Willis, Halifax: Alexander **McKAY** of Scotland and Mary Ann, 2nd dau of John **POTTS**, St. Margarets Bay, NS - *AR*, 24 May 1828.

Died 24 July 1828 at Sydney, NS: John **WHYTE**, Esq., 25, surgeon, native of Banff, Scotland - *AR*, 20 Sep 1828.

Died 21 Aug 1828 at St. Andrews, NB: James **TAIT**, 42, native of Glasgow, Scotland - *NBC*, 30 Aug 1828.

Died 4 Oct 1828 at Saint John: John **MILLER**, Sr., 66, late of Stirlingshire, Scotland - *MM*, 7 Oct 1828.

Died on board the brig *Despatch* on passage from Grenada to St. Andrews, NB: Staff Surgeon John **SIMSON**, native of Strathaven, Scotland - *CG*, 12 Nov 1828.

Died 18 Nov 1828 at Saint John: George **MACARA**, 28, native of Perth, Scotland - *NBC*, 22 Nov 1828.

Died 16 Dec 1828 at Port Maria, Jamaica: Capt. Alexander **TAYLOR** of the brig *Harriet* of Saint John, native of North Britain, leaving a widow and two children - *NBRG*, 28 Mar 1829.

Died in Dec 1828 at Poman, near Falkirk, Scotland: Elizabeth, wife of George **COATS**, formerly a merchant in Saint John - *NBC*, 1 Aug 1829.

Married 8 Jan 1829 by Rev. John Loughnan, [Catholic] Halifax: Peter **GRANT** and Isabella **SCOTT**, both of Keith, Scotland[35] - *AR*, 17 Jan 1829.

Died 20 Feb 1829 at Fredericton: Charles **DUFF**, 59, formerly of Perthshire, Scotland[36] - *NBC*, 7 Mar 1829.

---

[34] Matthew **DRIPPS** was born in Clydesdale, Scotland, and was a minister in Nova Scotia from 1797 until his death - *cf.*, A. E. Betts, *Our Fathers in the Faith* (Halifax, 1983), p.33.

[35] St. Peter's Catholic Church register says that Peter **GRANT**, carpenter, was a widower from Banffshire, Scotland, and that Isabella **CROSBY** from the Isle of Coll, Scotland, was the widow of John **SCOTT**. While Keith was partly in Banffshire, the Isle of Coll is in the Hebrides. This is an instance where "one cannot believe all that one reads in the paper." See also note 104 on page 71.

[36] Charles was born 5 June 1770 at the Mains of Kinnaird, Perthshire, a son of Charles and Isobel (**ROBERTSON**) DUFF. He settled in New Brunswick about 1801. His widow died 8 April 1836 (*infra*).

Died 3 Mar 1829 at Lunenburg: Jane, native of Lochaber, [Inverness-shire], Scotland, wife of Dr. John **BOLMAN**[37] - *AR*, 14 Mar 1829.

Died 17 May 1829 at Halifax: James **EDWARDS**, 32, native of Scotland - *AR*, 23 May 1829.

Died 21 May 1829 at Glasgow, Scotland: Capt. Walter **SIMPSON**, late of the brig *Forth* - *NBC*, 1 Aug 1829.

Married 1 June 1829 by Rev. Dr. George Burns, Saint John: Capt. Alexander **ELDER** of the brig *Saint George* of Saint John and Margaret, youngest dau of Thomas **RANKINE**, "all of Perthshire", Scotland - *NBC*, 6 June 1829.

Married 14 July 1829 at Neilsland, Scotland, by Rev. Dr. Meek Hamilton: Rev. Gavin **LANG**[38], minister of the Scottish Church at Shelburne, NS, to Ann Robertson, dau of John **MARSHALL**, Esq. - *NBC*, 24 Oct 1829.

Inquest in Sep 1829 on the body of Alexander **SIMPSON**, late of Saint John, native of Aberdeen, Scotland; came to NB in 1819 - *NBC*, 5 Sep 1829.

Died 5 Sep 1829 at Portland Bridge, NB: George **IRVING**, 60, native of Dumfries-shire, Scotland; for 10 years a butcher at Saint John - *NBC*, 12 Sep 1829.

Married 9 Sep 1829 by Rev. Frederick H. Carrington, St. John's, NL: Kenneth **McLEA** of Greenock, Scotland, agent of Mssrs. James **STEWART** & Co., Greenock and St. John's, and Elizabeth, 2nd dau of John **BRINE**, St. John's, NL - *RGNA*, 15 Sep 1829.

Married 1 Oct 1829 by Rev. John Brown, Londonderry, NS: George **WHITE**, Esq., of Dumfries, Scotland, and Margaret, widow of Capt. **COOK**, Lunenburg, NS - *AR*, 10 Oct 1829.

Married 20 Oct 1829 by Rev. John Martin, Halifax: William **TAYLOR**, Halifax, and Catharine **FERGUSON** from Scotland - *AR*, 24 Oct 1829.

Died in Nov 1829 in Springfield, [Kings County], NB: Duncan **McGREGOR**, 66, native of Perthshire, Scotland, leaving a widow [Janet] and "numerous" family - *NBC*, 28 Nov 1829.

Married 14 Nov 1829 by Rev. Edwin Gilpin, Aylesford, NS: James **CARRUTHERS** of Dumfries, Scotland, and Eliza **HARRIS**, Aylesford - *AR*, 12 Dec 1829.

Died 19 Nov 1829 at Halifax: George **BURGESS**, native of Gallowayshire, Scotland - *AR*, 21 Nov 1829.

---

[37] Johann Daniel **BOLLMAN**, surgeon from Saxony, married 14 Feb 1782 at St. John's Anglican Church, Lunenburg, NS, Johanna, or Jane, widow of Philip A. **KNAUT**. Jane was the eldest dau of Robert and Margaret (**STEWART**) **BREMNER** from Inverness-shire, Scotland.

[38] Gavin Scott **LANG** (ca. 1792 - 1869) was ordained at Paisley, Scotland, 11 May 1829. He served at Shelburne, NS, from 1829 to 1831, then he returned to Scotland. He was grandfather of Cosmo Gordon LANG (1864 - 1945), Archbishop of Canterbury from 1928 to 1942.

Married 24 Nov 1829 by Rev. Dr. George Burns, Saint John: John **GRAY** and Margaret **PURVIS**, both natives of Scotland and residents of Saint John - *NBC*, 28 Nov 1829.

Died 29 Nov 1829 at Saint John: Hugh **JOHNSTON**, Esq., 74, native of Morayshire, Scotland[39] - *NBC*, 5 Dec 1829.

Died 29 Nov 1829 at Halifax: Robert **ANDERSON**, 75, native of Scotland - *AR*, 5 Dec 1829.

Died 15 Dec 1829 at Saint John: John C. **McPHERSON**, 42, native of the Isle of Mull, Scotland - *NBC*, 19 Dec 1829.

Died in January 1830 at Demerara: Alexander **SUTHERLAND**, 33, native of Dornoch, Scotland; formerly of Halifax - *AR*, 20 Mar 1830.

Died 4 Jan 1830 at St. Andrews, NB: Angus **McDONALD**, Sr., 75, native of Glenroy, Lochaber, Inverness-shire, Scotland. He came to New Brunswick in 1805 - *NBRG*, 27 Jan 1830.

Married 29 Jan 1830 in Miramichi, NB, by Rev. Samuel Bacon: Thomas **SMITH**, merchant and tailor, Newcastle, NB, to Elizabeth **CARRUTHERS** of Langholm, Dumfries-shire, Scotland - *GNS*, 2 Feb 1830.

Died [3 Feb] 1830 at Shelburne, NS: Robert **GORDON**, 50, native of Gallowayshire, Scotland - *AR*, 20 Mar 1830.

Died 13 Feb 1830 at Charlottenburg, Upper Canada: Finlay **ROSS**, 90, native of Ross-shire, Scotland; came to New York in 1773, and to Canada in 1783 - *NBRG*, 10 Mar 1830.

Died 18 Feb 1830 at Nashwaak, York County, NB: Capt. Archibald **McLEAN**, half pay officer formerly of the New York Volunteers, native of "Isle of Mann" [Torrans, Isle of Mull], Scotland, leaving a widow [Susan] and [numerous] family - *CG*, 3 Mar 1830.

Died 24 Feb 1830 at Stewiacke, NS: James **CROCKET**, 64, native of Scotland, leaving a widow and four children - *AR*, 13 Mar 1830.

Died 11 Mar 1830 at Saint John: James **ROBERTSON**, Jr., 37, editor of *New Brunswick Courier*, native of Huntly, Aberdeenshire, Scotland, leaving three children [Alexander, Ann and Elizabeth]. He came to NB in 1815 - *CG*, 17 Mar 1830. [He was a widower.]

Married 22 Mar 1830 by Rev. Dr. George Burns, Saint John: Peter **KING** and Christy Ann **McCOLL**, both of Perthshire, Scotland - *NBC*, 27 Mar 1830.

Died in March 1830 at Berbice [in modern Guyana]: Francis **McDONALD**, native of Caithness, Scotland, and formerly of Halifax - *NS*, 3 June 1830.

Drowned 8 May 1830 two crewmen in the ship *Anna*: John **SHANKS**, native of Greenock, Scotland, and John **ROBINSON** - *NBC*, 22 May 1830.

Died 13 May 1830 at Shelburne: J. **MARTIN**, 71, native of Glasgow, Scotland - *NS*, 9 June 1830.

---

[39] Hugh was born 4 Jan 1756, a son of William and Isabel (**HEPBURN**) **JOHNSTON**. His second wife was Margaret **THORBURN**. Hugh had a large family from his two marriages.

Married 27 May 1830 at Glasgow, Scotland: George Johnson **HARDING**, MD, Saint John, NB, and Margaret, dau of Thomas **POLLOCK**, merchant, Glasgow - *NBC*, 31 July 1830.

Married 30 May 1830 at Halifax: James **HUMPHREY**[40] and Jane, youngest dau of late Rev. John **MACARA**, Perthshire, Scotland - *AR*, 3 June 1830.

Married 31 May 1830 by Rev. Dr. Burns, Saint John: Donald **GUNN** and Mary, 5th dau of late Duncan **McGREGOR** from Perthshire, Scotland - *NBC*, 5 June 1830.

Inquest on the body of Archibald **LITTLE** from Dumfries-shire, Scotland, who drowned 2 June 1830 at Wishart's Point, NB - *GNS*, 29 June 1830.

Died 6 June 1830 at Amherst, NS: James **KERR**, Esq., 76, native of Dumfries-shire, Scotland, leaving a widow and "11 or 12" children, and had lost three sons and one daughter. He served as a captain in the Queen's Rangers during the Revolutionary War - *NBRG*, 23 June 1830.

Died in June 1830 at Saint John: Donald **MUNN**, 45, native of Rothesay, [Isle of Bute], Scotland, leaving a widow and five children; lived 14 years at Saint John - *CG*, 30 June 1830.

Died 16 June 1830 at St. Andrews, NB: Daniel **McMASTER**[41], born 1753 in Galloway, Scotland. He was the last surviving brother of the firm James, Patrick, John and Daniel McMaster - *NBRG*, 30 June 1830.

Died 5 July 1830 at Antigonish, NS: William **THOMPSON**, 68, native of Elgin, Scotland, and a resident of Nova Scotia for 24 years - *HJ*, 12 July 1830.

Married 7 July 1830 by Rev. Dr. Lee, Edinburgh, Scotland: Samuel **CARSON**, MD, St. John's, NL, and Margaret, youngest dau of late Rev. William **SAWERS**, A.M. minister of Crookham, Northumberland, England - *RGNA*, 24 Aug 1830.

Died 8 July 1830 at Fredericton: Archibald **WRIGHT**, 66, native of Argyllshire, Scotland - *NBC*, 17 July 1830.

Died 17 July 1830 at Canso, NS, aboard the schooner *Margaret*, en route to Buren, NL: George **McINTOSH**, 33, of Miramichi, NB, native of Sutherlandshire, Scotland - *NBC*, 7 Aug 1830.

Died in July 1830 at Pictou, NS: George **JOHNSTON**, Esq., MD, 39, native of Aberdeen, Scotland - *AR*, 31 July 1830.

Died 9 Aug 1830 at St. Andrews, NB: John **CAMPBELL**, 66, native of Argyllshire, Scotland, who emigrated in 1784 - *NBC*, 14 Aug 1830. [He left a widow, Margaret.]

---

[40] Dr. James **HUMPHREY** died 15 Oct 1855 at Mexico City, age 47 - *AR*, 6 Dec 1856.

[41] **McMASTER**'s will, dated 2 March 1829, proved 17 July 1830, names his seven children: Ann Elizabeth, Samuel James, George Patrick, Jane **HASLUCK**, Edward Daniel, Thomas Edwin, and Martha Lucy [wife of Alexander] **STRACHAN**. McMaster was born at Kirkcudbright, in Galloway.

Died 11 Aug 1830 at Halifax: Capt. John **FLEMING**, late of Jamaica, and native of Greenock, Scotland - *AR*, 14 Aug 1830.

Died 18 Aug 1830 in Halifax: John **BLACK**, printer, native of Edinburgh, Scotland - *NBC*, 4 Sep 1830.

Died 20 Aug 1830 at Halifax: Mrs. Jane **HIGGINS**, 68, native of Edinburgh[42] - *AR*, 4 Sep 1830.

Died 25 Aug 1830 at Québec: James **THOMPSON**, 98, native of Thain [Tain, Sutherlandshire], Scotland - *NBC*, 11 Sep 1830.

Died 6 Sep 1830 at Bathurst, NB: Andrew **STRAWHORN**, 45, native of Argyllshire, Scotland, leaving a widow and seven children; about 14 years in NB - *GNS*, 21 Sep 1830.

Died 9 Sep 1830 at Boston: George **MILLER**, 55, clock and watchmaker formerly of Saint John; native of Dumfries, Scotland - *NBC*, 11 Sep 1830.

Married 19 Sep 1830 by Rev. Charles William Weeks, Guysborough, NS: Alexander **SINCLAIR**, St. Mary's River, NS, and Margaret **RAMSAY**, Edinburgh, Scotland - *AR*, 2 Oct 1830.

Married 6 Oct 1830 by Rev. George S. Jarvis, Saint John: Henry T. **PARTELOW**, merchant at Saint John, and Annie, 4th dau of the late Andrew **SCOULLAR**, Lanark, Scotland - *NBC*, 9 Oct 1830.

Married 25 Oct 1830 by Rev. John Martin, Halifax: Peter **McINTIRE**, Scotland, and Martha **BETTINSON**, Plymouth, England - *AR*, 30 Oct 1830.

Married 28 Oct 1830 by Rev. Charles William Weeks, [Anglican] Dartmouth, NS: Hector **ELLIOTT**, Scotland, and Catherine **ROBERTSON**, Lawrencetown, NS - *AR*, 6 Nov 1830.

Married 6 Dec 1830 by Rev. McGill, Glasgow, Scotland: William Boyd **KINNEAR**, recorder of Saint John, NB, and Janet, dau of James **MUIR**, Rose Bank, near Greenock, Scotland - *NBRG*, 5 Mar 1831.

Died 8 Dec 1830 at St. David, NB: Archibald **STEVENSON**, 72, killed by a falling tree; native of Wigtownshire, Scotland, and emigrated in 1824 to NB - *NBC*, 18 Dec 1830.

Married 10 Jan 1831 by Rev. John Scott, Halifax: Donald **SUTHERLAND**, Sutherlandshire, Scotland, and Mary Elizabeth, eldest dau of James **MERKEL**, Halifax[43] - *AR*, 15 Jan 1831.

Died 14 Jan 1831 at Saint John: William **TENNANT**, 52, native of Fifeshire, Scotland - *CG*, 19 Jan 1831.

Died 25 Jan 1831 at Halifax: John **MITCHELL**, 46, native of Aberdeen, Scotland - *AR*, 29 Jan 1831.

---

[42] She came to Halifax in 1818 as a widow, with sons Thomas (died 18 Sep 1818, age 24), and William Bell **HIGGINS**. She was also survived by a daughter, Mrs. John **DUFF** of Baltimore, MD.

[43] Donald **SUTHERLAND** died 30 Sep 1860 at Halifax, age 59. Mary Elizabeth was baptised on 7 Oct 1811 at St. Paul's Anglican Church, Halifax, eldest child of James and Elizabeth (**MIERS**) **MERKEL**.

Died in March 1831 at Pictou, NS: James **MOFFATT**, 60, native of Scotland - *Colonial Patriot*, 12 Mar 1831. [*AR*, 26 Mar 1831, gives the death date of 4 March, and his age as 40.]

Died 1 Mar 1831 at Liverpool, Kent County, NB: John **GRAHAM**, 38, timber merchant, native of Dumfries-shire, Scotland - *NBC*, 19 Mar 1831.

Died 2 Mar 1831 at Saint John: James **COWAN**, 44, stonecutter, native of Dumfries-shire, Scotland, who had lived in Saint John for twelve years - *NBC*, 12 Mar 1831.

Died 2 Mar 1831 in Nova Scotia: Daniel **MacDOUGALL**, 86, native of Inverness-shire, Scotland - *AR*, 12 Mar 1831.

Died 23 Mar 1831 at Saint John: Andrew **HUTCHINSON**, [carpenter], 55, native of Mauchlin, Ayrshire, Scotland - *NBC*, 26 Mar 1831. [He left a widow Elizabeth and a family.]

Died 1 Apr 1831 at Judique, NS: Peter **McARTHUR**, 47, native of Inverness, Scotland - *HJ*, 25 Apr 1831.

Died 16 Apr 1831 at Richibucto, NB, at the home of his uncle, R[obert] **JARDINE**: David **DUNBAR**, 21, native of Scotland - *GNS*, 26 Apr 1831.

Died 6 May 1831 at Saint John: Janet, 37, native of Port Glasgow, Scotland, wife of Edward **TAYLOR**, "formerly of this place". She left three children - *NBC*, 7 May 1831.

Died 7 May 1831 at Halifax: John **FRASER**, 53, native of Aberdeen, Scotland - *AR*, 14 May 1831.

Died 23 May 1831 at Old Ridge, St. Stephen, NB: William **GRANT**, 72, native of Strathspey[44], Scotland; formerly a Sgt. in the 71st Highland Regt., and an early settler of Charlotte County - *NBC*, 4 June 1831.

Died 25 May 1831 at Pictou, NS: Jane, 30, native of Moffat, Dumfries-shire, Scotland, widow of the late J. **PAGAN**, leaving six children. She emigrated in 1821 - *HJ*, 20 June 1831.

Died 3 June 1831 at Lancaster, Upper Canada [Stormont-Dundas-Glengarry County, Ontario]: Duncan **MURCHISON**, Esq., 86, native of Ross-shire, Scotland - *HJ*, 6 June 1831.

Died 9 June 1831 aboard the brigantine *Dove*, en route from Berbice to Halifax: Peter **PATTERSON**, seaman from Aberdeen, Scotland - *AR*, 2 July 1831.

Died 19 June 1831 aboard the brigantine *Dove*, en route from Berbice to Halifax: William **TAYLOR**, seaman from Morayshire, Scotland - *AR*, 2 July 1831.

Died 16 July 1831 at Springs, West River, Pictou, NS: Murdock **McKENZIE**, 88, native of Lochbroom, [Ross and Cromarty], Scotland - *NBRG*, 20 July 1831.

Died 17 July 1831 aboard the brig *Brisk*, en route to Halifax: J. **JUNIO** of Scotland - *AR*, 30 July 1831.

---

[44] William **GRANT** was born at Keith, Banffshire. He married Catherine **PATTON**, who survived him with a family.

Married in August 1831 at Leeds, Yorkshire, England: John Joseph **MacBRAIRE**, Esq., only son of James MacBraire, Esq., of Tweed Hill, Berwick on Tweed, and formerly of St. John's, NL, and Miss . . ., dau of B. **GOTT** of Leeds - *RGNA*, 25 Oct 1831.

Married 1 Sep 1831 by Rev. John Scott, Halifax: Rev. James **SOUTER**, pastor of St. James Church in Newcastle, NB, to Helen Ogilvie, eldest dau of James **DYCE**, Aberdeen, Scotland - *AR*, 3 Sep 1831.

Married 22 Sep 1831 at Aberdeen, Scotland: John **ANDERSON** of Miramichi, NB, and Mary, dau of John **GARRON**, manufacturer, and widow of Alexander **BRANSBY**, late of Elgin Academy - *GNS*, 7 Feb 1832.

Married 29 Sep 1831 by Rev. Anderson, Edinburgh, Scotland: James Compton **HUME**, surgeon, Halifax, NS, and Christian Blackhall, 5th dau of late Thomas **DENHAM** - *AR*, 12 Nov 1831.

Died 6 Oct 1831 at Halifax: Thomas **TROTTER**, stone mason, native of Leith, Scotland, leaving a widow and six children - *AR*, 15 Oct 1831.

Died 8 Oct 1831 at Halifax: Hon. Michael **WALLACE**[45] - *AR*, 8 Oct 1831.

Died 17 Oct 1831 at Chatham, NB: Robert **GRAHAM**, 33, native of Derwoodie-Green, Dumfries-shire, Scotland - *GNS*, 18 Oct 1831.

Married 12 Nov 1831 by Rev. Charles Milner at Dorchester Island, NB: George **SCOULLAR**, Lanark, Scotland, and Theodosia, 4th dau of James **SAYRE**, Dorchester Island - *NBC*, 19 Nov 1831.

Died 21 Nov 1831 at Loch Lomond, NB: Margaret, 55, native of Perthshire, Scotland, wife of James **McGREGOR** - *NBC*, 26 Nov 1831.

Died 25 Nov 1831 at Fishers Grant, NS: The wife of Hugh **ROSS**, who survived her with two children. She was a native of Ross-shire, Scotland - *AR*, 10 Dec 1831.

Died 30 Nov 1831 at Saint John: George, 34, son of Francis **McBEATH**. He was a native of Scotland and left a widow and two children - *NBRG*, 7 Dec 1831.

Married 12 Dec 1831 by Rev. Jerome Alley, St. Andrews, NB: Peter **STUBS**, cashier, Charlotte County Bank, and Matilda, 3rd dau of the later Peter **WARWICK**, Kirkcudbright, Scotland - *NBC*, 17 Dec 1831.

Died 13 Dec 1831 at Saint John: John **HUNTER**, 44, carpenter, native of Tranent, Haddingtonshire, Scotland - *NBC*, 17 Dec 1831.

---

[45] Michael **WALLACE** was born in Lanarkshire, Scotland, and emigrated to Norfolk, VA, in 1771, where he was a merchant. He came to Nova Scotia as a Loyalist, and was elected to the House of Assembly in 1785, becoming Provincial Treasurer in 1797, and appointed to the Legislative Council in 1802. His career is described by D. A. Sutherland in the *Dictionary of Canadian Biography*, VI, pp. 798-801.

Died in Dec 1831 at sea: James **SMITH** of the brig *Ann*, en route from Greenock, Scotland, to Saint John - *GNS*, 31 Jan 1832.

Died in January 1832 at Antigonish, NS: Mrs. Ann **CHISHOLM**, 98, native of Scotland - *NS*, 8 Feb 1832.

Died 29 Jan 1832 in Scotland: Hugh **McKAY**, 31, formerly of Pictou, NS - *HJ*, 7 May 1832.

Died 5 Feb 1832 at the house of Mr. **STOTHARD**, Newcastle, NB: Walter **GLENDENNING**, native of Scotland - *GNS*, 7 Feb 1832.

Died 11 Feb 1832 at Halifax: Barbara, 62, wife of Donald **SUTHERLAND**, Dornoch, Scotland - *AR*, 18 Feb 1832.

Died 24 Feb 1832 at Middle River, Pictou, NS: Hector **McINNIS**, native of Argyllshire, Scotland, leaving a widow and nine children - *HJ*, 26 Mar 1832.

Died 7 Mar 1832 at Wallace, NS: John **McLEOD**, 47, native of Ross-shire, Scotland - *HJ*, 26 Mar 1832.

Died 7 Mar 1832 at Rogers Hill, NS: Andrew **McCARA**, Esq., 76, native of Scotland - *HJ*, 26 Mar 1832.

Died 6 May 1832 at Halifax: James **HERKES**, native of Inervisk [Innerwick, East Lothian], Scotland - *AR*, 12 May 1832.

Died 14 May 1832 at Albion Mines, NS: Dr. Alexander **PATRICK**, native of Scotland, and formerly surgeon in the packet *Lady Wellington* - *AR*, 26 May 1832.

Died 16 May 1832 at Halifax: Thomas **ROSS**, 99, native of Morayshire, Scotland - *AR*, 19 May 1832.

Died 16 May 1832 at Londonderry, NS: Mary, 37, wife of James **IRVING**, who survived her with five children. They emigrated from Dumfries-shire, Scotland in 1819 - *HJ*, 2 July 1832.

Died in May 1832 at Clyde River, NS: Mrs. Janet **MORRISON**, 85, native of Scotland - *HJ*, 2 July 1832.

Died 21 May 1832 at Loch Lomond, Saint John County, NB: James **McGREGOR**, 67, native of Perthshire, Scotland - *NBC*, 26 May 1832.

Died 3 June 1832 at Shelburne, NS: Mrs. Mary **LIGHTBODY**, 74, native of Scotland[46] - *HJ*, 2 July 1832.

Died 16 June 1832 at Halifax: James **THOMPSON**, 33, native of Ross-shire, Scotland - *AR*, 23 June 1832.

Died 17 June 1832 at Montréal, of cholera: Dr. John Leitch **SMITH**, late of Glasgow, Scotland - *AR*, 14 July 1832.

---

[46] She was the widow of Andrew **LIGHTBODY**, who died 21 June 1816 at Shelburne, NS, age 71 - *AR*, 13 July 1816. The newspaper assigned him no place of birth.

Died 11 July 1832 at Lower Clements, NS: Thomas **RUSSELL**, 43, born near Glasgow, Scotland - *NBC*, 14 July 1832.

Married 14 July 1832 by Rev. J. W. D. Gray, Saint John: Daniel **JOHNSTON**, merchant, Wakefield, Carleton County, NB, and Janet, 3rd dau of Robert **CHESTNUT** of Hamilton, Lanarkshire, Scotland - *NBC*, 14 July 1832.

Died 19 July 1832 at Montréal: Archibald **WATT**, Esq., of Glasgow, Scotland - *AR*, 21 July 1832.

Married 14 Aug 1832 by Rev. John Scott, Halifax: Alexander **HENRY**, Greenock, Scotland, and Jean, eldest dau of James **REID**, Edinburgh, Scotland - *AR*, 25 Aug 1832.

Died 15 Aug 1832 at Halifax: Rev. Robert **ELLIOT** of Preston, NS, 38, native of Roxburghshire, Scotland - *AR*, 18 Aug 1832.

Died 20 Aug 1832 at St. Andrews, NB: Mary, 74, native of Beith, near Glasgow, Scotland, wife of David **CRAIG**, early settler of Charlotte County, NB - *WO*, 28 Aug 1832.

Died 21 Aug 1832 at Halifax: James **WILKIE**, 44, native of Fifeshire, Scotland - *AR*, 25 Aug 1832.

Died 9 Sep 1832 at Trout Brook, St. Nicholas River, NB: James **WALKER**, 46, native of Dumfries-shire, Scotland[47] - *GNS*, 2 Oct 1832.

Died 16 Sep 1832 at Bathurst, NB: Capt. William T. **MILLER**, native of Saltcoats, [Ayrshire], North Britain, and late master of the brig *Margaret Ritchie* - *NBC*, 13 Oct 1832.

Married 2 Oct 1832 by Rev. John Scott, Halifax: John **WRIGHT**, Royal Engineers, and Mary, 2nd dau of James **REID**, all of Edinburgh, Scotland - *AR*, 6 Oct 1832.

Married 14 Oct 1832 by Rev. Donald Allen Fraser, Pictou, NS: Charles **MARTIN**, Esq., member of the Royal College of Surgeons, Edinburgh, and Margaret, 2nd dau of James **SKINNER**, M.D., of Pictou, NS - *AR*, 1 Dec 1832.

Died 23 Oct 1832 at the Almshouse, Saint John: Thomas **JOHNSTON**, native of Scotland, who had "lately arrived from New York in last stage of consumption" - *NBC*, 27 Oct 1832.

Died 24 Oct 1832 at Halifax: Capt. James **OSWALD** of the brig *Aberdeenshire*, native of Aberdeen, Scotland - *AR*, 10 Nov 1832.

Died 7 Nov 1832 at Saint John: Ann, 59, late of Hamilton, Scotland, widow of William **TAYLOR**, adjutant, 27th Regt. - *NBC*, 10 Nov 1832.

Died 27 Nov 1832 at Carleton, NB: John **McKENZIE**, 85, who served as a Sgt. in the 42rd (Royal Highland) Regt. in the Revolutionary War. He settled at Nashwaak, York County, when disbanded, later moving to Carleton County - *NBC*, 1 Dec 1832.

---

[47] James **WALKER** married Mary **COWDEN** of Urr Parish, Kirkcudbrightshire, and emigrated to New Brunswick about 1826 with his wife and a family of several children, including Jean, Agnes and Sarah.

Died 10 Dec 1832 at Beaverbank, NS: Henry **OLIVES**, 37, native of Selkirkshire, Scotland
  - *AR*, 15 Dec 1832.

Died 27 Dec 1832 aboard the brig *H. N. Binney*, en route from Jamaica to Halifax: Capt.
  Alexander **HENDERSON**, from Greenock, Scotland - *HJ*, 21 Jan 1833.

Died aboard the *Mary Elizabeth* from Falmouth, Jamaica: Allan **McMASTER**, from Scotland
  - *HJ*, 31 Dec 1832.

Died 31 Dec 1832 at Saint John: John **CLARK,** private, 34th Regt., "native of Ayrshire near
  Irvin[e]" - *NBC*, 5 Jan 1833.

Died 3 Feb 1833 at Union St., Saint John: Mrs. Elizabeth **FRASER**, "at an advanced age",
  native of Scotland - *WO*, 5 Feb 1833.

Married 6 Feb 1833 by Rev. Dr. Benjamin Gerrish Gray at Saint John: Alexander **McEACHY** of
  Campbeltown, [Argyllshire], Scotland, and Elizabeth, 2nd dau of the late Thomas **KING**,
  Sussex Vale, NB, and stepdau of Capt. W. J. **STOCKTON** - *WO*, 12 Feb 1833.

Married 9 Feb 1833 by Rev. John Scott, Halifax: James **GRE[I]G**, from Scotland[48], and Mrs.
  Amelia **SMITH**, Halifax - *HJ*, 18 Feb 1833.

Died 2 Mar 1833 at Sydney, Cape Breton, NS, when they froze to death: Laughlan, Alexander and
  Dugald **McMULLEN**, brothers, and recent immigrants from Scotland. Survived by their widowed
  mother, several sisters and a married brother - *CG*, 28 Mar 1833.

Died 23 Mar 1833 at Montréal: James **MACKIE**, late merchant and ship owner in Aberdeen,
  Scotland - *GNS*, 7 May 1833.

Died 26 Mar 1833 at Halifax: Adam **MILLER**, 43, native of Roxburghshire, Scotland
  - *HJ*, 1 Apr 1833.

Died 30 Mar 1833 at Gardner's Creek, NB: Andrew **CUNNINGHAM**, Jr., 25, native of Dumfries-
  shire, Scotland - *WO*, 16 Apr 1833.

Died 5 Apr 1833 at Saint John: William **BAIRD**, [carpenter], 83, native of Stirling, Scotland, an early
  settler - *WO*, 9 Apr 1833.

Died 13 Apr 1833 at Stirling, Scotland: Susannah, 71, widow of Colin **CAMPBELL**, Esq., late
  H. M. Customs, Saint John - *WO*, 2 July 1833.

Died 16 Apr 1833 at Digdeguash River, St. Patrick Parish, Charlotte County, NB: Alexander
  CAMERON, 89, native of the Scottish Highlands; served during the American Revolution with
  the 74th Regt. He settled in NB in 1783, and left a widow and twelve grown children
  - *WO*, 7 May 1833.

---

[48] James **GREIG** died at Halifax, 18 Apr 1850, age 59.

Died 29 Apr 1833 at Saint John: John **PAUL**, 82, formerly of the Royal Artillery and lately of the Ordnance Dept., a native of Lanark, Scotland; came to NB in 1783 - *WO*, 30 Apr 1833. He fought at the battles of Lexington, Bunker Hill, Brandywine, Long Island and Germantown, being wounded at Lexington. He landed at Saint John on 25 July 1783 - *WO*, 7 May 1833.

Married [7 May] 1833 by Rev. John Scott, Halifax: Alexander **STEWART** and Eliza **STEPHEN**[49], both of Morayshire, Scotland - *AR*, 11 May 1833.

Died 7 May 1833 at Saint John: David **KILPATRICK**, 28, native of Dumfries-shire, Scotland - *NBC*, 7 May 1833.

Married 7 May 1833 by Rev. C. Porter, Newport, NS[50]: William **SHEARER** and Eliza **HOPE**, both natives of Morayshire, Scotland - *HJ*, 13 May 1833.

Married 12 June 1833 by Rev. Cunningham, Greenock, Scotland: Hon. Judge **DesBARRES**, St. John's, NL, and Isabella, only dau of J. **STEWART**, Belltrees, Scotland - *AR*, 27 July 1833.

Died 14 June 1833 at Newcastle, NB: Jesse, 5 months 23 days old, son of Marcus **GUNN**, formerly a merchant in Thurso, [Caithness], North Britain - *GNS*, 25 June 1833.

Died 22 June 1833 at St. Patrick, NB: Walter **McFARLANE**, 80, native of Scotland[51], leaving a family of nine; served in the 74th Regt., and came to Digdeguash in 1783 - *WO*, 2 July 1833.

Drowned out of a canoe at Southampton, York County, NB: Havander **CALDER**, 25, a native of Sutherlandshire, Scotland - *WO*, 9 July 1833.

Died 7 July 1833 at Lower Stewiacke, NS: William **ANNAND**, 29, native of Aberdeen, Scotland - *AR*, 13 July 1833.

Died 9 July 1833 at the forks of the Marsh Road [Portland Parish, Saint John County], NB: David **ANDERSON**, [innkeeper], 51, native of New Abbey, "Shire of Galloway", Scotland, leaving a widow [Margaret] and nine children - *NBC*, 13 July 1833.

Married 4 Sep 1833 by Rev. Robert Fitzgerald Uniacke, [Anglican] Halifax: Peter **TULLOCH**, North Scotland, and Jane **SMITH**, Halifax - *AR*, 14 Sep 1833.

Married 23 Sep 1833 by Rev. Robert Fitzgerald Uniacke, Halifax: Robert **HARDIE** and Margaret **GILLIS**, both from Mid Lothian, Scotland - *HJ*, 30 Sep 1833.

---

[49] Elizabeth **STEPHEN** or **STEVENS** died 10 Apr 1854 at Lake Thomas, NS, age 41.

[50] In its following issue, 20 May 1833, the *Halifax Journal* denied this marriage. It was a hoax.

[51] Walter **McFARLANE** was a native of Bonhill, Dumbartonshire. Among his children were sons named John, Robert and Walter.

Died 30 Oct 1833 at Edinburgh, Scotland: Rev. Andrew **BROWN**, professor at the University of Edinburgh and "for some time Minister of St. Matthew's Church, Halifax, NS"[52] - *NBRG*, 15 Jan 1834.

Died 1 Nov 1833 at Halifax: James C. **MacKAY**, 23, native of Scotland - *AR*, 2 Nov 1833.

Died 2 Nov 1833 at Halifax: James **CARMICHAEL**, 44, native of Scotland - *AR*, 2 Nov 1833.

Married 21 Nov 1833 by Rev. John Scott, Halifax: James **MAITLAND**, Aberdeen, Scotland, and Elizabeth **BOUZIE** of Germany - *AR*, 30 Nov 1833.

Died 23 Nov 1833 at Fredericton: John **OGLEVY**, 42, stone cutter, native of Scotland, leaving a widow and five children. He formerly served in the Royal Artillery - *NBC*, 30 Nov 1833.

Died 28 Dec 1833 at St. Andrews Parish, NB: Daniel **GRANT**, 82, native of Sutherland, Scotland - *NBC*, 18 Jan 1834.

Died 31 Dec 1833 at Chester, NS: Alexander **PATILLO**, 92, from [Aberdeen], Scotland - *HJ*, 13 Jan 1834.

Died 20 Jan 1834 at Martintown, Upper Canada: A. **McINTOSH**, 92, and his wife, C—, 80, natives of Glengarry, Scotland, who emigrated to Canada in 1793 - *FP*, 18 Feb 1834.

Died 24 Jan 1834 at Halifax: Andrew **ANGUS**, 63, native of Dunfermline, Scotland - *AR*, 25 Jan 1834.

Died 4 Feb 1834 at the house of W[illiam] H. **STREET**, Esq., Saint John: Mrs. . . ., widow of James **BRUCE**, Naval Officer at Leith, Scotland - *NBC*, 8 Feb 1834.

Married 7 Feb 1834 by Rev. William Cogswell, Halifax: William **STEWART** and Jessie **McLEOD**, both from Scotland - *AR*, 8 Feb 1834.

Married 12 Feb 1834 by Rev. Benjamin Gerrish Gray, Saint John: James **PROVEN** of Glasgow and Elizabeth, 3rd dau of late Henry **FROST** of Saint John - *NBC*, 15 Feb 1834.

Died in February 1834 in Scotland: James **HUNTER**, Esq., 60, of Denoon, Scotland, a former partner in Mssrs. Hunter & Co., St. John's, NL - *Times, Newfoundland*, 30 Apr 1834.

Died 14 Mar 1834 at Sydney, NS: Alexander **CAMPBELL**, 68, native of Argyllshire, Scotland - *HJ*, 7 Apr 1834.

---

[52] Rev. Andrew **BROWN** was born 22 Aug 1763 at Biggar, Scotland, a son of Richard and Isabella (**FORREST**) Brown. George Shepperson, in the *Dictionary of Canadian Biography*, VI, pp. 87-89, states that he died on 19 Feb 1834 at Primrose Bank, Carrington, Scotland. Since the newspaper issued on 15 January contained news of Brown's death, Sheppertson must be mistaken. Brown served at St. Matthew's in Halifax from 1787 to 1795.

Married in March 1834 by Rev. Somerville at Bathurst, NB: George **CURRIE**, Aberdeen, Scotland, and Lucy **PALMER** of Prince Edward Island - *GNS*, 1 Apr 1834.

Died 16 Apr 1834 at Portland, NB: James **McVETE**, native of Scotland, leaving a widow and family - *NBC*, 19 Apr 1834.

Died 22 Apr 1834 at Halifax: James **REA**, 25, native of Morayshire, Scotland - *AR*, 26 Apr 1834.

Married 26 Apr 1834 by Rev. William Cogswell at St. Paul's Anglican Church, Halifax, NS: Dr. Frederick A. **WEBSTER** of Yarmouth, NS, and Margaret, 3rd dau of John **McNAUGHT**, Glasgow, North Britain - *NBC*, 2 May 1834.

Married 2 May 1834 by Rev. John Martin, St. Andrew's Church, Halifax: James **MALCOLM** [from Scotland] to Jean **ANDERSON** of Edinburgh, Scotland - *AR*, 10 May 1834.

Married 11 May 1834 by Rev. Frederick H. Carrington, St. John's, NL: Richard **PERCHARD**, Jr., merchant at St. John's, NL, and Jane, eldest dau of William **OLIPHANT**, Esq., of Leith, Scotland - *RGNA*, 20 May 1834.

Married 19 May 1834 by Rev. Robert Wilson, Saint John: James **WALES** of Portland Parish, NB, and Clementina **JAMIESON**, lately from Scotland - *NBC*, 24 May 1834.

Died 19 May 1834 at Barneys River, NS: William **McKENZIE**, 62, native of Sutherlandshire, Scotland - *HJ*, 26 May 1834.

Died in 1834 at Aberdeen, Scotland: James **THOM** who carried on business in Nova Scotia and New Brunswick for nearly 40 years - *NBC*, 9 Aug 1834.

Married 16 June 1834 by Rev. Robert Wilson, Saint John: Hugh **REED** and Christiana **GRAHAM**, lately from Scotland - *NBC*, 21 June 1834.

Died 22 June 1834 at Mount Stewart, PE: John **STEWART**, 75, emigrated from Kintyre, Scotland, 68 years before - *NBC*, 12 July 1834.

Died 26 June 1834 at the home of Colin **CAMPBELL** near St. Andrews, NB: Hugh **HENDERSON**, 103, native of Argyllshire, Scotland - *NBC*, 12 July 1834.

Died 4 July 1834 at Halifax: Mrs. Ann **STEWART**, 79, native of Banffshire, Scotland - *AR*, 5 July 1834.

Died 5 July 1834 at Campobello, NB: William, 25, acting sub-collector of H. M. Customs, West Isles, son of William **HARLEY**, Glasgow, Scotland - *NBC*, 12 July 1834.

Died 21 July 1834 at Saint John: Alexander **KIRK**, 47, native of Grangemouth by Falkirk, Scotland - *NBC*, 26 July 1834.

Died 28 July 1834 at Wilmot, NS: George **INNES**, 53, native of Banffshire, Scotland - *NBC*, 23 Aug 1834.

Died 1 Aug 1834 at Halifax: Donald **SUTHERLAND**, 61, native of Sutherlandshire, Scotland - *AR*, 2 Aug 1834.

Died 4 Aug 1834 at Annapolis Royal, NS: William **CROSS**, Sr., 83, native of Paisley, Scotland, leaving a widow. He came to Nova Scotia at the end of the Revolutionary War - *NBC*, 23 Aug 1834.

Died in August 1834 at Oak Bay, Charlotte County, NB: Bryce **CHALMERS**[53], 38, native of Scotland - *NBC*, 16 Aug 1834.

Died 11 Aug 1834 at Halifax: Robert **MILLNE**, [74], native of Aberdeen, Scotland - *AR*, 16 Aug 1834.

Died 11 Aug 1834 at Montréal: John **JAMIESON**, Esq., 36, native of Glasgow, Scotland, "but a resident of Pictou, NS, for the last 8 years" - *AR*, 20 Sep 1834.

Died 20 Aug 1834 at Halifax: Robert **WILSON**, 58, native of Elgin, Scotland - *AR*, 23 Aug 1834.

Died 29 Aug 1834 at Clyde River, NS: John **STALKER**, 84, native of Inverness-shire, Scotland - *HJ*, 15 Sep 1834.

Died 6 Sep 1834 at Halifax: Neil **STEWART**, 30, native of Thurso, Scotland. He left a widow and four children - *AR*, 13 Sep 1834.

Died 13 Oct 1834 at Nappan, NS: John **RAE**, 58, native of Dumfries-shire, Scotland, leaving a widow and seven children. He "arrived in country only a few months ago and commenced superintendance of school" at Nappan - *NBC*, 15 Nov 1834.

Died 25 Oct 1834 at West River, Pictou, NS: Rev. Duncan **ROSS**[54], 64, native of Ross-shire, Scotland - *HJ*, 10 Nov 1834.

Died 26 Oct 1834 at Portland Parish, NB, of Asiatic cholera: Duncan **MacKAY**, ship carpenter, son of Rupert MacKay of Caithness, Scotland - *NBC*, 1 Nov 1834.

Died 29 Oct 1834 at Bathurst, NB: James **ROBERTSON**, 98, native of Banffshire, Scotland. He emigrated to NB about 1764, and was master cooper to Commodore **WALKER**. He visited Scotland for the last time in 1775 "when he married and returned to this parish with his wife" - *NBC*, 29 Nov 1834.

Married 30 Oct 1834 by Rev. Robert Wilson, Saint John: Robert **JARDINE** of Saint John and Euphemia **REID**, Kildonan, [Sutherlandshire], Scotland - *NBC*, 1 Nov 1834.

---

[53] The will of Bryce **CHALMERS**, innkeeper, was dated 30 July 1834, and proved 20 Sep 1834. His wife was Mary. He provided for £30 to be sent to his mother Margaret, care of James **WEATHER** of Carriwell, Parish [sic] of Stonacher, Galloway, Scotland.

[54] Duncan **ROSS** was born at Tarbert, Ross-shire. He same to Nova Scotia in 1795, and married at New Glasgow, NS, 28 Sep 1796, Isabella **CREELMAN** of Stewiacke, NS, and had a large family - *cf.*, A. E. Betts, *Our Fathers in the Faith* (Halifax, 1983), p. 113.

Died 11 Dec 1834 at Bartibog, NB: Lt. Col. Alexander **McDONALD**, 72, native of Argyllshire, Scotland. He came to Miramichi in 1784 and left a family[55] - *GNS*, 30 Dec 1834.

Died 20 Dec 1834 at Rossbank, Greenock, Scotland: James **MUIR**, Esq. - *NBC*, 12 Feb 1835.

Died 26 Dec 1834 at Saint John: James **TAYLOR**, Sr., Esq., 79, native of Port Glasgow, Scotland, whence he emigrated to New York early in life. He was active as a Loyalist during the Revolutionary War and came to NB in 1783. He was long vice president of the Society of St. Andrew - *NBRG*, 31 Dec 1834.

Died 31 Dec 1834 at Toronto, Upper Canada: Hon. John **McGILL**[56], Member of the Legislative Council of Upper Canada; 'for several years a resident in [New Brunswick]' - *NBC*, 31 Jan 1835.

Died 13 Jan 1835 at Tower Hill, St. David Parish, Charlotte County, NB: William **TOWERS**, 84, native of Stirlingshire, Scotland.[57] He served in the Engineer Dept. of the British Army during the American Revolution, then came with the Loyalists "who built the first houses at St. Andrews" and later moved to St. David "where he raised a large family" - *NBC*, 31 Jan 1835.

Died 18 Jan 1835 at Glasgow, Scotland: J., wife of Robert **WALLACE**[58], painter, formerly of Saint John, and eldest dau of William **BELL**, Dumfries, Scotland - *CG*, 30 Apr 1835.

Married 23 Jan 1835 by Rev. Samuel Joll, Wesleyan Missionary, at Wakefield, NB: Nathan **JOHNSTON** of Wakefield and Margaret, dau of Robert **CHESTNUT** of Hamilton, [Lanarkshire], Scotland - *NBC*, 31 Jan 1835.

Married 10 Feb 1835 by Rev. James D. Drummond, [Catholic] Halifax: James **DOYLE**, County Carlow, Ireland, and Jannet **FRASER**, Inverness-shire, Scotland[59] - *AR*, 14 Feb 1835.

Died 2 Mar 1835 near Ledge, St. Stephen, NB: Daniel **BROWN**, Sr., 91, native of the Scottish Highlands, and leaving "upwards of 200 descendants". He emigrated to America "at an early period of his life" and settled at Castine, ME, but removed to NB after the peace of 1783 - *NBC*, 25 Apr 1835.

Died 6 Mar 1835 at Halifax: Elspet, 39, from Morayshire, Scotland, wife of James **FINDLAY**[60] - *AR*, 7 Mar 1835.

---

[55] Alexander was born at Ardnamurchan, Argyllshire. He married Grace **MacLEAN** from the Isle of Eigg. She died at Bartibog, NB, 31 Dec 1834, age 62 - *NBRG*, 21 Jan 1835.

[56] He was born at Auckland, Wigtonshire, in March 1752. His career is traced by S. R. Mealing in the *Dictionary of Canadian Biography*, VI, pp. 451-3.

[57] William was baptised 24 Feb 1751 at Kirkton, Stirlingshire, a son of John and Janet **(SIMPSON) TOWERS**.

[58] Married 6 Oct 1822 by Rev. Dr. Burns, Presbyterian, Saint John: Robert **WALLACE** and Jessie **BELL**.

[59] James **DOYLE** came from Borris, County Carlow. Jannet was a dau of John and Elizabeth **FRASER**, of Crow End, Inverness-shire, Scotland.

[60] James **FINDLEY** married Elizabeth **FRASER** at St. Andrew's Presbyterian Free Church in Halifax, 8 Nov 1831.

Married 25 Mar 1835 by Rev. John Martin, Halifax: John A. **MANN** and Catherine **SUTHERLAND**, native of Scotland - *AR*, 4 Apr 1835.

Married 14 Apr 1835 at Gartferry House, [Lanarkshire], Scotland: John **ROBERTSON**, Esq., merchant, of Saint John, and Sophia, youngest dau of David **DOBIE**, Esq., Gartferry - *NBRG*, 17 June 1835.

Died 15 Apr 1835 at St. Andrews, NB: Agnes, 39, native of Dumfries, Scotland, wife of William **DOUGLAS**. She emigrated to NB with her husband "about 18 years ago" - *NBC*, 25 Apr 1835.

Died 5 May 1835 at Black River, NB: John **GUNN**, 74, native of Scotland, who emigrated from Caithness in 1802 - *GNS*, 12 May 1835.

Died 11 May 1835 at Saint John: Lt. John **CAMERON**, 41, native of Scotland and on half pay from the 3rd Regt. of Foot - *NBC*, 16 May 1835.

Married 11 May 1835 at Montréal: Alfred **SAVAGE**, druggist, Québec, and Jane, dau of late Capt. John **DONALDSON**, St. Stephen, NB, and formerly of Greenock, Scotland - *NBC*, 30 May 1835.

DIED 13 MAY 1835 AT BATHURST, NB: JOHN RONALDS, 43, PILOT, NATIVE OF FALKIRK, SCOTLAND. THE DECEASED WITH FOUR OTHER PERSONS PUT OFF FROM THE SOUTH OF THE HARBOUR IN ORDER TO BOARD SOME OF THE VESSELS THAT CAME TO ANCHOR IN THE BAY THE DAY PREVIOUS, AND GOT ENTANGLED WITH THE ICE, WHICH WAS IN GREAT ABUNDANCE BETWEEN THE INNER AND OUTER BAR. AFTER ABOUT TEN HOURS ARDUOUS STRUGGLE IN GETTING THE BOAT OVER AND THROUGH THE ICE, THE DECEASED WAS SPEECHLESS WHEN TAKEN ON BOARD THE *SCEPTRE* AND DIED 15 MINUTES AFTERWARDS - *NBRG*, 24 June 1835.

Died 29 May 1835 at Sydney, NS: Anne, 34, widow of James **BROWN** of Scotland - *Times*, 16 June 1835.

Died at sea in the schooner *Henry Robert* on passage from Montego Bay, Jamaica, to Saint John, NB: Daniel **THOMSON**, mate, native of Rothesay, Scotland - *CG*, 17 June 1835.

Died 4 July 1835 at Halifax: James **YOUNG**, 41, native of Edinburgh, Scotland, leaving a widow and three children - *AR*, 4 July 1835.

Married 26 Aug 1835 by Rev. Charles Jenkins, Charlottetown, PE: George R. **MORGAN** of the firm **BENNETT** & Morgan, St. John's, NL, and Eliza Brenton, youngest dau of William **OLIPHANT**, Leith, Scotland, and formerly of Bonnington Park, near Edinburgh - *AR*, 5 Sep 1835.

Married 22 Sep 1835 by Rev. John Martin, Halifax: Rev. John **STEWART**[61], St. Georges Channel, Cape Breton, NS, and Alicia Murray, youngest dau of late William **DRYSDALE**, Edinburgh, Scotland - *AR*, 26 Sep 1835.

---

[61] John **STEWART** was born in Perthshire, Scotland, about 1800 and died 4 May 1860 at New Glasgow, NS - *cf.*, A. E. Betts, *Our Fathers in the Faith* (Halifax, 1983), p. 125.

Died 10 Oct 1835 at Little Snorke, Chaleur Bay, NB: Sarah, 39, wife of Edward **BRADLEY** of Scotland, and 4th dau of John [and Mary] **NEWTON**, Nova Scotia - *AR*, 9 Jan 1836.

Died 23 Oct 1835 at Halifax: Mrs. Janet **THOMPSON**, 84, native of Banffshire, Scotland - *AR*, 24 Oct 1835.

Drowned 31 Oct 1835 at Carleton, NB: Wallace **CAMPBELL**, 32, native of [Inver]ness, Scotland - *NBC*, 7 Nov 1835.

Died 14 Nov 1835 at Halifax: Thomas **BROWN**, 38, native of Scotland - *NSRG*, 18 Nov 1835.

SHIPWRECK! THE SCHOONER *REVENGE* OWNED BY SAMUEL **SOLEY** FROM TRURO, NS . . . AND BOUND TO SAINT JOHN WAS TOTALLY LOST ON THE NORTH SHORE NEAR CAPE MISPECK ABOUT 12 OR 14 MILES FROM SAINT JOHN DURING THE SNOW STORM ON MONDAY NIGHT [23 NOV 1835]. OF TEN PERSONS ON BOARD, SIX FOUND A WATERY GRAVE. . . . THE PERSONS ON BOARD AT THE TIME OF THE ACCIDENT WERE THREE SONS OF MR. SOLEY COMPOSING THE CREW; AND SEVEN PASSENGERS, VIZ. JOHN **BISHOP** OF ONSLOW, MR. **FULTON** OF NS, MRS. **McFARLANE** AND HER FOUR CHILDREN. DROWNED: JAMES SOLEY, MR. FULTON, MRS. McFARLANE AND HER THREE YOUNGEST CHILDREN.

THE CASE OF MRS. McFARLANE IS PARTICULARLY DISTRESSING. SHE HAD RECENTLY COME FROM SCOTLAND TO PICTOU, NS, AND WAS WITH HER FAMILY ON THE WAY TO JOIN HER HUSBAND IN SAINT JOHN, AND HAD ACTUALLY ENGAGED PASSAGE IN ANOTHER VESSEL FROM TRURO TO SAINT JOHN (WHICH ARRIVED HERE SOME DAYS SINCE) WHEN, IN HOPES OF MAKING A MORE SPEEDY PASSAGE, SHE WAS INDUCED TO EMBARK IN THE *REVENGE*. - *NBC*, 28 Nov 1835.

Died 30 Nov 1835 at St. Stephen, NB: Peter **McDIARMAID**, 83, native of the Highlands of Scotland. He came to America in 1778 as a Sgt. in the 74th Regt. - *NBC*, 18 Jan 1836.

Died 14 Dec 1835 in St. Patrick Parish, Charlotte County, NB: James **STEWART**, 78, native of Fifeshire, Scotland. He came to America in 1778 with the 74th Regt., and was at the Battle of Castine [Maine] - *NBC*, 19 Dec 1835.

Died 18 Dec 1835 at Montréal: William **BLACK**, about 43, "a stranger supposed to be a native of Ayrshire", Scotland - *AR*, 30 Jan 1836.

Died 30 Dec 1835 at Halifax: W[illiam] **MACARA**, druggist, 45, native of Scotland[62] - *NBRG*, 13 Jan 1836.

Married in January 1836 at Edinburgh, Scotland: Thomas Cochran **HUME**[63] and Isabella, 2nd dau of William **SINCLAIR** of Tuswick, Caithness, Scotland - *AR*, 22 Feb 1836.

---

[62] The inquest at Halifax determined that he had shot himself - NSARM, RG 41 "C", Vol. 11. He was a native of "Pert Sruie Hill", perhaps a hilly location in Perthshire.

[63] Thomas Cochran **HUME** was baptised 18 Oct 1811 at St. Matthew's Presbyterian Church, Halifax, a son of Dr. Robert and Augusta Sophia (**HEAD**) **HUME** of Halifax, NS. He died 3 Mar 1846 at Hamilton, Bermuda. His wife Isabella died 28 Jan 1840 at Edinburgh, Scotland. They had two children.

Died 28 Jan 1836 at St. Andrews, NB: George **MILLAR**, Esq., 40, cashier of Charlotte County Bank, native of Scotland. He left a widow and large family - *NBRG*, 10 Feb 1836.

Died 1 Mar 1836 at Sussex Vale, NB: Arthur **McARTHUR**, 51, native of Perthshire, Scotland, "and for last 30 years in Sussex Parish" - *NBC*, 12 Mar 1836.

Married 10 Mar 1836 by Rev. James McIntosh, Halifax: James **FINDLAY**, Morayshire, Scotland, and Mrs. Margaret Ann **GRAY**, Halifax - *AR*, 12 Mar 1836.

Died 11 Mar 1836 at Margaree, Cape Breton, NS: Margaret, 27, wife of William **ROSS**, and dau of Capt. George **McKAY**, formerly of Archliney, Sutherlandshire, Scotland[64]. She left a husband and four children. Capt. McKay emigrated to NS from Scotland in 1800 - *GNS*, 3 May 1836.

Died 17 Mar 1836 at Newcastle, NB: Lewis **HENRY**, 58, native of Aberdeenshire, Scotland, and for many years a merchant at Newcastle - *GNS*, 22 Mar 1836.

Died 24 Mar 1836 at Bellville, [Pictou, NS]: Hugh **DENOON**[65], Esq., 90, Judge of the Court of Common Pleas, deputy recorder, magistrate, collector of imports and excise for the Port of Pictou, a native of Red Castle Parish, Inverness-shire, Scotland - *NBC*, 16 Apr 1836.

Died 2 Apr 1836 at Halifax: Robert, 17, youngest son of the late James **HUTTON**, Aberdeenshire, Scotland - *NSRG*, 6 Apr 1836.

Died 8 Apr 1836 at St. Mary's, Nashwaak, NB: Barbara, 57, native of Perthshire, Scotland, widow of Charles **DUFF**. She emigrated to NB with her husband in 1801 - *NBRG*, 13 Apr 1836.

Died 18 Apr 1836 at Saint John: Hugh **McMILLAN**, 72, native of Scotland, and for the past 36 years a resident of Saint John - *NBC*, 23 Apr 1836.

Married 21 Apr 1836 by Rev. Henderson, Murtel, Aberdeenshire, Scotland: Robert **YOUNG**, Esq., of Elgin, and Isabella Turburn, 3rd dau of Hugh **JOHNSTON**, Esq., of Saint John, NB - *NBRG*, 22 June 1836.

Died 14 May 1836 at Halifax: William **McKINLEY**, 42, native of Ayrshire, Scotland, leaving a widow and four children - *AR*, 21 May 1836.

Married 16 May 1836 by Rev. F. Stanislas, Carleton, Chaleur Bay: John **CLAPPERTON** of Scotland and Felicity **DUGAS**, Bay Chaleur - *NS*, 8 June 1836.

Married 27 May 1836 by Rev. Campbell, at New York: John **WILSON** and Catherine **GLEN**, both from Scotland but "late of Halifax" - *AR*, 2 July 1836.

---

[64] The *Halifax Journal*, 9 May 1836, gives **McKAY**'s birthplace as Arichteing. His widow, Catherine **FRASER**, died 11 Nov 1838 at Pictou (*Acadian* Recorder 17 Nov 1838).

[65] Hugh **DENOON** was born 18 Sep 1762, a son of David and Mary (**INGLIS**) Denoon. His rather spotty career as an immigrant contractor is detailed by J. M. Bumsted in the *Dictionary of Canadian Biography*, VII, pp. 244-246.

Died 1 June 1836 in Lanarkshire, Scotland: Robert **LINDSAY**, 77, father of John Lindsay, Pictou, NS - *AR*, 24 Sep 1836.

Died 22 June 1836 at St. George, NB: Andrew **SUTHERLAND**, 53, native of Ross-shire, North Britain - *NBC*, 23 July 1836.

Died 11 July 1836 at Gartferry House, Lanarkshire, Scotland: David **DOBIE**, Esq. - *WC*, 9 Sep 1836.

Inquest at Westfield, Kings County, NB, 22 July 1836 on the body of William **READ**, native of Scotland, believed to have fallen out of a boat and drowned - *NBC*, 30 July 1836.

Died 7 Aug 1836 at Glengary, Upper Canada: John **McDONALD**, 90, native of Inverness, Scotland. He was one of the last survivors of the 500 Highlanders who emigrated in 1784 with the late Allan McDonald, Esq., of Glengary - *WC*, 23 Sep 1836.

Died 22 Aug 1836 at the home of her dau, Mrs. **CHAMBERS**, Waterloo Place, Edinburgh[60]: Janet, 86, widow of Robert **NOBLE**, Peebles, Scotland - *AR*, 22 Oct 1836.

Married 8 Sep 1836 by Rev. James McIntosh, [Presbyterian] Halifax: Capt. James **BERWICK** from Scotland and Lucy **ANDERSON** of Halifax - *AR*, 10 Sep 1836.

Married 17 Sep 1836 by Archdeacon Robert Willis, Halifax: David **McAINSH** and Janet **GLEN**, both natives of Scotland - *AR*, 24 Sep 1836.

Died 25 Sep 1836 at Saint John: Capt. James **DRIVER**, 48, native of Scotland - *WC*, 30 Sep 1836.

Married 12 Oct 1836 by Rev. John Martin, Halifax: William **ROBERTSON**, Esq., collector of H.M. Customs at Shelburne, and Catherine, only dau of James **MILLER** of Glasgow, Scotland - *NBRG*, 27 Dec 1836.

Died 15 Oct 1836 at Union St., Saint John: John **KEVAND**, 80, cabinetmaker, native of Galloway, Scotland - *WC*, 21 Oct 1836.

Died 29 Oct 1836 at Halifax: John **TULLOUGH**, 33, native of Scotland - *AR*, 29 Oct 1836.

Died 21 Nov 1836 at St. Andrews, NB: David **CRAIG**, 88, native of Scotland; emigrated to NB in 1783. He left seven children, 57 grandchildren and 37 great-grandchildren - *WC*, 16 Dec 1836.

Died 24 Nov 1836 at Dalkeith, near Edinburgh, Scotland: David **NOBLE**, 41, leaving a widow and five children - *HJ*, 9 Jan 1837.

Died 1 Dec 1836 at the home of John **SINCLAIR**, Saint John: Peter **PEDDIE**, 73, native of Perthshire, Scotland - *WC*, 2 Dec 1836.

---

[60] Mrs. **NOBLE** was the mother of Robert Noble (1791 - 31 Jan 1872), merchant at Halifax, NS.

Died 14 Dec 1836 in the Parish of Minnigaff [Kirkcudbrightshire], Scotland: Mrs. **McNAIRN**, 99 years 10 months. "She remembered Prince Charles, the Pretender" - *Times*. 17 Jan 1837.

Died 23 Dec 1836 at Halifax: Alexander **MITCHELL**, 88, native of Dundee, Scotland - *AR*, 24 Dec 1836.

Died 30 Dec 1836 at Quaco, NB: Allan **McLEAN**, 91, native of Nairn, Scotland, who emigrated to [Cornwallis], Nova Scotia, in 1784, and resided in Quaco since 1787 - *NBC*, 14 Jan 1837.

Died 3 Jan 1837 at Saint John: Thomas **ADDISON**, schoolmaster, 71, native of Forfarshire, Scotland, leaving a widow and eight children. He was "an able Mathematician and scholar". He emigrated to British America 43 years ago - *NBC*, 7 Jan 1837.

Died 15 Jan 1837 at Halifax: John **SIMMONDS**, 53, native of Fochabers, [Morayshire], Scotland - *AR*, 21 Jan 1837.

Died in January 1837 at Liverpool, NS: William **JOHNSTON**, 84, native of Scotland - *AR*, 4 Feb 1837.

Died 10 Feb 1837 at Green Harbour, NS: John **McKENZIE**, 92, leaving a widow age 91. "They were married 72 years ago, and came to this country from Inverness, Scotland, about 50 years ago" - *AR*, 18 Mar 1837.

Married 16 Feb 1837 by Archdeacon R. Willis, Halifax: William R. **CROIL** from Glasgow, Scotland, and Caroline Mary Ann, 5th dau of Matthew **RICHARDSON**, Halifax[67] - *AR*, 18 Feb 1837.

Married 14 Mar 1837 by Rev. Alexander Gibson, Glasgow, Scotland: John **HOGAN**, merchant of Saint John, NB, and Eliza, dau of James **BLACK,** manufacturer - *NBC*, 29 Apr 1837.

Married 20 Apr 1837 at Edinburgh, Scotland: Capt. Charles **DUNDAS**, eldest son of Capt. Dean Dundas, and Janet Lindsay, dau of John **JARDINE** - *AR*, 13 May 1837.

Died 29 Apr 1837 at Saint John: Mary, 22, wife of Charles **HUMPHREYS**, and dau of the late James **COWAN**, formerly of Dumfries, Scotland - *NBC*, 6 May 1837.

Died 13 May 1837 at Musquodoboit, NS: James **BENVIE**, 83, native of Banffshire, Scotland - *AR*, 17 June 1837.

Married 3 June 1837 by Rev. John Loughnan, RC, Halifax: Thomas **CROCKET**, Dumfries, Scotland[68], and Ellen, 2nd dau of James **SANDERS**, Halifax - *AR*, 10 June 1837.

---

[67] This was a marriage of first cousins. The groom's mother and the bride's father were brother and sister. William Richardson **CROIL** (1812 - 1873) was a son of James Croil of Cargill Parish, Perthshire, Scotland, and his wife Jane, dau of William **RICHARDSON**, brother of Matthew Richardson (1771 - 1860). Caroline, born 17 Dec 1816 at Halifax, died 14 Feb 1891 at Montréal, was a daughter of the said Matthew Richardson and his second wife, Louise Ann **McINTOSH** of Halifax, NS.

[68] Thomas **CROCKET**, mariner, was a son of Robert and Ellen (**KILPATRICK**) Crocket of Dumfries, Scotland. Ellen was the dau of James and Joanna (**EVOY**) **SAUNDERS** of Halifax.

Married 6 June 1837 at Corse [Aberdeenshire]: Alexander **THOM**, Aberdeen, Scotland, and Margaret Udney, only dau of John **HENRY** of Watchmount - *HJ*, 21 Aug 1837.

Married 13 June 1837 by Rev. John J. Baxter, Onslow, NS: Alexander **CHRISTIE**, Onslow, NS, and Margaret, only dau of Joseph **LAIDLAW**, lately from Scotland - *Times*, 11 July 1837.

Died 13 June 1837 at Black River, NB: Elizabeth, 69, wife of William **McBEATH** [69] - *GNS*, 20 June 1837: "AFTER A UNION OF 46 YEARS, DISTINGUISHED BY INCREASING LOVE AND VIRTUE, DEATH HAS AT LENGTH TORN ASUNDER THE VENERABLE PAIR. THE HOMES OF THEIR PARENTS HAVING BEEN CONTIGUOUS, THEY SPENT THE MORNING OF THEIR DAYS, ENJOYING THE SOCIETY OF EACH OTHER, IN THE LAND OF THEIR BIRTH, SUTHERLAND, NORTH BRITAIN. 28 YEARS AFTER THEIR UNION, THEY EMIGRATED WITH THEIR THREE SONS AND TWO DAUGHTERS TO MIRAMICHI AND SETTLED IN BLACK RIVER WHERE THEY SINCE DWELT IN PEACE TOGETHER."

Married 22 June 1837 by Rev. Joseph F. Bent, Sackville, NB: Robert **BOWSER** , Sackville, and Jane, only dau of the late Alexander **KIRK**, formerly of Edinburgh, North Britain - *NBC*, 22 July 1837.

Died in June 1837 at St. John's, NL: Robert **DOBIE**, Esq., 28, surgeon, native of Kirkaldy, [Fifeshire], Scotland - *RGNA*, 27 June 1837.

Died 26 June 1837 at Musquodoboit, NS: Mary, widow of James **BENVIE**. She "survived her husband one month" - *AR*, 1 July 1837. [They were natives of Banffshire.]

Died 5 July 1837 at Creetown, [Dumfries-shire], Scotland: William, son of Samuel **McKEAN**, late of Richibucto, Kent County, NB - *GNS*, 5 Sep 1837.

Married 11 July 1837 by Rev. W. R. Taylor, at Thurso, Caithness, Scotland: Donald **MANSON** and Jessie, eldest dau of Alexander **BAIN** - *NSRG*, 6 Sep 1837.

Married 22 July 1837 by Rev. Bayard, New York: LeBaron **BOTSFORD**, MD, of Woodstock, NB, and Margaret, eldest dau of the late James **MAIN**, Esq., Glasgow, Scotland - *NBC*, 12 Aug 1837.

Married 22 July 1837 by Rev. Bayard, New York: Henry A. **HARTT**, MD, Fredericton, NB, and Jessie, 2nd dau of the late James **MAIN**, Esq., Glasgow, Scotland - *NBC*, 12 Aug 1837.

Died 6 Aug 1837 at Milton, Perthshire, Scotland: John **ROBERTSON**, 68 - *NBC*, 28 Oct 1837.

Died 6 Aug 1837, suddenly off New Orleans of yellow fever: Capt. James **SIMPSON** of the schooner *Samuel Gould* of Saint John. "Two of the crew died on passage from Montego Bay and two others were sick." Capt. Simpson was a native of Grangemouth, [Stirlingshire], Scotland - *NBC*, 16 Sep 1837.

---

[69] See note under his death, 13 Aug 1840 (*infra*).

Married 16 Aug 1837 by Rev. Richard Shepherd, Saint John: Henry J. **THORNE**, merchant, Saint John, and Agnes, youngest dau of Robert **CHESTNUT** of Scotland - *NBC*, 19 Aug 1837.

Died 20 Aug 1837 at Glasgow, Scotland: W. S., youngest son of David **RAIT** of St. Andrews, NB - *STA*, 28 Sep 1837.

Died 26 Aug 1837 at Shelburne, NS: Sarah **HOUSTON**, 86, native of Galloway, Scotland - *AR*, 9 Sep 1837.

Died 31 Aug 1837 at Windsor, NS: James **CLARKE**, 61, native of Banffshire, Scotland - *AR*, 30 Sep 1837.

Died 8 Sep 1837 at Saint John: James **McGLASHAN**, cooper, 40, native of Perthshire, Scotland. Burial from house of Charles **KAY**, Nelson Street - *NBC*, 9 Sep 1837.

Died 13 Sep 1837 at Woodstock, NB: William **CARMONT**, native of Scotland. "His death [was] occasioned by his falling from a cart on his return from the Poll on Friday previous, the wheel passing over and lacerating one of his legs in the most shocking manner." - *NBC*, 23 Nov 1837.

Died in September 1837 at Halifax: William **STEWART**, 37, native of Scotland - *AR*, 30 Sep 1837.

Died in September 1837 at Halifax: John **HECYER**, 64, native of Scotland - *AR*, 30 Sep 1837.

Died 6 Oct 1837 at *Willow Park*, Halifax: John **YOUNG**[70], Esq., Member of the Assembly for Sydney County [now Antigonish County] - *NBC*, 14 Oct 1837.

Died 8 Nov 1837 at Greenock, Scotland: James **STEWART**, Esq., of James & William Stewart, merchants at St. John's, NL, and Greenock - *RGNA*, 2 Jan 1838.

Died 17 Nov 1837 at Saint John: Jane, 23, wife of Jonathan **McDOUGALL**, late from Scotland. She lived at York Point, Saint John County - *NBC*, 18 Nov 1837.

Died 23 Nov 1837 at Halifax: Mrs. Jane **BOYD**, Sr., 72, native of Elgin, Morayshire, Scotland[71] - *AR*, 25 Nov 1837.

Died 29 Nov 1837 at Sydney, NS: John **LYONS**, native of Scotland - *AR*, 16 Dec 1837.

Married 14 Dec 1837 at Dorchester, NB: James **SCOULLAR**, 52, and Joan **McRAE**, both natives of Scotland - *NBC*, 6 Jan 1838.

Died 27 Dec 1837 at Halifax: Alexander **PHILIPS**, 83, native of Elgin, Scotland[72] - *AR*, 30 Dec 1837.

---

[70] John **YOUNG** was born 1 Sep 1777 at Falkirk, Scotland, the son of William and Janet YOUNG. He emigrated to Nova Scotia in 1814 with his wife Agnes **RENNY** and four sons. His work in promoting scientific methods of agriculture earned him the nickname *Agricola*. His career is written up by R. A. MacLean in the *Dictionary of Canadian Biography*, VII, pp. 930-935.

[71] Married 24 July 1785 at St. Matthew's Presbyterian Church, Halifax: Errol **BOYD** and Jean **WILLSON**. Errol Boyd died 20 Feb 1828 - *AR*, 23 Feb 1828. His burial entry gives his age as 76.

[72] Married 3 Nov 1787 at St. Matthew's Presbyterian Church, Halifax: Alexander *PHILIPS* and Agnes **GEORGE**, who died 5 May 1848 at Halifax, age 76.

Died 29 Dec 1837 at Halifax: Mrs. Crawford **FINDLAY,** 91, native of Edinburgh, Scotland
  - *AR*, 30 Dec 1837.

Died 31 Dec 1837 at Halifax: Duncan **McPHERSON**, 78, native of Nairn, Scotland
  - *HJ*, 1 Jan 1838.

Died 5 Jan 1838 at Saint John: Hugh **REED**, 28, master of the schooner *Elizabeth*, native of Alloa,
  [Clackmannan], Scotland. Buried from Mrs. **DRIVER**'s house, York Point - *NBC*, 6 Jan 1838.

Died 5 Jan 1838 at Saint John: John **BROWN**, 72, native of Glasgow, Scotland
  - *AR*, 24 Feb 1838.

Married 17 Jan 1838 by Rev. John Loughnan, RC, Halifax: Charles **LAMONT**, native of
  Aberdeenshire, Scotland, and Mary Frances **GRANT**, Halifax[73] - *HP*, 27 Jan 1838.

Died 21 Jan 1838 on passage from Jamaica to Norfolk: Capt. Matthew **KAVAND**, 35, shipmaster
  of the brig *La Plate* of Saint John. He was a native of Edinburgh, Scotland and left a widow and
  two children - *NBC*, 10 Mar 1838.

Died 25 Jan 1838 at Port Stanley, London District, Upper Canada: Charles, son of late David
  OGILVY, Esq., Port Common, Montrose, Scotland - *NBC*, 10 Mar 1838.

Died 30 Jan 1838 at Halifax: William **McDONALD**, 75, Ordnance Dept., native of Inverness,
  Scotland - *AR*, 3 Feb 1838.

Married 19 Feb 1838 by Rev. William Cogswell, Halifax: Andrew **OSWALD**, Grangemouth,
  Stirlingshire, Scotland, and Charlotte, 3rd dau of Robert **SNOOK**, St. John's, NL - *AR*, 24 Feb
  1838.

Died 6 Mar 1838 at Halifax: James **CRUIKSHANKS**, 51, native of Banffshire, Scotland, leaving a
  widow - *AR*, 10 Mar 1838.

Married 21 Mar 1838 by Rev. Alexander Romans, Dartmouth, NS: Thomas **ELLIOT** and
  Christianna **LAIDLAW**, both of Roxburghshire, Scotland - *AR* 24 Mar 1838.

Died 21 Mar 1838 at Londonderry, NS: William **CUMMINGS**, 68, native of Scotland
  - *HJ*, 9 Apr 1838.

Died 29 Mar 1838 at Halifax: Malcolm **NICHOLSON**, 88, native of Inverness, Scotland
  - *AR*, 31 Mar 1838.

Died 7 Apr 1838 at Rome: Charles Andrew, 19, native of Roxburghshire, Scotland, only remaining
  son of William and Alicia **SCOTT**, and grandson of the late Hon. Richard J. **UNIACKE**, Halifax
  - *AR*, 16 June 1838.

---

[73] Charles was a son of Malcolm and Janet (**McDONALD**) **LAMONT** of Aberdeenshire, Scotland.
Mary was a dau of Peter and Margaret (**TAILOR**) **GRANT** of Halifax.

Married 12 Apr 1838 at Edinburgh, Scotland: Valentine H. **NELSON** of Saint John, NB, and Margaret, eldest dau of William **RODGER**, Esq., 12 Leopold Place, Edinburgh - *NBC*, 16 June 1838.

Died 12 Apr 1838 at Drummond, West Branch, East River, Pictou, NS: James **FRASER**, 84, native of Inverness, Scotland - *AR*, 28 Apr 1838.

Died 15 Apr 1838 at Fredericton: Mrs. Sarah **BEVERLY**, 69, late of Aberdeen, Scotland - *NBC*, 21 Apr 1838.

Died 15 Apr 1838 at Chatham, NB: John **CHAMBERS**, 71, native of Dumfries-shire, Scotland - *NBC*, 28 Apr 1838.

Died 21 Apr 1838 at Saint John: John **BLACK**, 50, native of Aberdeen, Scotland - *NBC*, 28 Apr 1838.

Died 8 May 1838 at his son's house, St. Andrews, NB: David **RAIT**, Esq., 66, native of Fifeshire, Scotland, and resided many years in Edinburgh before emigrating to join his son's family in New Brunswick. "He was taking an airing in his chaise, accompanied by his granddaughter, when the horse became unmanageable, ran off and at the turn coming into town, broke the carriage into pieces. Fortunately the young lady escaped unhurt but Mr. Rait received a concussion which hastened the termination of his life." - *STA*, 12 May 1838.

Died 26 May 1838 at Halifax: Samuel **ADAMSON**, 42, leaving a widow and two children.[74] [He was a native of Scotland] - *AR*, 26 May 1838.

Died 26 May 1838 at the home of Thomas **MUSGRAVE**, Sussex Vale, NB: David **SHAW**, 80, native of Aberdeenshire, Scotland, "one of the first traveling gospel preachers in the province" - *NBC*, 9 June 1838.

Died in May 1838 at St. John's, NL: James **BLAIKIE**, Esq., 62, native of Roxburghshire, Scotland, clerk of the Supreme Court and for 28 years Police Magistrate at St. John's - *RGNA*, 4 June 1838.

Married 9 June 1838 by Archdeacon Robert Willis, Halifax: John **BAXTER** from Scotland, and Eliza, 2nd dau of Robert **PENGILLY**, Biddeford, England - *AR*, 16 June 1838.

Married 17 June 1838 by Rev. John Loughnan, RC, Halifax: Angus **CAMPBELL**, Inverness-shire, Scotland, and Margaret, youngest dau of Peter **GRANT**[75] - *AR*, 23 June 1838.

Murdered 28 June 1838 at Sydney, NS: Roderick **McISAAC**, "a Scotchman residing at Bras d'Or Lake" - *Times*, 17 July 1838.

Died 1 July 1838 at Chatham, NB: James **HUNTER**, 41, tailor, native of Dumfries, Scotland. He left a widow and five children - *GNS*, 3 July 1838.

---

[74] Married at St. Matthew's Presbyterian Church, Halifax, 19 July 1832: Samuel **ADAMSON** and Ann **NICHOL**.

[75] Angus was a son of John and Christiana (**CAMPBELL**) CAMPBELL. Margaret was a dau of Peter and Margaret **GRANT**.

Married 5 July 1838 by Rev. Churchill, Halifax: David **FALCONER** and Ann, dau of late Dr. **MILLER** of Wick, Caithness, Scotland - *HP*, 13 July 1838.

Died 11 July 1838 at Joppa, NB: Sgt. John **WRIGHT**, 110, "Commenced military career in 21st Fusiliers commanded by Col. **HAMILTON**. Witnessed death of General **WOLFE** on Plains of Abraham during French Canadian War, served under General **BURGOYNE** and Earl **CORNWALLIS** during American War of Independence, left son, a Roman Catholic priest at Montréal, Québec. He was a native of Edinburgh, Scotland" - *STA*, 14 July 1838.

Died 4 Aug 1838 at Halifax: Ann, 38, native of Inverness, Scotland, wife of A[lexander] **FRASER** - *HP*, 10 Aug 1838.

Inquest 29 Aug 1838 near Campbellton, NB, on the body of John **DRYNAN**, native of Scotland "who met his death by the accidental discharge of a gun which he had with him" - *GNS*, 25 Sep 1838.

Married 2 Sep 1838 by Rev. John Scott, Halifax: Angus **McLELLAN**, North Uist, Inverness-shire, Scotland, and Sarah **PHILIPS**, Halifax - *AR*, 8 Sep 1838.

Died 7 Oct 1838 at Halifax: Peter **McEWEN**, 30, turner, native of Edinburgh, Scotland - *AR*, 13 Oct 1838.

Died 9 Oct 1838 at 98 West George Street, Glasgow, Scotland: Hugh **DOHERTY**, Esq., 28, merchant late of Strabane, Ireland, "had a mercantile establishment in Saint John" - *STA*, 8 Dec 1838.

Married 9 Oct 1838 by Rev. Dr. Benjamin Gerrish Gray, Saint John: John **GALLAGHER**, Esq., Town Major, and Jean, dau of James **IRWIN** of Edinburgh, Scotland - *NBC*, 13 Oct 1838.

Died 19 Oct 1838 at Edinburgh, Scotland: Clementina, 26, 4th dau of late Rev. Thomas **GRAY** of Kirkaldy, and sister of professor Gray of King's College - *NBRG*, 16 Jan 1839.

Married 24 Oct 1838 at Bathurst, NB: George **DeBLOIS**, Halifax, and Jane, youngest dau of late John **MILLER**, Esq., Stirlingshire, Scotland - *NS*, 25 Oct 1838.

Died 2 Nov 1838 at Dalhousie, NB: Charles **STEWART**, Esq., 81, senior magistrate, colonel 1st Battalion of Militia. He was a native of Campbeltown, Argyllshire, Scotland "from whence he emigrated with his father and family in 1771" - *GNS*, 20 Nov 1838.

Died 15 Nov 1838 at Pictou, NS: Rev. Kenneth John **McKENZIE**[1], 39, recently pastor of St. Andrew's Church in that town - *NBC*, 24 Nov 1838.

Died in November 1838 at Halifax: James **MORTEN**, 40, of the ship *Thalia*, a native of Scotland - *Times*, 20 Nov 1838.

---

[1] Mr. **McKENZIE** was born at Stornaway, Isle of Lewis, Scotland - *cf.*, A. E. Betts, *Our Fathers in the Faith* (Halifax, 1983), p. 80.

Died 20 Nov 1838 at Saint John: Richard, youngest son of Joseph **GRAHAM**, merchant, late of Glasgow, Scotland - *NBC*, 24 Nov 1838.

Died 8 Dec 1838 at Pictou, NS: Rev. James **ROBSON**[77], 63 - *NBC*, 22 Dec 1838.

Died 11 Dec 1838 at Anderston, [Lanarkshire], Scotland: Catherine Glen, 85, widow of W[illiam] **KIDSTON**, "for many years a resident of Halifax" - *AR*, 2 Mar 1839.

Died 26 Dec 1838 at Douglas, NS: Alexander **SCOTT**, 80, native of Aberdeenshire, Scotland - *NS*, 17 Jan 1839.

Died 3 Jan 1839 at Chatham, NB: Alexander **GERRIE**, 57, native of Scotland - *GNS*, 8 Jan 1839.

Died 6 Jan 1839 at Mount Dalhousie, NS: Alexander **McKENZIE**, 39, native of Dornoch, [Sutherlandshire], Scotland, leaving a widow and eight children - *NSRG*, 23 Jan 1839.

Died 8 Jan 1839 at Aylesford, NS: Jane, 63, widow of John **CARRUTHERS**, both from Scotland - *NS*, 17 Jan 1839.

Died 18 Jan 1839 at Saint John: Euphemia Auld, 1 year 11 months, only dau of Rev. John G. **McGREGOR**, licentiate of the Church of Scotland, and granddau of late Rev. Alexander **STIRLING**, minister of Tillecoultry, North Britain - *NBRG*, 30 Jan 1839.

Died 21 Jan 1839 at Chatham, NB: Adam Dixon **SHIRREFF**, Esq., 55, native of Leith, Scotland; emigrated to Halifax[78], thence to Chatham "where he has resided many years" - *STA*, 16 Feb 1839.

Married 22 Jan 1839 by Rev. John Scott, Halifax: B[enjamin] D. **CROW** and Margaret, 2nd dau of the late Alexander **BAIRD**, Edinburgh, Scotland - *AR*, 2 Feb 1839.

Died in January 1839 at Halifax: Edward **BURKE**, 62, from Scotland - *AR*, 2 Feb 1839.

Died 16 Feb 1839 at his residence, *The Hermitage*, Bermuda: Gilbert **SALTON**, Esq., 70, for 23 years collector of customs in Bermuda, native of Edinburgh, Scotland - *AR*, 23 Mar 1839.

Died in February 1839 at St. George Parish, Charlotte County, NB: John **DICK**, 95, native of Scotland. He "came to this Province with Loyalists" - *STA*, 2 Mar 1839.

Married 2 Mar 1839 by Rev. John Martin, Halifax: David **CALDER**, Caithness, Scotland, and Maria, only dau of William **CALDWELL**, Halifax - *AR*, 9 Mar 1839.

Died 9 Mar 1839 at Cornwallis, NS: James **BLACK**, 50, native of Stirlingshire, Scotland, leaving a widow and nine children - *AR*, 16 Mar 1839.

---

[77] Mr. **ROBSON** was born at Kelso, Scotland, and came to Nova Scotia in 1811 - *cf.*, A. E. Betts, *Our Fathers in the Faith* (Halifax, 1983), p. 111.

[78] Married 6 June 1820 at St. Paul's Anglican Church, Halifax: Adam Dixon **SHIRREFF** and Jane **HUNTER**.

Killed 17 Apr 1839 by lightning on board schooner *Loyalist* during its voyage from Wilmington to Saint John: Peter **WHITY**, seaman, native of Argyllshire, North Britain - *STA*, 27 Apr 1839.

Died 5 May 1839 at Mount Hope, near Shelburne, NS: Elizabeth, 81 years 6 months, native of Hamilton, [Lanarkshire], Scotland, widow of John **MARTIN** - *HJ*, 27 May 1839.

Died 4 July 1839 at Highland Hill, NB, at the residence of Joseph **WALTON**, Esq., "where he had resided upwards of 24 years as a faithful servant: John **McCOLL**, over 84 years old, native of Argyllshire, Scotland, and one of those disbanded from the 74th Regt. at the end of the Revolutionary War and located on the Digdeguash River under the grant to Archibald **WILLIAMSON** and others. There are only three of that fine old class remaining in Charlotte Co." - *NBC*, 13 July 1839.

Died 15 July 1839 at Halifax: James **FRASER**, 70, native of Aberdeenshire, Scotland - *AR*, 20 July 1839.

Married 27 July 1839 by Rev. E. B. Ramsay, Edinburgh, Scotland: Roderick Charles **McDONALD**, Castle Farm, PE, grandson of *"The Glenaladale"* of 1745 [The Jacobite Rising], and Elizabeth, eldest dau of the late *"Glengarry"* - NSRG, 18 Sep 1839.

Died 9 Aug 1839 at Red Head, Saint John: William **SCOTT**, 46, native of Lanarkshire, Scotland, leaving a widow and eight children - *NBC*, 10 Aug 1839.

Died 6 Sep 1839 at St. Andrews, NB: Peter **HYSLOP**, 96, native of Scotland - *NBC*, 21 Sep 1839.

Died in September 1839 at Halifax: Isabel **WOODS**, 34, native of Scotland - *AR*, 21 Sep 1839.

Died 18 Sep 1839 at Wolfe Islands, Kingston, Upper Canada: Donald **McDONALD**, 97, native of Glengary, Scotland, leaving a large family. "He came to America with the McDonells in 1772; and in 1773 joined the British Standard under Sir John **JOHNSON** in whose regiment he served 7 years" - *NBC*, 12 Oct 1839.

Died 24 Sep 1839 on board the brig *Gambia* on passage from Jamaica to Saint John: Magnus **MYRRIMENT**, 22, mate of the vessel, a native of Scotland - *NBC*, 26 Oct 1839.

Died 25 Sep 1839 at Truro, NS: John **HENDERSON**, 95, native of Scotland - *AR*, 5 Oct 1839.

Died 7 Oct 1839 at Nerepis Settlement, NB: David **MATHER**, 49, native of Kincairn [Kincardine], Scotland - *NBC*, 12 Oct 1839.

Married 4 Nov 1839 by Rev. Robert Archibald, Miramichi, NB: Capt. Francis J. **McALPINE**, Halifax, and Martha, youngest dau of S. **RAINNIE**, Esq., of Aberdeen, Scotland - *NBC*, 30 Nov 1839.

Died 24 Nov 1839 at Halifax: Isabella **COOPER**, 26, native of Aberdeenshire, Scotland, leaving her husband and three children - *AR*, 30 Nov 1839.

Died 8 Dec 1839 at Fredericton: James **DOBIE**, Esq., 33, eldest son of late David Dobie of Gartferry, Scotland. Buried at Saint John - *NBC*, 14 Dec 1839.

Died 17 Dec 1839 at Saint John: John **SMITH**, native of Caithness, Scotland, leaving a widow and four children - *NBC*, 28 Dec 1839.

Died 22 Dec 1839 at Rochester, New York: Elizabeth, 90, widow of Daniel **McKENZIE** of Gleashee, Highlands of Perth, Scotland, and mother of William Lyon McKenzie[79], formerly of Toronto, "for last six months prisoner in Monroe County Jail" - *MCN,* 15 Jan 1840.

Died 28 Dec 1839 at Saint John: Thomas **WALLACE**, 25, merchant, eldest son of Thomas Wallace of Fenwick, [Ayrshire], near Kilmarnock, Scotland - *NBC,* 4 Jan 1840.

Died early 1840 in the Republic of Texas: Hugh **GREY**, 43, from Kilmarnock, Scotland; "late of Wallace, NS", left a widow and family - *NSRG,* 4 Mar 1840.

Died 4 Jan 1840 in Halifax: Alexander **THOMPSON**, 36, native of Dunfermline, [Fifeshire], Scotland - *CP,* 4 Jan 1840.

Married 9 Jan 1840 by Rev. Donald McConnachie at Rogers Hill, NS: John **MURRAY** of Rogart, Sutherlandshire, Scotland, and Christy, dau of Hugh **McLEOD**, Hardwood Hill, Pictou, NS - *Times,* 28 Jan 1840.

Died 26 Jan 1840 at Morris Street, Saint John: John **THOMPSON**, 63, late merchant at Saint John. "For upwards of 30 years conducted well known establishment in Dumfries, Scotland, and was a large exporter to this city" - *MCN,* 29 Jan 1840.

Died 5 Feb 1840 at Shelburne, NS: John **FRASER**, 87; "left Scotland before the first American War [i.e., before 1775], resided some time in New York, and came to this province at its first settlement [i.e., with Loyalists who founded Shelburne in 1783]" - *AR,* 22 Feb 1840.

Died in February 1840 at Tabisuntac, Northumberland County, NB: John **SUTHERLAND**, native of Scotland - *GNS,* 18 Feb 1840.

Died 9 Feb 1840 at Cornwallis, NS: Rev. William **FORSYTH**, 66[80] - *AR,* 22 Feb 1840.

Died 29 Feb 1840 in Nova Scotia: Donald Og **CHISHOLM**, 84 yrs. 4 mos., from Clachan, Strathglass, Inverness-shire, Scotland - *NS,* 4 Mar 1840.

Died in March 1840 at Sussex, NB: Mary, wife of John **McQUEEN**, schoolmaster, formerly of Paisley, Scotland - *NBC,* 7 Mar 1840.

Died 4 Apr 1840 at Saint John: Lillias McCorkendale, 12, 4th dau of James **MUIR** of Ayr, Scotland - *NBRG,* 8 Apr 1840.

Died 16 Apr 1840 at Halifax: Sinclair **OAL**, 22, native of Caithness, Scotland - *NS,* 23 Apr 1840.

Died 25 Apr 1840 at Portland, Saint John: Margaret, 53, widow of David **ANDERSON**, formerly of Dumfries, Scotland. She was survived by her aged father and numerous family - *NBC,* 25 Apr 1840.

---

[79] William Lyon **McKENZIE** was a leader of the abortive Rebellion in Upper Canada in Dec 1837. He was born 12 Mar 1795 at Springfield, Dundee, Scotland, the only son of Donald and Elizabeth (MacKenzie) **McKENZIE**, natives of Kirkmichael, Perthshire. W. L. McKenzie died at Toronto, 28 Aug 1861. His grandson, William Lyon McKenzie **KING**, was prime minister of Canada several times between 1921 and 1948. W.L.McKenzie was imprisoned by the American authorities in Monroe County, New York, for violating American neutrality by launching an attack from American soil against British North America.

[80] He was a native of Ecclefechan, Dumfries-shire. Came to Nova Scotia about 1800 - A. E. Betts, *Our Fathers in the Faith* (Halifax, 1983), p. 39.

Died 2 May 1840 at Shelburne: Capt. Charles **McLEAN**, 71, native of Argyllshire, Scotland, son of Hugh McLean - *AR*, 23 May 1840.

Died 4 May 1840 at residence of John **WALKER**, Esq., Saint John: Barbara **CAMPBELL**, 93, native of Caithness, Scotland - *NBC*, 9 May 1840.

Died 7 May 1840 at Portuguese Cove, NS: John **MUNRO**, 70, native of Morayshire, Scotland - *CP*, 9 May 1840.

Inquest 22 May 1840 at Saint John on the body of William **GIBB**, carpenter in the bark *Eliza* of Irvine, Scotland, a native of Trune [Troon, Ayrshire], Scotland. Gibb, "in endeavouring to get on board . . .vessel, fell overboard Friday, drowned" - *GNS*, 26 May 1840.

Died 26 May 1840 at Cornwallis, NS: William **CAMPBELL**, Esq., 80; emigrated from Argyllshire, Scotland, in 1783 - *NS*, 4 June 1840.

Died in June 1840 at Halifax: Peter **REED**, 38, native of Leith, Scotland - *CP*, 20 June 1840.

Died in June 1840 at Halifax: Robert **FRASER**, 48, native of Scotland - *CP*, 20 June 1840.

Died 15 June 1840 at Halifax: David **McTIER**, 38, native of Wigtownshire, Scotland, leaving a widow and four children - *HJ*, 22 June 1840.

Died 30 June 1840 at Windsor Road [Sackville], NS: Andrew **BLAIR**, 86, native of Glasgow, Scotland - *AR*, 11 July 1840.

Died 18 July 1840 at Earltown, NS: J[ohn] **SUTHERLAND**, 103, native of Sutherlandshire, Scotland - *HJ*, 10 Aug 1840.

Died 6 Aug 1840 at South Brookfield, Colchester County, NS: John **DUFFUS**, 61, native of Scotland - *AR*, 12 Oct 1840.

Died 13 Aug 1840 at Black River, NB: William **McBEATH**, 73, native of Sutherlandshire, Scotland, who "emigrated here in 1819 where he made a comfortable living for himself and family."[81] He was an elder of St. Stephen's Church at Glenelg, NB - *GNS*, 25 Aug 1840.

Died 13 Aug 1840 at Saint John: Jane, 29, dau of Thomas **POLLOCK**, Esq., Glasgow, Scotland, and niece of James **MAXWELL**, Esq., collector of customs, Campbeltown, [Argyllshire], Scotland - *NBC*, 15 Aug 1840.

Died 13 Aug 1840 at Fredericton: Peter **FRASER**, Esq., 74, native of Forres, Morayshire, Scotland. He was Member of the Assembly for York County, a Justice of Common Pleas and Justice of the Peace , also colonel in the 3rd Battalion, Carleton County Militia. For many years he was president of the Fredericton Society of Saint Andrew - *NBC*, 22 Aug 1840.

Died 25 Aug 1840 at St. Andrews, NB: Thomas **McFARLANE**, 51, native of Alloa, [Clackmannan], Scotland - *NBC*, 5 Sep 1840.

---

[81] William was born 8 Mar 1767, the son of John and Barbara (**GUNN**) **McBEATH**, He married 4 Apr 1792 at Kildonan, Sutherlandshire, Elizabeth, born 12 Aug 1768, died 13 June 1837, dau of John and Barbara **GUNN**. They emigrated with children Margaret, Alexander, John, Donald and Barbara in 1819.

Died 25 Aug 1840 at New York: Andrew **McKENZIE**, 17, native of Ross-shire, Scotland, and formerly of Saint John, NB - *NBC*, 19 Sep 1840.

Died 25 Aug 1840 at Richmond, VA: Rev. Archibald **McQUEEN**, 59, native of Ayrshire, Scotland, father of Mrs. **BLACKADAR**[82] - *Times*, 29 Sep 1840.

Died 6 Oct 1840 at Halifax: J[ohn] **McINTYRE**, 79, from the Highlands of Scotland - *HMP*, 10 Oct 1840.

Died 30 Oct 1840 at Kirkcudbright, Scotland: Peter **STUBS**, Esq., 57, formerly a merchant at St. Andrews, NB - *STA*, 27 Nov 1840.

Died 1 Nov 1840 at Rogers Hill, NS: Ewan **McLACHLANE**, 26, lately from Scotland - *HJ*, 11 Jan 1841.

Died 25 Nov 1840 at Mount Thom, NS: Elizabeth **McDONALD**, 51, native of Sutherlandshire, Scotland, wife of Angus **MURRAY**, leaving husband and nine children - *NS*, 24 Dec 1840.

Died 25 Dec 1840 at Halifax: George **FAIRWEATHER**, native of Scotland - *AR*, 26 Dec 1840.

Died 8 Jan 1841 at Montego Bay, Jamaica: Robert **WAIT**, Esq., 68, native of Scotland, but had resided in Jamaica for 50 years. He was a magistrate and member of the Legislature - *NBC*, 20 Feb 1841.

Died 28 Jan 1841 at West River, Pictou, NS: John **GUNN**, 47, native of Caithness, Scotland - *HJ*, 8 Feb 1841.

Died 18 Feb 1841 at Meaghers Grant, NS: Duncan **CALDER**, 76, from Inverness-shire, Scotland - *HJ*, 15 Mar 1841.

Died in February 1841 at Musquodoboit, NS: Henry **HOLLANDWORTH**, 85; and George **WATSON**, 97, "from the mother country" [Scotland] - *AR*, 27 Feb 1841.

Died 28 Feb 1841 at Saint John: Elizabeth Ann, 51, native of Kirkconnel, Dumfries-shire, Scotland, wife of Charles **BOWATSON**[83] - *STA*, 5 Mar 1841.

---

[82] "Mrs. Blackadar" was Rev. **McQUEEN**'s eldest dau Catherine who married 17 Oct 1825, Henry Nichol **BLACKADAR** (1803 - 1852) of Halifax, NS, who was a Conservative Member of the Nova Scotia House of Assembly for Pictou, 1840-43 and 1845-51.

[83] This man's name should be **HOWATSON**. The *NBC*, 19 July 1845, reported that an inquest had been held at St. Andrews, Charlotte County, on 16 July, on the body of Julia Ann **HATT** who "destroyed herself by taking poison. The deceased had been living the last 3 or 4 years with Charles **HOWATSON** and had occasionally been addicted to drinking. The day before her death she purchased a sixpence worth of arsenic, a portion of which she mixed with tea which caused death in 9 hours. Charles Howatson was in the room at the time, saw the deceased take the poison, knowing it to be such and did not . . . prevent her and did not call in medical or other assistance. He was committed to jail to stand trial, being considered an accessory to the death."

Died 2 Mar 1841 at Boston: William Russell **MASON**, 50, native of Edinburgh, and formerly of Halifax, NS - *HJ*, 22 Mar 1841.

Died 8 Mar 1841 at the Beaches, Pictou, NS: David **MURDOCH**, 73, native of Perthshire, Scotland, who emigrated to Pictou in 1801 - *NS*, 25 Mar 1841.

Died 10 Mar 1841 at Salt Springs, Upham Parish, Kings County, NB: Peter **McDOUGALD**, 50, native of Perthshire, Scotland, leaving a widow and five children. He emigrated to New Brunswick 20 years before - *NBC*, 3 Apr 1841.

Died 1 Apr 1841 at Tabisuntac, NB: Mrs. Jane **HARKNESS**, 71, native of Dumfries, Scotland, who emigrated here about 18 months ago - *STA*, 27 Apr 1841.

Died 3 Apr 1841 at Halifax: William J. **McLEOD**, 38, native of Caithness, Scotland, leaving a widow and four children - *AR*, 10 Apr 1841.

Died in April 1841 at Halifax: Charles **HAY** and James **OSBURN**, natives of Scotland - *AR*, 17 Apr 1841.

Died 20 Apr 1841 at Saint John: John **MOYES**, 45, native of Dumfries-shire, Scotland, leaving a widow and two children - *NBC*, 24 Apr 1841.

Died 21 Apr 1841 at Halifax: William **PARKER**, 55, native of Scotland - *AR*, 24 Apr 1841.

Died 24 Apr 1841 at Halifax: Isabella, 74, widow of James **WILSON**, Bolton, Haddingtonshire, Scotland - *AR*, 1 May 1841.

Married 27 Apr 1841 by Rev. George Almond at Garnett Hill, Glasgow, Scotland: Robert **BELL**, Esq., banker at Edinburgh, and Mary Elizabeth, 2nd dau of James **PETERS**, Esq., Saint John, NB - *NBC*, 22 May 1841.

Died 2 May 1841 at Musquodoboit, NS: Alexander **STEWART**, native of Banffshire, Scotland - *AR*, 22 May 1841.

Died 11 May 1841 at Burton, Sunbury County, NB: James **BLAIN**, 42, native of Ayrshire, Scotland - *NBC*, 22 May 1841.

Died 14 May 1841 at Glasgow, Scotland: George A., son of Enoch **BARKER**, Esq., of Sheffield, Sunbury County, NB, a medical student and a clerk at the Glasgow Royal Infirmary. He had studied in the Baptist Seminary at Fredericton, then at the Grammar School in Saint John, where he gained the school's highest honour, Corporate Gold Medal - *NBC*, 12 June 1841.

Died 14 May 1841 at Halifax: James **McNEVEN**, 30, from Great Britain - *AR*, 15 May 1841.

Died in May 1841 at Jordan Bay, NS: William **McKAY**, leaving a widow and large family. He emigrated from Scotland about 20 years ago - *AR*, 22 May 1841.

Married 16 June 1841 by Rev. J. W. D. Gray at Saint John: Ira **MOSHER** of Saint John and Catherine, dau of late Capt. H. **CHISHOLM** of the Royals and latterly Fort Major of Fort Augustus, Inverness-shire, Scotland - *NBC*, 3 July 1841.

Died 5 July 1841 on board the barque *Hope* in St. Andrews Harbour, NB: Peter **SMART**, 36, chief mate, a native of Scotland - *STA*, 9 July 1841.

Married 11 July 1841 by Rev. Somerville at Bathurst, NB: William **PALLEN** and Margaret, eldest dau of the late John **RONALDS** of Aberdeen, Scotland - *STA*, 30 July 1841.

Died 11 July 1841 at Grand Manan, Charlotte County, NB: George **THOMSON** of Saint John, 54, shipbuilder. He was "superintending the raising of the ship *Wallace* recently stranded on the Murr Ledges". He was a native of Dumfries-shire, Scotland, and had lived 24 years in New Brunswick. "To his orphan daughter (who, only a week since, during her father's absence, returned home from Liverpool, whither she had accompanied her mother, whose health was declining and where she witnessed her demise - an event unknown to Mr. Thomson), the loss is indeed irreparable." - *NBC*, 17 July 1841.

Died 2 Aug 1841 at Wallace, NS: John **MacFARLANE**, 94, native of Perthshire, Scotland - *HJ*, 16 Aug 1841.

Married 3 Sep 1841 by Rev. William Harrison, Saint John: Capt. Thomas **SIMS** of Liverpool, England, and Mary Ann **FOREST**, Annan, Scotland - *NBC*, 18 Sep 1841.

Died 17 Sep 1841 at St. Andrews, NB: Elizabeth, 24, native of Ballantrae, Ayrshire, Scotland, eldest dau of Robert **PEACOCK** - *NBC*, 25 Sep 1841.

Married 1 Oct 1841 by Rev. James Hannay, Richibucto, NB: Capt. Thomas **LEAPER** of the barque *Intrepid*, Liverpool, and Mary **MILLER**, Lochmahan, Dumfries-shire, Scotland - *HJ*, 1 Nov 1841.

Died 16 Oct 1841 at Barneys River, Merigomish, NS: Jane **JEFFERYS**, 73, native of the Parish of Edrom, Berwickshire, Scotland, wife of John **SMITH** - *HJ*, 15 Nov 1841.

Died in November 1841 en route from Jamaica to Alexandria: Capt. William **HODGE** of the brig *Helen and Elizabeth*, Halifax; native of Ayrshire, Scotland, leaving a widow and child - *AR*, 20 Nov 1841.

Died 5 Nov 1841 at Arichat, NS: Alexander **WRIGHT**, 33, native of Kincardinshire, Scotland - *AR*, 13 Nov 1841.

Died 8 Nov 1841 at Cariboo Meadows, NS: Andrew **MURRAY**, 76, native of Sutherlandshire, Scotland - *HJ*, 13 Dec 1841.

Died 12 Nov 1841 at Pictou, NS: Alexander **THOM**, native of Scotland - *AR*, 20 Nov 1841.

Died 12 Dec 1841 at Edinburgh, Scotland: Alicia, widow of William **SCOTT**, and 3rd dau of the late Hon. Richard John **UNIACKE** of Nova Scotia - *AR*, 22 Jan 1842.

Died 14 Dec 1841 at Musquodoboit, NS: Peter **GORDON**, 65, native of Inverness, Scotland - *HJ*, 27 Dec 1841.

Died 22 Dec 1841 at Portland, NB: Charles **WATT**, 88, native of Montrose, Angus-shire, Scotland. Came to New Brunswick at the end of the Revolutionary War with Capt. Campbell's Company, 74th Regt. Buried from the residence of William Watt - *NBC*, 25 Dec 1841.

Died 28 Dec 1841 at Montego Bay, Jamaica: James **RAIT**, Esq., 43, late of St. Andrews, NB, a native of Glasgow, Scotland. He was a Justice of the Inferior Court of Common Pleas - *NBC*, 12 Feb 1842.

Died 30 Dec 1841 at Kingsclear, York County, NB: David **GOOD**, 95, native of Dundee, Scotland, came to New Brunswick as a Loyalist in 1783. He was survived by his wife of 60 years, five children, sixty grandchildren and forty-six great-grandchildren, 111 living descendants in all.[84] He was a Presbyterian - *NBC*, 29 Jan 1842.

Died 11 Jan 1842 at Glenelg, Northumberland County, NB: Angus **McDONALD**, native of the Isle of Lewis; an early settler who had been a soldier in the American Revolutionary War. He left a widow and family - *NBC*, 22 Jan 1842.

Died 20 Jan 1842 at Miramichi [Chatham Head, NB]: Catherine, 39, wife of Alexander **FRASER**, Jr., Esq., and dau of the late James B. **FRASER**, Esq., of Gorthleck, all of Stratherrick [by Loch Ness]. She left a husband and seven children - *NBC*, 29 Jan 1842; *Times*, 8 Feb 1842.

Died in January 1842 at Shubenacadie, NS: David **MILNE**, about 50, native of Scotland - *AR*, 26 Feb 1842.

Died 8 Feb 1842 at Scotch Hill, NS: Charles **McDONALD**, 81, who emigrated from Moulin, Perthshire, Scotland, about 39 years before - *HJ*, 21 Mar 1842.

Married 14 Feb 1842 at Jersey, Great Britain, by Rev. Dean: David **REID**, Esq., Glenshiel, [Ross and Cromarty], Scotland, and Sarah Jane, eldest dau of D. J. **McQUEEN**, late major, 74th Regt. - *WC*, 8 Apr 1842.

Died 18 Feb 1842 at Dalhousie, NB: Elizabeth **SILLER**, 100 years, 11 months old, native of the Isle of Arran, Scotland, widow of D. M. **NEISH** - *HJ*, 28 Mar 1842.

Married 23 Feb 1842 by Rev. Harrison, Portland, NB: Charles J. **WATERBERY**, Portland, NB, and Ann, 3rd dau of Thomas **PHILIPS**, Esq., Dysart, Fifeshire, Scotland - *NBC*, 26 Feb 1842.

Married 1 Mar 1842 by Rev. J. Eachie, Edinburgh, Scotland: Thomas **FENE[R]TY**, Halifax, NS, and Isabella, dau of James **LEISHMAN**[85] - *AR*, 26 Mar 1842.

Died in March 1842 at Hillsborough River, PE: John **FERGUSON**, 80, who emigrated from Perthshire, Scotland, in 1807 - *HJ*, 28 Mar 1842.

---

[84] David was baptised 23 Apr 1749 in Fifeshire, opposite Dundee, a son of James and Barbara (**BERRY**) **GOOD**. He emigrated to America in 1770 and married Jane . . . His five surviving children were Elizabeth, James, Francis, Catherine and Solomon.

[85] Thomas Joseph **FENERTY** died 29 Nov 1868 age 50. He was a son of Samuel W. and Catherine Fenerty of Halifax. Isabella was a dau of James **LEISHMAN** and Elizabeth **SMITH** who were married at St. Matthew's Presbyterian Church, Halifax, 12 May 1814.

Died 17 Mar 1842 "on the ice" at Richibucto, NB: William **McGAVIE**, 37, from Scotland, "who practiced the medical profession during the last year". He left a widow and three children - *NBC*, 9 Apr 1842.

Died 18 Mar 1842 at Toronto, Upper Canada: William Alexander **McDONELL**, 60, native of Inverness, Scotland, formerly speaker of the Upper Canadian House of Assembly[86] - *WC*, 15 Apr 1842.

Died 19 Mar 1842 at Halifax: John **ROBB**, 49, native of Borharm, Banffshire, Scotland, leaving a widow and seven children[87] - *HJ*, 21 Mar 1842.

Died 4 Apr 1842 at Lunenburg, NS: John **McGRIGOR**, 84, native of Aberdeen, Scotland[88] - *AR*, 16 Apr 1842.

Died 10 Apr 1842 at Merigomish, NS: John **SUTHERLAND**, 115 [sic], native of Clyne Parish, Sutherlandshire, Scotland - *AR*, 28 May 1842. He was commonly called the "kilty man" - *WC*, 20 May 1842.

Died 12 Apr 1842 at Halifax: James **ARMSTRONG** from Stirling, Scotland - *AR*, 16 Apr 1842.

Died 17 Apr 1842 at Halifax: Duncan **McFARLANE**, 60, native of Aberfoyle, [Perthshire], Scotland - *AR*, 23 Apr 1842.

Married 14 May 1842 by Rev. Prof. Alexander Romans, Halifax: Robert Duncan **CLARKE**, Dumbarton, Scotland, and Margaret, 4th dau of the late Andrew **CRAWFORD**, Halifax - *HMP*, 17 May 1842.

Married 1 June 1842 by Rev. John Loughnan, RC, Halifax: William **JAMESON**, Ayrshire, Scotland, and Marion, eldest dau of the late Samuel **LAWRENCE**, Halifax[89] - *AR*, 4 June 1842.

Died 3 June 1842 at Halifax: Adam **CARR**, 53, native of Berwick-upon-Tweed, "for many years a merchant in New Glasgow" - *AR*, 4 June 1842.

---

[86] Alexander **McDONELL** was born 16 Apr 1762 at Fort Augustus, Scotland, a son of Allen McDonell of Collachie and Helen **MacNAB**. His career was written up by J. M. Bumsted, in the *Dictionary of Canadian Biography*, Vol. VII, pp. 554-556.

[87] The 1838 census reports John **ROBB** was a measurer, and at that time had a son and six daughters.

[88] John, shoemaker, son of George and Barbara **McGREGOR**, married 23 Aug 1789 in the Dutch Reformed Church, Lunenburg, NS, Johanna, dau of Johann Georg and Regina **BOEHNER**, and had twelve children.

[89] The church register is more informative. The married couple were William, son of James **JAMISON** and Ann **FOLLES** of Lochinnock, Ayrshire, and Marion, dau of the late Samuel **LAWRENCE** and Ellen **SULLIVAN**, Halifax. Marion was baptised on 14 Feb 1823, age 2 months, the dau of Samuel Lawrence from Wiltshire, England, and Eleanor Sullivan from Buttevant, County Cork, Ireland.

Died 13 June 1842 at Halifax: Adam **BLACK**, 44, native of Kilmarnock, Scotland[90]
- *AR*, 18 June 1842.

Died 15 June 1842 at Saint John: Capt. John **STEWART** from Alloa, [Clackmannan], Scotland, late master of the brig *Retreat* - *NBC*, 18 June 1842.

Died 11 July 1842 at Newcastle, NB: Joseph **HOME**, Esq., 79, native of Berwick-upon-Tweed, and for many years J.P. for Northumberland County - *NBC*, 30 July 1842.

Married 19 July 1842 at New Annan, NS, by Rev. Robert Blackwood: John **DUNCAN** and Margaret **RAMSAY**, "lately from Scotland" - *AR*, 6 Aug 1842.

Married 24 July 1842 at Halifax by Rev. John Thomas Twining: William **MILLARD**, Bristol, England, and Charlotte Adelaide, widow of Capt. William **CATTERNICH**, Aberdeen, Scotland - *AR*, 30 July 1842.

Died 31 July 1842 at Halifax: Mary, 56, wife of John **SMITH**, blacksmith and engineer "late of Scotland" - *AR*, 6 Aug 1842.

Married 2 Aug 1842 at Collean Cottage, Ayrshire: W. H. **DOBIE**, Esq., Glasgow, and Ann Elleison[91], eldest dau of the late A. **McDOWAL**, Esq., Two Mile Wood, Jamaica - *NBC*, 10 Sep 1842.

Died 4 Aug 1842 at Halifax: William **FINDLAY**, 76, native of Rothes, [Morayshire], Scotland - *AR*, 6 Aug 1842.

Died in August 1842 in the brig *Diamond*, en route from Berbice to St. Andrews, NB: James **GILAN**, 22, native of Perth, Scotland - *STA*, 26 Aug 1842.

Died 26 Aug 1842 at the Marine Hospital, Saint John: John R. **WILSON**, 69, of the brig *Reliance*, native of Saltcoats, [Ayrshire], Scotland - *STA*, 2 Sep 1842.

Died 31 Aug 1842 at Saint John: Capt. Alexander **BLACK**, late of the ship *Crown*, a native of Fittenwiem [Pittenweem], Fifeshire, Scotland - *NBC*, 3 Sep 1842.

Died 1 Sep 1842 at Merigomish, NS: Alexander **FORBES**, 62, native of Inverness-shire, Scotland - *HMP*, 13 Sep 1842.

Died 27 Sep 1842 at Halifax: John **ANDERSON**, 75, of the Ordnance Dept., native of Fifeshire, Scotland; lived 56 years in Halifax[92] - *AR*, 1 Oct 1842.

Died 28 Sep 1842 at Dunoon, Argyllshire: Margaret Birkmyre, 74, wife of David **MILLER**, Esq. - *NBC*, 12 Nov 1842.

---

[90] The 1838 Census shows Adam **BLACK** as a grocer, with a wife and two sons aged 6 to 14.

[91] Ann E., wife of William H. **DOBIE**, died 3 Apr 1853 at Royal Crescent, Glasgow, Scotland - *NBC*, 23 Apr 1853.

[92] John **ANDERSON** married 25 Dec 1800 at Brunswick Street Methodist Church, Halifax, Lavinia, youngest dau of Thomas and Sarah (**WICKHAM**) **SELLON** of Halifax.

Married 3 Oct 1842 at Halifax by Rev. Prof. Alexander Romans: John **SMITH** and Mrs. **DAVIDSON**, both from Sutherlandshire, Scotland - *AR*, 8 Oct 1842.

Married 20 Oct 1842 at Halifax by Rev. Prof. Alexander Romans: Rev. William **McCULLOCH**, Truro, NS[93], and Jane, dau of Andrew **McCULLOCH**, Lanarkshire, Scotland - *AR*, 22 Oct 1842.

Married 1 Nov 1842 at St. John's, NL, by Rev. T. F. H. Bridge: Andrew **MILROY**, Esq., manager of the Bank of British North America, and Susanna S., 2nd dau of the late Joseph S. **NIXON**, Edinburgh, Scotland, and niece of Dr. S. **CARSON** and Judge [W. Q.] **SAWERS**, Halifax - *AR*, 26 Nov 1842.

Died 18 Nov 1842 at Musquash, Saint John, NB: Alexander **HEPHBURN**, 67, native of Scotland, leaving a widow and children[94] - *NBC*, 19 Nov 1842.

Died 23 Dec 1842 at Halifax: Robert **WATSON**, 21, native of Perthshire, Scotland - *AR*, 31 Dec 1842.

Died in January 1843 at Halifax: Walter **HIBBURN**, 28, native of Scotland - *HJ*, 16 Jan 1843.

Died 20 Jan 1843 at Johnston, Queens County, NB: Jane, 27, native of Hamilton, Lanarkshire, Scotland, wife of Thomas **SHEARER**, Saint John, NB - *NBC*, 4 Feb 1843.

Died 26 Jan 1843 at Balls Creek, Cape Breton, NS: Neil **CAMPBELL**, 98, native of South Uist, Scotland - *Times*, 14 Feb 1843.

Married 6 Feb 1843 at Glenelg, Northumberland County, NB, by Rev. Angus McMaster: James **McKAY**, from Wick, Caithness-shire, and Catherine **McRAE**, Black River, NB - *MN*, 15 Feb 1843.

Married 21 Feb 1843 at Saint John, by Rev. J. M. Brooke: Thomas **TORRANCE**, Loudon, Ayrshire[95], and Isabella, widow of James **BLAIN**, Oromocto, NB - *NBC*, 18 Mar 1843.

Died 26 Feb 1843 at his son's home, St. John's, NL: Hon. William **CARSON**, MD, 72, late Speaker of the NL Assembly[96] - *Royal Gazette & Newfoundland Advertiser*, 28 Feb 1843.

Died 24 Mar 1843 at Halifax: Archibald **HART**, 52, native of Scotland - *HJ*, 27 Mar 1843.

Died 1 Apr 1843 at Liverpool, NS: David **GRIEVE**, Esq., 44, member of the Royal College of Surgeons, Edinburgh, eldest son of Thomas Grieve, merchant at Edinburgh - *STA*, 13 Apr 1843. The *Times*, 4 Apr 1843, adds that he left a widow and had been 26 years in Liverpool.

---

[93] William **McCULLOCH** was born in 1811 at Pictou, NS, and died 14 July 1895. He was a son of the distinguished Rev. Dr. Thomas McCulloch from Renfrewshire, Scotland.

[94] Married 24 Nov 1802 at Saint John, by Rev. Dr. Mather Byles: Alexander **HEPHBURN** and Mabel, dau of Daniel **BELDING**, Saint John - *SJG*, 27 Nov 1802. The widow, Mabel, died 12 Oct 1866 at Griffin St., Carleton, Saint John, age 85 - *Morning News*, 15 Oct 1866.

[95] Thomas **TORRANCE** died at Fredericton, NB, 18 Nov 1882, age 72 - *Fredericton Evening Capital*, 21 Nov 1882. James **BLAIN** died 11 May 1841 (*supra*).

[96] **CARSON** was baptised 4 June 1779 at Kelton, Kirkcudbrightshire, Scotland, a son of Samuel and Margaret (**CLACHERTIE**) Carson. Written up by Patrick O'Flaherty in the *DCB*, Vol. VII, pp. 151-156.

Married 1 Apr 1843 at Halifax, by Rev. Alexander Romans: John **COOPER**, from Aberdeen, Scotland, and Mary Hardwood, 3rd dau of Joseph **JENNINGS**, Halifax, merchant[97] - *NS*, 3 Apr 1843.

Died 19 Apr 1843 at Halifax: Catherine, native of Stromness [Orkney Isles], Scotland, wife of Capt. John **WILLIS** - *HMP*, 20 Apr 1843.

Died 3 May 1843 at Hillsborough, NB: Duncan **SHAW**[98], 75, native of Forfarshire, Scotland, who came to New Brunswick about 1790 - *NBC*, 20 May 1843.

Died 23 May 1843 at Maitland Village, NS: James **DOUGLAS**, Sr., 73, native of Dumfries-shire, Scotland, leaving a widow and large family - *NSRG*, 8 June 1843.

Died 1 June 1843 at Halifax: Lewis **KEITH**, 37, Elgin, Morayshire, Scotland - *Times*, 6 June 1843.

Died 17 June 1843 at Saint John: Alexander **WEDDERBURN**, Esq., 47, a native of Aberdeen, Scotland.[99] He was Chief Emigration Agent for New Brunswick - *NBC*, 24 June 1843.

Died 22 June 1843 at Vera Cruz, Mexico: Capt. Evan **HALLIDAY** of the barque *Lady Mary* of Liverpool, a native of Edinburgh, Scotland, formerly a ship master out of Saint John, NB - *NBC*, 2 Sep 1843.

Died 3 July 1843 at Campbelltown, NB: Sarah **CAMPBELL**, 35, native of Glenelg, Inverness-shire, Scotland, leaving a husband, Laughlin **SINCLAIR**, and six children - *GNS*, 4 Aug 1843.

Died 1 Aug 1843 at Pictou, NS: James, 74, son of the late Rev. James **MUNROE** of Cromarty, Scotland - *STA*, 17 Aug 1843.

Married 8 Aug 1843 at Chatham, NB, by Rev. Richard Shepherd [Methodist]: John **FRASER**, merchant from Inverness, Scotland, and Margaret, 5th dau of John **McARTHUR**, Esq., Sussex Vale, NB - *NBC*, 19 Aug 1843.

Died 10 Aug 1843 at Saint John: Donald **ROSS**, 38, trader, native of Fort Charlotte, Lerwick, Shetland Isles, leaving a wife and family - *NBC*, 12 Aug 1843.

---

[97] The bride's proper name was Margaret Harriet. She was born 28 Nov 1824 and baptised, 1 Jan 1825 at St. Paul's Anglican Church, Halifax, third dau of Joseph **JENNINGS**, grocer, and Ann **DENNET**. Joseph Jennings married Ann Dennet, 8 Sep 1819 at St. Paul's Church. At that time he was a private in the British Army.

[98] Duncan was born 29 Feb 1768 at Glenelg, Angus, son of Farquhar and Susan (**RATTRAY**) **SHAW**. He married 17 July 1800 at Sackville, NB, Martha, dau of Capt. **HAMM** of Portland, ME. Martha, 40, wife of Duncan **SHAW**, died 2 Dec 1818 at Sackville, NB - *CG*, 23 Dec 1818.

[99] **WEDDERBURN** settled in New Brunswick in 1815. On 15 Jan 1823 at Saint John, he married Jane, dau of Thomas and Elizabeth (**DEAN**) **HEAVISIDE**. His career is presented by William A. Spray in the *Dictionary of Canadian Biography*, Vol. VII, p. 898.

Died 27 Aug 1843 at Nappan, NS: Hugh Fraser **CHISHOLM**, 28, native of Inverness, Scotland, "for some time resident of Saint John" - *NBC*, 2 Sep 1843.

Died 6 Sep 1843 at Halifax: George M. **BARTON**, 49, [mason], native of Dumfries, Scotland[100] - *Times*, 12 Sep 1843.

Died 7 Sep 1843 at Halifax: Mrs. Grassie **CAMPBELL**, 80, native of Grandholm, near Aberdeen, Scotland - *Times*, 12 Sep 1843.

Died 27 Sep 1843 at Yarmouth, NS: Capt. Robert **DIXON**, 60, native of Fifeshire, Scotland - *Times*, 17 Oct 1843.

Married 16 Oct 1843 at Halifax, by Rev. William Cogswell: Dr. [Lawrence] **TREMAIN**[101], Prince Edward Island, and Margaret Gordon, dau of late Eneas **MORRISON**, Esq., Perthshire, Scotland - *Times*, 31 Oct 1843.

Died 17 Oct 1843 at Douglastown, Northumberland County, NB: . . ., [76], widow of Malcolm **RAMSAY**, Indian River, PE, and native of Kintyre, Scotland. She was brought to Prince Edward Island in 1770 when she was three years old - *NBC*, 4 Nov 1843.

Married 19 Oct 1843 at Harvey Settlement, NB, by Rev. John McCurdy: Andrew **LITTLE**, Kingsclear Parish, NB, and Mrs. Janet **FORSYTH**, lately from Dumfries-shire, Scotland - *The Loyalist*, 26 Oct 1843.

Married 28 Oct 1843 at Halifax, by Rev. Prof. James McIntosh: William **SINCLAIR**, Caithness, Scotland, and Elizabeth **WHESTON**, Halifax - *Times*, 7 Nov 1843.

Died 31 Oct 1843 at Saint John: Alexander **McDONALD**, Little Brook, Black River, Northumberland County, NB, age 68, native of Ross-shire, Scotland, who came to Cape Breton, NS, in 1803, and later moved to New Brunswick[102] - *WC*, 17 Nov 1843.

Died 8 Nov 1843 at Canning, Queens County, NB: Alexander **McDONALD**, 53, native of North Britain[103] - *NBC*, 8 Nov 1843.

Died 8 Nov 1843 at Chatham, NB: William **WATSON**, 38, native of Scotland. His eldest son James, 5, died the following day - *WC*, 17 Nov 1843.

------

[100] Married 17 Oct 1817 at St. Paul's Anglican Church, Halifax: George M. **BARTON** and Charlotte **McGREGOR**. Their first child was James Lettett Barton, born 2 May, baptised 16 Dec 1819 at St. Paul's Anglican Church, Halifax.

[101] Dr. **TREMAIN** died 19 Apr 1891 at Tryon, PE, age 80. Margaret, his wife, died 15 Oct 1880 at Crapaud, PE. His eldest son, Dr. William Scott Tremain, was a doctor in the U.S. Army and died, 9 Jan 1898 at Buffalo, NY.

[102] Alexander **McDONALD** was born in the Parish of Assynt, Sutherlandshire. His wife was Grace **MacASKILL**.

[103] His wife was Catherine **STILWELL**.

Died 20 Nov 1843 at Digby, NS: William **FOREST**, 43, native of Dumfries, Scotland - *NBC*, 9 Dec 1843.

Died 25 Nov 1843 at Carleton Village, near Shelburne, NS: Isabella, 80. She was the wife of Donald **McDONALD**, who died 26 Nov 1843, age 78. Both were natives of Sutherlandshire, Scotland, where they were married about 55 years earlier. They came to Nova Scotia in 1807 - *Times*, 12 Dec 1843.

Died 29 Nov 1843 at Halifax: Isabel, 47, native of Keith, Banffshire, Scotland, wife of Peter **GRANT**[104] - *HJ*, 4 Dec 1843.

Died 14 Dec 1843 at residence of John **KING**, Studholm, Kings County, NB: James **McMILLAN**, 92, native of Perthshire, Scotland - *NBC*, 13 Jan 1844.

Died 22 Dec 1843 at Aberdeen, Scotland: James **KNIGHT**, 40, brother of Alexander Knight of Halifax - *Times*, 23 Jan 1844.

Married 23 Dec 1843 at Halifax, by Rev. J. Scott: Godfrey M. **SCHWARTZ**, Halifax[105], and Mary **JAMIESON**, Banffshire, Scotland - *Times*, 26 Dec 1843.

Died 28 Dec 1843 at Loch Lomond, Saint John, NB: Daniel **ROBERTSON**, 69, native of Perthshire, Scotland. He came to New Brunswick nearly 27 years before - *NBC*, 30 Dec 1843.

Comments

Readers will have noticed a few things in these newspaper notices which may have aroused their curiosity. First of all, there seems to have been a fad at the time among middle-class Scottish families to give girls middle names that were prominent, but not necessarily related, surnames, e.g., Mary Stewart Black. The numbers of clergy and medical doctors is larger than one would expect, but this reflects the newspapers' interest at the time of reporting events relating to the professional and commercial classes, so that farmers and craftsmen appear well below their true proportion in the community. This bias, if one may call it that, helps to explain the seemingly large number of Maritime Scots who returned to Scotland to marry or to die. They had the means to do so, which others lacked.

-The author

---

[104] Peter **GRANT** died 18 Dec 1870, age 83. Married 8 Jan 1829 at Halifax, RC: Peter Grant, carpenter from Banffshire, widower, and Isabella **CROSBY**, from the Isle of Coll, Scotland, widow of John George **SCOTT**, shoemaker, who died on 9 Feb 1824, age 32, leaving four children (*AR*, 14 Feb 1824). See note 35 on page 33 regarding Isabella's birthplace. Peter Grant's marital history is confusing, but interesting, as he was married four times. On 20 Jan 1814 at St. Paul's Anglican Church he married Margaret **TAYLOR** from the Parish of Grange in Banffshire. She died on 18 Feb 1827, age 40, having had seven children. Peter married, secondly, on 2 June 1827, Hannah **GAY**, who died on 21 Oct 1828, age 27. Their only child died soon after birth. Peter married, thirdly, Isabella Crosby, as above. He married, fourthly, 23 May 1844, in St. Mary's Catholic church, Halifax, Margaret **ROBINSON**, from England, who died 31 Aug 1874, age 80. She was the widow of Rev. Robert **ELLIOT**, a Presbyterian minister from Roxburghshire, Scotland, who died 15 Aug 1832 at Preston, NS, age 38 (*AR*, 18 Aug 1832).

[105] Godfrey M. **SCHWARTZ** died at Halifax, 15 Dec 1856, age 58. Mary, his widow, was living in Halifax as late as 1884.

CAPE BRETON CENSUS OF 1818: THE SCOTS

Cape Breton Island was separated in 1784 from Nova Scotia until 1820 when the two were reunited. The surviving portions of a census taken in Cape Breton in June 1818 were published by the Public Archives of Nova Scotia as Appendix B to *Holland's Description of Cape Breton Island and Other Documents*. The census noted the birthplace of the head of each family as well as that of their parents. This permits us to find the Scottish population of much of Cape Breton at the time.

The census asked the head of each household how long he had been in Cape Breton, which enables us to see when immigration occurred. In the district of St. Andrews the time in Cape Breton was expressed in years and months. I have rounded this information off to the nearest half year. In all, 436 households appear of which the head of the family had Scottish-born parents. Of these, 366 were themselves Scottish-born, 34 were born in mainland Nova Scotia (one specified Pictou), 21 were natives of Prince Edward Island, and 9 had been born in Cape Breton. Two were born in Ireland, two in the United States (one cited Georgia) and one in England, of Scottish parentage. Ninety-nine had been less than four years (i.e., came after 1814) in Cape Breton, while seventy-eight had resided there seventeen or more years (i.e., since before 1801).

There is a dearth of passenger lists for the early period. We know few even of the names of vessels bringing Scots to Cape Breton before 1818. The *Northern Friends of Clyde* took 340 Scots from the western Highlands and the isles to Sydney in 1802, while the *Polly* sailed from Scotland to the Gut of Canso in 1805 with Scottish passengers. The Napoleonic Wars reduced emigration until 1815. The *Hope* and the *William Tell*, both out of Greenock, reached Sydney, Cape Breton, in late July 1817. The *Hope* had 161 Scottish emigrants aboard, while the *William Tell* transported 221 souls. The latter also called at the Gut of Canso at the other end of the island. Some of those below as being only one or two years in Cape Breton may have been among their passengers.

Since thirty-four natives of Nova Scotia and twenty-one of Prince Edward Island appear in Cape Breton in 1818, it is evident that a considerable number of the Scots in Cape Breton had not landed there initially, but were moving about one, several, or even many, years after reaching the Gulf of St. Lawrence region at Pictou or Charlottetown. The information presented allows us to hypothesize, but not actually establish, kinship and migratory patterns. For instance, in the lower settlement of River Inhabitants we find these entries together:

	Age	Yrs. in CB	Birthplace	Parents from	Trade	Married	Children
Dugald McCORMICK	65	5	Scotland	Scotland	Farmer	M	7
Hugh McCORMICK	28	5	Scotland	Scotland	Farmer	M	1
John McCORMICK	26	5	P. E. Island	Scotland	Farmer	S	
Archibald McCORMICK	23	5	P. E. Island	Scotland	Farmer	S	
Norman McCORMICK	18	5	P. E. Island	Scotland	Farmer	S	

It seems that Dugald McCormick, 65, was the patriarch of a family group that settled in Cape Breton five years before (1813), after spending some years in Prince Edward Island where John, Archibald and Norman were born between 1792 and 1800. Since Hugh was born in Scotland in about 1790, the original emigration from Scotland was to Prince Edward Island between 1790 and 1792[1]. We see that Dugald had seven children in his household in 1818, and the oldest son, Hugh, was married with a child by then. A glance at the 1838/39 census of the area reveals the presence of four McCormick households in the Port Hawkesbury vicinity in Richmond County: Dougald, Hugh, Donald and Norman. This is not proof, but suggests a line for further enquiry.

---

[1] Possibly he was the Dugald **McCORMICK** from Grulin, Isle of Eigg, who crossed to Prince Edward Island from Druimindarroch, Inverness-shire, Scotland in the summer of 1790 in the ship *Jane*.

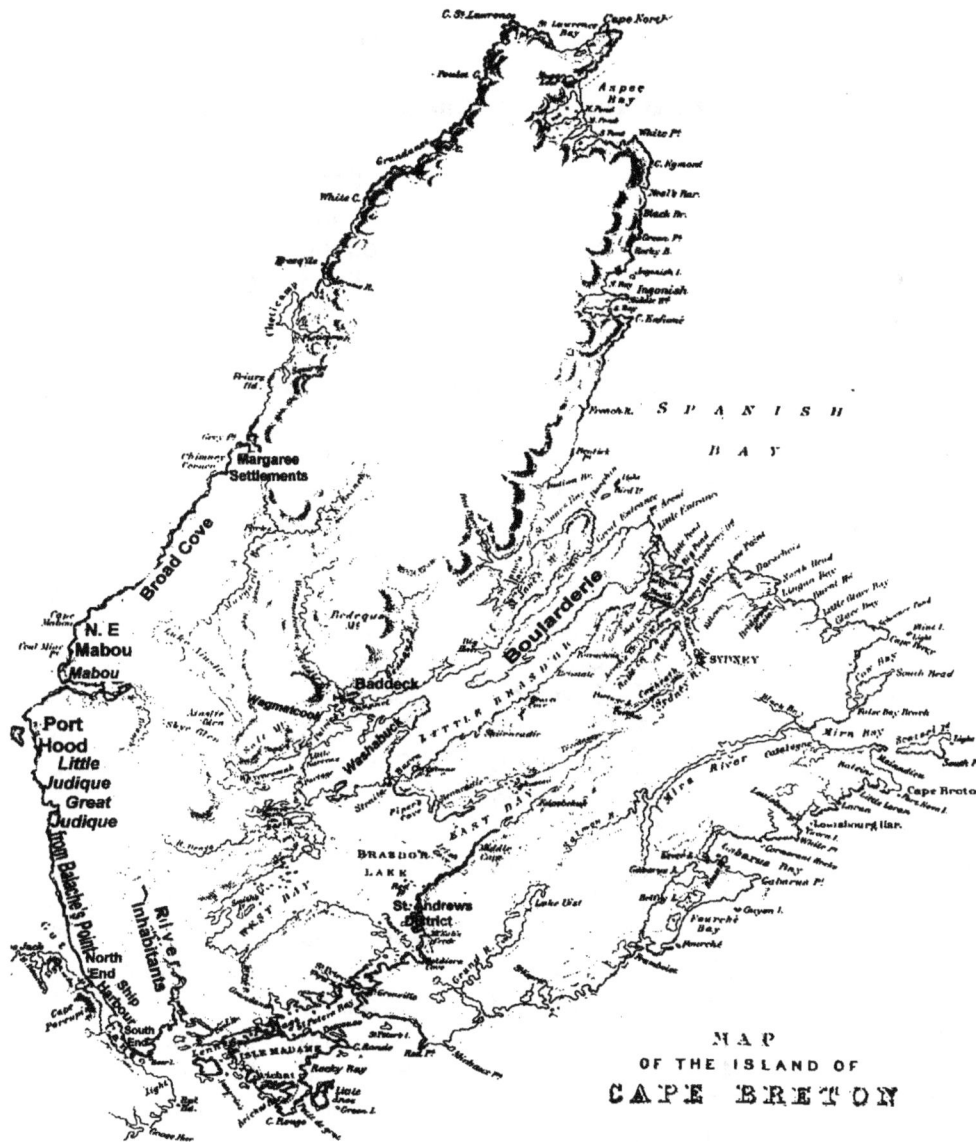

Map 5 - Census Districts of Cape Breton in 1818
Adapted from map in Richard Brown, *A History of the Island of Cape Breton* (London, 1869).

The information below is presented in the order: name, age, time in Cape Breton, country of birth, parents' country, trade, Married (M), Single (S) or Widowed (W), and number of children. In some districts country of birth was given as "North Britain", which is simply Scotland, and I have listed them as such. Since settlement patterns may be reflected in the original census, the names have in general been left in the order originally written with no attempt on my part to alphabetize the names. Reference to Map 5 (above) will suggest where the census districts were in 1818. By comparing this map to a modern map, the present locations and names of each should appear. The extant portion of the 1818 census accounts for 1,674 people in "Scottish" households.

Ship Harbour, Gut of Canso (1 household)

Angus GRANT, Esq.	41	17	Scotland	Scotland	....	M	6

North end of the Gut of Canso (5 households)

John McLEAN	23	2	Scotland	Scotland	Cooper	S	
Donald NICKLESON	36	3	Scotland	Scotland	Fisherman	S	
Hector McQUARRY	62	7	Scotland	Scotland	Farmer	M	3
Donald McQUARRY	23	7	Scotland	Scotland	Labourer	S	
Hector McQUARRY, Jr.	21	7	Scotland	Scotland	Labourer	S	

From Balache's Point in Gut of Canso to Grand Judique (158 households)

John McKINNON, Sr.	42	7	Scotland	Scotland	Farmer	M	3
John McKINNON, Jr.	24	16	Scotland	Scotland	Farmer	M	1
Angus McCORMICK	34	7	Scotland	Scotland	Farmer	M	3
Hugh McDOUGALD	25	2	Scotland	Scotland	Farmer	S	
Hector CAMERON	45	2	Scotland	Scotland	Farmer	M	3
John McEACHERN	46	18	Scotland	Scotland	Farmer	M	8
Angus McDONALD	47	17	Scotland	Scotland	Farmer	M	8
Colin CHISHOLM	55	17	Scotland	Scotland	Farmer	M	8
William CHISHOLM	48	17	Scotland	Scotland	Farmer	M	2
Colin CHISHOLM	22	6	Scotland	Scotland	Farmer	S	
Alexander CHISHOLM	27	17	Scotland	Scotland	Farmer	S	
Colin CHISHOLM	20	17	Scotland	Scotland	Farmer	S	
William CHISHOLM	21	2	Scotland	Scotland	Farmer	S	
John CHISHOLM	52	17	Scotland	Scotland	Farmer	M	4
John CHISHOLM	25	17	Scotland	Scotland	Farmer	S	
Alexander CHISHOLM	23	17	Scotland	Scotland	Carpenter	S	
Colin CHISHOLM	21	17	Scotland	Scotland	Farmer	S	
Donald CHISHOLM	19	17	Scotland	Scotland	Farmer	S	
Alexander CHISHOLM	42	17	Scotland	Scotland	Farmer	M	5
John McLEAN	33	14	Scotland	Scotland	Farmer	M	3
Donald McLEAN	72	14	Scotland	Scotland	Farmer	M	1
Hugh McLEAN	21	14	Nova Scotia	Scotland	Farmer	S	
John GILLIES	34	13	Scotland	Scotland	Farmer	M	5
Hugh McEACHERN	33	16	Scotland	Scotland	Farmer	M	4
Alexander McEACHERN	22	16	Scotland	Scotland	Farmer	S	
Alexander GILLIES	46	16	Scotland	Scotland	Farmer	M	5
John GILLIES	42	16	Scotland	Scotland	Farmer	S	
Allan McINNES	21	2	Scotland	Scotland	Farmer	S	
Niel McMILLAN	48	13	Scotland	Scotland	Farmer	M	4
Donald McMILLAN	18	13	Scotland	Scotland	Farmer	S	
John McDONALD	55	15	Scotland	Scotland	Farmer	M	4
Donald McDONALD	17	15	Scotland	Scotland	Farmer	S	
John McDONALD	28	2	Scotland	Scotland	Farmer	M	4
John GILLIES	40	7	Scotland	Scotland	Farmer	M	3

John O'HANLEY	30	19	Scotland	Scotland	Farmer	M	3
John McDONALD	30	13	Scotland	Scotland	Farmer	M	4
John McDONALD	24	19	Nova Scotia	Scotland	Farmer	S	
Donald McDONALD	26	19	Nova Scotia	Scotland	Farmer	S	
Colin McDONALD	28	19	Scotland	Scotland	Farmer	M	1
William McDONALD	1[9]	19	Nova Scotia	Scotland	Farmer	[S]	
Duncan McDONALD	87	19	Scotland	Scotland	Farmer	M	
Hugh McDONALD	26	19	P. E. Island	Scotland	Farmer	S	
Archibald McDONALD	30	19	Scotland	Scotland	Farmer	M	
John McDONALD	48	19	Scotland	Scotland	Farmer	M	5
James McDONALD	16	16	Cape Breton	Scotland	Farmer	S	
Alexander McDONALD	64	18	Scotland	Scotland	Farmer	M	6
Alexander McDONALD	23	18	Scotland	Scotland	Farmer	S	
James McDONALD	30	18	Scotland	Scotland	Farmer	M	
Allan McDONALD	36	16	Scotland	Scotland	Farmer	M	7
Ronald McDONALD	52	18	Scotland	Scotland	Farmer	M	6
James McDONALD	20	18	Scotland	Scotland	Farmer	S	
Hugh McMILLAN	....	....	Scotland	Scotland	Farmer	M	7
Hector McQUARRIE	64	....	Scotland	Scotland	Farmer	M	1
George SAWERS	26	6	Scotland	Scotland	Farmer	M	2
Hugh SKINNER	34	13	Scotland	Scotland	Farmer	M	3
John McDONALD	46	15	Scotland	Scotland	Farmer	M	5
Norman McISAAC	52	18	Scotland	Scotland	Farmer	M	4
John McLEAN	55	16	Scotland	Scotland	Farmer	M	2
Charles McKINNON	30	7	Scotland	Scotland	Farmer	M	2
Lauchan McQUARRIE	60	2	Scotland	Scotland	Farmer	M	1
Roderick McLEAN	62	16	Scotland	Scotland	Farmer	M	5
Duncan McLEOD	35	7	Scotland	Scotland	Farmer	M	4
John McINTYRE	46	16	Scotland	Scotland	Farmer	M	8
Robert McINTYRE	49	5	Scotland	Scotland	Farmer	M	1
William CHISHOLM	60	1	Scotland	Scotland	Farmer	M	4
William McKAY	40	2	Scotland	Scotland	Farmer	M	3
John McDONALD	35	19	Scotland	Scotland	Farmer	M	2
Alexander McDONALD	56	19	Scotland	Scotland	Farmer	M	6
John McNEIL	34	9	Nova Scotia	Scotland	Farmer	M	4
John McDONALD	26	19	P. E. Island	Scotland	Farmer	M	2
Allan McEACHERN	37	19	Scotland	Scotland	Farmer	M	5
Angus McDONALD	70	16	Scotland	Scotland	Farmer	M	1
Roderick McDONALD	32	16	Scotland	Scotland	Farmer	M	5
Alexander McDONALD	25	16	Scotland	Scotland	Farmer	M	2
John McISAAC	41	19	Scotland	Scotland	Farmer	M	4
Dugald McDONALD	60	16	Scotland	Scotland	Farmer	W	
John McDONALD	60	17	Scotland	Scotland	Farmer	M	1
Hugh McDONALD	27	2	Scotland	Scotland	Farmer	M	2
James McDONALD	27	17	Scotland	Scotland	Farmer	M	1
Roderick McISAAC	24	1	Scotland	Scotland	Farmer	M	2
Allan McDONALD	58	19	Scotland	Scotland	Farmer	M	1
Lauchan McKINNON	27	7	Scotland	Scotland	Farmer	M	1

Donald CAMPBELL	44	1	Scotland	Scotland	Trader	M	1
Hugh McDONALD	52	16	Scotland	Scotland	Farmer	M	4
Donald McMASTER	54	16	Scotland	Scotland	Farmer	M	3
John McMASTER	46	16	Scotland	Scotland	Farmer	M	9
John McINNES	27	18	Scotland	Scotland	Farmer	M	
John CAMERON	70	18	Scotland	Scotland	Farmer	W	6
Alexander CAMERON	30	18	P. E. Island	Scotland	Farmer	M	
Colin CAMERON	38	2	Georgia	Scotland	Tailor	M	3
Alexander McINNES	29	16	Scotland	Scotland	Farmer	M	2
John McINNES	50	1	Scotland	Scotland	Farmer	M	4
Donald McDONALD	48	16	Scotland	Scotland	Farmer	M	7
Hugh McEACHERN	27	16	Scotland	Scotland	Cooper	S	
Duncan McEACHERN	70	16	Scotland	Scotland	Farmer	M	
Ronald McEACHERN	30	16	Scotland	Scotland	Farmer	M	3
Angus McEACHERN	27	16	Scotland	Scotland	Farmer	M	
Alexander McDONALD	30	2	Scotland	Scotland	Farmer	M	2
Archibald McDOUGALD	30	2	Scotland	Scotland	Farmer	M	3
Donald McDOUGALD	38	2	Scotland	Scotland	Farmer	M	
John McDOUGALD	32	2	Scotland	Scotland	Farmer	M	5
John McEACHERN	25	1	Scotland	Scotland	Farmer	S	
Rory McDONALD	60	10	Scotland	Scotland	Farmer	M	4
Angus McDONALD	23	19	Scotland	Scotland	Farmer	S	
Archibald McDONALD	20	19	Scotland	Scotland	Farmer	S	
John McINNES	58	16	Scotland	Scotland	Farmer	M	6
Hugh McINNES	21	16	Scotland	Scotland	Farmer	S	
John McDONALD	27	12	Scotland	Scotland	Farmer	M	
Duncan McMASTER	27	16	Scotland	Scotland	Farmer	M	2
Donald McEACHEN	27	14	Scotland	Scotland	Farmer	M	1
Malcolm McEACHEN	29	14	Scotland	Scotland	Farmer	M	4
Angus McEACHEN	60	14	Scotland	Scotland	Farmer	M	5
John McEACHEN	64	16	Scotland	Scotland	Farmer	M	6
Lachlin McEACHEN	32	16	Scotland	Scotland	Farmer	M	3
Angus McEACHEN	27	16	Scotland	Scotland	Farmer	....	
Donald McEACHEN	60	16	Scotland	Scotland	Farmer	M	5
Donald McISAAC	70	16	Scotland	Scotland	Farmer	M	6
Hector McISAAC	23	16	Scotland	Scotland	Farmer	[S]	
Donald McEACHEN	23	16	Scotland	Scotland	Farmer	[S]	
John McEACHEN	18	16	Scotland	Scotland	Farmer	[S]	
Donald GILLIES	35	16	Scotland	Scotland	Farmer	M	5
Donald McINNES	45	24	P. E. Island	Scotland	Farmer	M	6
Alexander McINNES	42	24	P. E. Island	Scotland	Farmer	M	6
Donald GILLIES, Sr.	65	22	Scotland	Scotland	Farmer	M	
Angus McDONALD	24	[23]	Scotland	Scotland	Farmer	....	
Allan McDONALD	26	25	Scotland	Scotland	Farmer	....	
Donald CAMERON	40	10	Scotland	Scotland	Farmer	M	6
Angus McMASTER	35	16	Scotland	Scotland	Farmer	M	5
Donald McMASTER	74	16	Scotland	Scotland	Farmer	M	1
Donald McMASTER, Jr.	29	16	Scotland	Scotland	Farmer	M	3

John McMASTER	28	2	Scotland	Scotland	Farmer	M	2
Hugh McMASTER	30	2	Scotland	Scotland	Farmer	M	
Donald McMASTER	26	2	Scotland	Scotland	Farmer	S	
Rory HENL[E]Y	60	19	Scotland	Scotland	Farmer	M	2
Stephen HENL[E]Y	20	19	Pictou, NS	Scotland	Farmer	[S]	
Angus HENLEY	17	17	Cape Breton	Scotland	Farmer	[S]	
Alexander McDONALD	46	7	Scotland	Scotland	Farmer	M	8
John GRAHAM	65	23	Scotland	Scotland	Farmer	M	2
Alexander GRAHAM	21	21	Cape Breton	Scotland	Farmer	[S]	
Hugh GILLIES	48	21	Scotland	Scotland	Farmer	M	7
Duncan GILLIES	50	21	Scotland	Scotland	Farmer	M	6
Angus GILLIES	18	18	Cape Breton	Scotland	....	[S]	
John McDONALD	18	18	Cape Breton	Scotland	Farmer	S	
Ronald McDONALD	16	16	Cape Breton	Scotland	Farmer	S	
Maxwell McISAAC	19	17	Scotland	Scotland	Farmer	S	
John McISAAC	17	17	Nova Scotia	Scotland	Farmer	S	
Alan McQUARRIE	26	2	Scotland	Scotland	Farmer	S	
Hector McLEAN	19	16	Scotland	Scotland	Farmer	S	
John McLEAN	17	16	Scotland	Scotland	Farmer	S	
Donald McISAAC	19	19	Cape Breton	Scotland	Farmer	S	
Hugh McMASTER	18	18	Cape Breton	Scotland	Farmer	S	
Donald CAMERON	26	18	P. E. Island	Scotland	Farmer	S	
Angus CAMERON	22	18	P. E. Island	Scotland	Farmer	S	
Hugh McINNES	18	1	Scotland	Scotland	Farmer	S	
John McINNES	16	1	Scotland	Scotland	Farmer	S	
John McDONALD	18	16	Scotland	Scotland	Farmer	S	
John CAMPBELL	51	1	Scotland	Scotland	Farmer	M	4
Donald SUTHERLAND	24	2	Scotland	Scotland	Farmer	S	

District of Port Hood (85 households)

Little Judique (9 households):

John McNIEL, Sr.	63	10	Scotland	Scotland	Farmer	M	8
John McNIEL, Jr.	31	11	Scotland	Scotland	Farmer	M	4
Hugh McNIEL	28	11	Scotland	Scotland	Farmer	M	
Alexander McNIEL	40	10	Scotland	Scotland	Farmer	M	5
Alexander McDONALD	23	1	Scotland	Scotland	Farmer	S	
John LIVINGSTON	45	15	Scotland	Scotland	Weaver	M	6
Angus GILLIES	60	12	Scotland	Scotland	Farmer	M	
Donald GILLIES	30	12	Scotland	Scotland	Farmer	M	3
John GILLIES	27	12	Scotland	Scotland	Farmer	M	3

Great Judique (12 households):

Angus McDOUGAL	23	18	Scotland	Scotland	Farmer	S	
Angus McINNIS	44	16	Scotland	Scotland	Farmer	M	7
Donald McINNIS	55	18	Scotland	Scotland	Farmer	M	8
Alexander McINNIS	23	18	Nova Scotia	Scotland	Farmer	S	
Allan McINNIS	20	18	Nova Scotia	Scotland	Farmer	S	
Angus McINNIS	18	17	Nova Scotia	Scotland	Farmer	S	
Angus BEATON	41	12	Scotland	Scotland	Farmer	M	4

Findley BEATON	28	12	Scotland	Scotland	Farmer	M	
Hugh McLEAN	61	19	Scotland	Scotland	Farmer	M	7
Alexander McLEAN	26	19	Scotland	Scotland	Farmer	S	
Niel McDOUGAL	57	18	Scotland	Scotland	Farmer	M	6
Thomas McDONALD	40	8	Scotland	Scotland	Farmer	M	7

Coal mines Northeast Mabou (9 households):

Archibald McFEE	40	9	Scotland	Scotland	Farmer	M	5
Donald BEATON	25	12	Scotland	Scotland	Farmer	S	
John McDONALD	25	2	Nova Scotia	Scotland	Blacksmith	S	
Alexander BEATON	62	12	Scotland	Scotland	Farmer	M	7
John BEATON	23	9	Scotland	Scotland	Farmer	S	
Findly BEATON	55	9	Scotland	Scotland	Farmer	M	6
Angus BEATON	47	2	Scotland	Scotland	Farmer	M	4
John CAMPBELL	32	2	Scotland	Scotland	Farmer	M	2
Niel McNIEL	37	2	Scotland	Scotland	Farmer	M	4

Port Hood (7 households):

Ranal McDONALD	23	14	Scotland	Scotland	Trader	S	
Loughlan McDONALD	17	14	Scotland	Scotland	Farmer	S	
[blank name]	64	14	Scotland	Scotland	Farmer	M	4
Donald BEATON	25	12	Scotland	Scotland	Farmer	S	
Donald McDONALD	27	6	Nova Scotia	Scotland	Farmer	M	2
Ranal McDONALD	36	20	Scotland	Scotland	Farmer	M	2
William WATTS	42	32	England	Scotland	Farmer	M	6

Little Mabou (5 households):

Niel McQUARRY	30	14	Scotland	Scotland	Farmer	M	2
John McDONALD	45	14	Scotland	Scotland	Tailor	M	3
Lauchlin McQUARRY	21	14	Scotland	Scotland	Farmer	S	
Alexander McEACHRAN	39	14	Scotland	Scotland	Farmer	S	
Hugh McEACHRAN	41	14	Scotland	Scotland	Tailor	M	2

"Mawboo" - Mabou (43 households):

Malcolm McLEAN	42	14	Scotland	Scotland	Farmer	M	7
Donald McDONALD	50	14	Scotland	Scotland	Farmer	M	5
John McNIEL	29	1	Scotland	Scotland	Farmer	M	
John BEATON	17	9	Scotland	Scotland	Farmer	S	
Angus McINTIRE	48	9m.	Scotland	Scotland	Farmer	M	5
Robert BROWNLEY	65	37	Scotland	Scotland	Cooper	S	
Rory McNIEL	25	16	Scotland	Scotland	Farmer	S	
Alexander McEACHRAN	45	6	Scotland	Scotland	Farmer	M	4
Alexander McNIEL	18	6	Scotland	Scotland	Farmer	S	
James McNIEL	22	9m.	Scotland	Scotland	Fisherman	S	
. . . . McNIEL	20	9m.	Scotland	Scotland	Boat builder	S	
Archibald McDONALD	40	10	Scotland	Scotland	Farmer	M	2
John CAMMERON	40	12	Scotland	Scotland	Farmer	M	5
Angus CAMMERON	50	12	Scotland	Scotland	Farmer	M	4
Daniel BEATON	40	12	Scotland	Scotland	Farmer	M	4
John BEATON	33	12	Scotland	Scotland	Farmer	M	1
Alexander BEATON	36	2	Scotland	Scotland	Farmer	M	1
Daniel BEATON	32	2	Scotland	Scotland	Farmer	M	1

Name	Age		Birthplace	Father's Birthplace	Occupation	Status	
Angus BEATON	46	2	Scotland	Scotland	Farmer	M	4
William CLARK	22	2	Scotland	Scotland	Farmer	S	
Alexander McDONALD	40	12	Scotland	Scotland	Farmer	M	5
Alexander McDONALD	50	2	Scotland	Scotland	Farmer	M	3
Alexander McDONALD	21	2	Scotland	Scotland	Farmer	S	
Duncan GILLIS	17	13	Scotland	Scotland	Farmer	S	
Donald McLEOD	60	15	Scotland	Scotland	Farmer	M	5
Donald McLEOD	20	15	Scotland	Scotland	Farmer	S	
Alexander McDONALD	43	1	Scotland	Scotland	Tailor	M	1
Findley McDONALD	45	12	Scotland	Scotland	Farmer	M	5
John McNIEL	23	1	Scotland	Scotland	Farmer	M	3
Rory MORRISON	31	16	Scotland	Scotland	Farmer	M	3
Malcom McLEAN	45	12	Scotland	Scotland	Farmer	M	3
Hugh McLEAN	39	15	Scotland	Scotland	Farmer	M	7
Robert SINCLARE	26	4	Orkney Is.	Orkney Is.	Farmer	M	1
Daniel MORRISON	57	14	Scotland	Scotland	Farmer	M	9
Allan MORRISON	23	14	Scotland	Scotland	Farmer	S	
Patrick MORRISON	21	14	Scotland	Scotland	Farmer	S	
John ADAMS	29	21	Scotland	Scotland	Farmer	S	
Donald CAMPBELL	35	6	Scotland	Scotland	Farmer	W	5
Dougal McCORMICK	50	14	Scotland	Scotland	Farmer	M	
Angus CAMMERON	36	12	Scotland	Scotland	Farmer	M	3
Niel McEACHRAN	28	14	Scotland	Scotland	Farmer	M	
John GILLIS	28	8	Scotland	Scotland	Farmer	M	3
Donald McNIEL	21	8	Scotland	Scotland ·	Farmer	S	

Broad Cove (43 households)

Name	Age		Birthplace	Father's Birthplace	Occupation	Status	
Alexander McISAAC	24	6	Scotland	Scotland	Farmer	S	
Angus McISAAC 5th	22	6	Scotland	Scotland	Farmer	S	
John McISAAC	36	10	Scotland	Scotland	Farmer	M	4
Donald McISAAC 4th	22	10	P. E. Island	Scotland	Farmer	S	
Alexander McISAAC 2nd	19	10	P. E. Island	Scotland	Farmer	S	
Donald McISAAC 5th	19	6	Scotland	Scotland	Farmer	S	
Duncan McDOUGALD	50	5	Scotland	Scotland	Farmer	M	7
Archibald McDOUGALD	34	6	Scotland	Scotland	Farmer	M	4
Alexander McDOUGALD	23	6	P. E. Island	Scotland	Farmer	S	
John McINTYRE 1st	48	3	Scotland	Scotland	Farmer	M	8
John McINTYRE 2nd	20	3	P. E. Island	Scotland	Farmer	S	
Allan McDONALD	49	2	Scotland	Scotland	Farmer	M	6
Ranald McDONALD	19	2	Scotland	Scotland	Farmer	S	
Hugh McLEAN	29	18	Scotland	Scotland	Farmer	M	3
Niel McINNES	27	15	Scotland	Scotland	Farmer	M	2
Ranald McLEAN	30	2	Scotland	Scotland	Farmer	M	4
Donald McDONALD	28	2	Scotland	Scotland	Farmer	M	4
John McDONALD 1st	37	12	Scotland	Scotland	Farmer	M	
Alexander McNIEL	35	6	Scotland	Scotland	Farmer	M	6
John McDONALD 2nd	25	12	Scotland	Scotland	Farmer	M	1

Name	Age		Born	Origin	Occupation	Status	
Alexander GILLES	32	12	Scotland	Scotland	Farmer	M	4
Alack McDONALD	38	9	Scotland	Scotland	Farmer	M	5
Dunken McLOUD	25	9	Nova Scotia	Scotland	Farmer	S	
Rodrick MacLEAN	68	6	Scotland	Scotland	Farmer	M	7
William McLEAN	40	6	Scotland	Scotland	Farmer	M	
Niel McLEAN	30	6	Scotland	Scotland	Carpenter	S	
Murdoch McLEAN	28	2	Scotland	Scotland	Farmer	S	
Charles McLEAN	26	6	Scotland	Scotland	Farmer	M	2
John McLEAN	32	6	Scotland	Scotland	Farmer	M	2
Allan McLEAN	24	6	Scotland	Scotland	Carpenter	S	
Donald McLEAN	22	6	Scotland	Scotland	Farmer	S	
Donald KENNEDY	26	2	Nova Scotia	Scotland	Farmer	S	
Angus McISAAC 1st	48	13	Scotland	Scotland	Schoolmaster	M	8
Angus McISAAC 2nd	23	13	Nova Scotia	Scotland	Farmer	S	
Donald McISAAC 1st	21	13	Nova Scotia	Scotland	Farmer	S	
Donald McISAAC 2nd	50	13	Scotland	Scotland	Farmer	M	7
Angus McISAAC 3rd	18	13	Scotland	Scotland	Farmer	S	
Donald McISAAC 3rd	22	13	Scotland	Scotland	"Nothing"	S	
Hector McKINNON	50	13	Scotland	Scotland	Farmer	M	6
John McKINNON	22	13	Nova Scotia	Scotland	Farmer	S	
Angus McKINNON	19	12	Nova Scotia	Scotland	Farmer	S	
Angus McISAAC 4th	64	6	Scotland	Scotland	Farmer	M	4
Murdoch McISAAC	28	6	Scotland	Scotland	Farmer	M	1

Settlements at Margaree – Broad Cove (26 households)

Margaree (12 households):

Name	Age		Born	Origin	Occupation	Status	
Ranald McKINNON	32	12	Scotland	Scotland	Farmer	M	4
James ROSS	61	35	Ireland	Scotland	Farmer	M	2
James McDONALD	32	6	Scotland	Scotland	Farmer	S	
Martin CAMERON	20	12	Nova Scotia	Scotland	Farmer	S	
Angus CAMERON	24	12	Nova Scotia	Scotland	Farmer	S	
Donald CAMERON	24	12	Nova Scotia	Scotland	Farmer	S	
Donald McDONALD	50	13	Scotland	Scotland	Farmer	M	6
Alexander McDONALD	36	2	Nova Scotia	Scotland	Farmer	M	1
Daniel McWATT	50	30	Scotland	Scotland	Farmer	M	
David ROSS	46	15	Nova Scotia	Scotland	Farmer	M	10
Edward ROSS	48	15	Nova Scotia	Scotland	Farmer	M	8
John MOWATT	88	33	Scotland	Scotland	Farmer	W	

Broad Cove (14 households)

Name	Age		Born	Origin	Occupation	Status	
William McLEAN	39	8	Scotland	Scotland	Farmer	M	
Hector McKAY	65	8	Scotland	Scotland	Farmer	M	1
John McKAY	17	8	Scotland	Scotland	Farmer	S	
James SMITH	27	11	Scotland	Scotland	Farmer	M	1
Angus SMITH	60	11	Scotland	Scotland	Farmer	M	9
Hector McKENZIE	62	2	Scotland	Scotland	Farmer	M	9
Murdoch McKENZIE	25	2	Scotland	Scotland	Farmer	S	
Donald McKENZIE	23	2	Nova Scotia	Scotland	Farmer	S	

Niel McLELLAN	30	2	Scotland	Scotland	Farmer	M	1
Alexander McLELLAN	28	2	Scotland	Scotland	Farmer	S	
Niel MacQUILLAN	30	3	Scotland	Scotland	Farmer	M	1
Hugh MacKINNON	60	8	[Scotland]	Scotland	Farmer	M	3
John MacKINNON	21	8	Scotland	Scotland	Farmer	S	
Niel McKINNON	27	8	Scotland	Scotland	Farmer	S	

South end of the Gut of Canso (7 households)

Samuel McCARTER	60	20	Scotland	Scotland	. . . . . .	M	
Fenly McLEOD	47	1	Scotland	Scotland	. . . . . .	S	
Fenly McLIATTERN	47	7	Scotland	Scotland	Farmer	M	7
Alexander McLEOD	26	1	Scotland	Scotland	. . . . . .	S	
David McPHERSON	27	24	Scotland	Scotland	Farmer	M	1
Andrew McLEOD	23	1	Scotland	Scotland	. . . . . .	S	
Collen McEACHRAN	31	4	Scotland	Scotland	Carpenter	M	4

Lower Settlement, River Inhabitants (12 households)

Dugald McCORMICK	65	5	Scotland	Scotland	Farmer	M	7
Hugh McCORMICK	28	5	Scotland	Scotland	Farmer	M	1
John McCORMICK	26	5	P. E. Island	Scotland	Farmer	S	
Archibald McCORMICK	23	5	P. E. Island	Scotland	Farmer	S	
Norman McCORMICK	18	5	P. E. Island	Scotland	Farmer	S	
Donald McCORMICK	30	4	Scotland	Scotland	Farmer	M	1
John MORISON	49	16	Scotland	Scotland	Farmer	M	9
Lachlin MORISON	19	16	Nova Scotia	Scotland	Farmer	S	
John STEEL	36	5	Scotland	Scotland	Farmer	M	3
Mary GRANT, widow	...	...	. . . . .	[Scotland]	. . . . . .	W	10
John GRANT	23	14	Nova Scotia	Scotland	. . . . . .	S	
Robert GRANT	16	14	Nova Scotia	Scotland	. . . . . .	S	

Baddeck Division (26 households)

Baddeck (4 households):

William WATSON	42	30	U. S. A.	Scotland	. . . . . .	M	8
Robert ANDERSON	58	32	Scotland	Scotland	Joiner	M	8
Alexander ANDERSON	20	20	Cape Breton	Scotland	. . . . . .	S	
Magnes LOUTTET	39	7m.	Scotland	Scotland	Blacksmith	S	

Washabuck (7 households)

William MATTHEWSON	33	3	Scotland	Scotland	. . . . . .	M	1
Daniel CARMICHAEL	31	9	Scotland	Scotland	Stonecutter	M	2
Allen MUNROW	33	4	Scotland	Scotland	. . . . . .	M	4
George CAMPBELL	67	4	Scotland	Scotland	. . . . . .	M	2
Collin CAMPBELL	27	3	Scotland	Scotland	. . . . . .	M	3
Daniel McALLA	33	4	Scotland	Scotland	. . . . . .	M	5
Daniel McNEIL	33	1	Scotland	Scotland	. . . . . .	M	5

Wagmatcook (14 households):

Kanaugh McLEOD	64	6	Scotland	Scotland	Blacksmith	M	5
John McLEOD	26	6	Scotland	Scotland	. . . . . .	M	1
Kanaugh McLEOD, Jr.	23	6	Scotland	Scotland	. . . . . .	S	
Rodrick McKENZEY	40	6	Scotland	Scotland	. . . . . .	M	5
Daniel McREA	58	6	Scotland	Scotland	. . . . . .	M	8
John McREA	33	6	Scotland	Scotland	. . . . . .	M	4
Finley McREA	30	6	Scotland	Scotland	. . . . . .	M	2
Dunken McREA	25	6	Scotland	Scotland	. . . . . .	S	
Daniel McREA, Jr.	20	6	Scotland	Scotland	. . . . . .	S	
Alexander McREA	16	6	Scotland	Scotland	. . . . . .	S	
Patrick CAMPBELL	66	6	Scotland	Scotland	. . . . . .	M	5
John CAMPBELL	25	6	Scotland	Scotland	. . . . . .	M	2
Angus CAMPBELL	22	6	Scotland	Scotland	. . . . . .	S	
Rodrick CAMPBELL	19	6	Scotland	Scotland	. . . . . .	S	

St. Patricks Channel (1 household):

William ROSS	50	28	Ireland	Scotland		M	13

District of Little Bras d'Or (10 households)

Boularderie Village (3 households)

Thomas DAVIDSON	40	....	Scotland	Scotland	Servant	S	
Robert GAMMELL	48	....	Scotland	Scotland	Farmer	W	5
William GAMMELL	46	....	Scotland	Scotland	Farmer	W	

Southern Shore (2 households)

Alexander McDONALD	30	....	Scotland	Scotland	Farmer	M	4
Peter MORISON	28	....	Scotland	Scotland	Farmer	M	

Boularderie (5 households)

James WALKER	43	....	Scotland	Scotland	Farmer	M	5
Thomas MATHEWS	48	....	Scotland	Scotland	Farmer	M	3
Hugh McKINNON	60	....	Scotland	Scotland	Farmer	M	
Alexander McKINNON	28	....	Scotland	Scotland	Farmer	M	1
Allan McFEE	20	....	Scotland	Scotland	Servant	S	

District of St. Andrews (63 households)

Lewis Cove (10 households)

Allen McDONALD	63	1	Scotland	Scotland	Farmer	M	4
Angus CAMPBELL	48	1½	Scotland	Scotland	Farmer	M	4
Donald CAMPBELL	24	1½	Inverness	Scotland	Farmer	S	
John SUTHERLAND	34	1	Scotland	Scotland	Farmer	M	3
Ronald McDONALD	30	1	Scotland	Scotland	Farmer	S	
Hugh McDONALD	22	1	Scotland	Scotland	Farmer	S	
Donald WHITE	45	1	Scotland	Scotland	Weaver	M	
Charles McNAB	52	8	Scotland	Scotland	Farmer	M	3
Dougall B. McNAB	23	8	Scotland	Scotland	Farmer	S	
Robert McNAB	21	8	Scotland	Scotland	Farmer	S	

Red Islands (19 households)

Name	Age		Birthplace	Origin	Occupation		
Hector McNIEL	48	16	Scotland	Scotland	Farmer	M	9
John McNIEL	23	9	Scotland	Scotland	Farmer	S	
Donald McNIEL	19	9	Scotland	Scotland	Farmer	S	
Niel McNIEL	17	9	Scotland	Scotland	Farmer	S	
John B. McNIEL	56	9	Scotland	Scotland	Farmer	M	7
Hector McNIEL	35	6½	Scotland	Scotland	Farmer	M	1
James McNIEL	22	9	Scotland	Scotland	Farmer	S	
Michael McNIEL	19	9	Nova Scotia	Scotland	Farmer	S	
Roderick McNIEL	17	9	Nova Scotia	Scotland	Farmer	S	
Alexander JOHNSON	40	11½	Scotland	Scotland	Farmer	M	8
Niel McKINNON	19	13	Scotland	Scotland	Farmer	S	
Duncan CAMPBELL	37	6½	Scotland	Scotland	Farmer	M	8
Angus JOHNSON	48	11	Scotland	Scotland	Farmer	M	5
Niel McKENZIE	37	11	Scotland	Scotland	Farmer	M	9
Donald JOHNSON	50	11	Scotland	Scotland	Farmer	M	6
Donald JOHNSON, Jr.	17	11	Scotland	Scotland	Farmer	S	
Hector CAMPBELL	40	11	Scotland	Scotland	Farmer	M	8
John McMULLEN	67	10½	Scotland	Scotland	Farmer	M	4
Niel McMULLEN	34	10½	Scotland	Scotland	Farmer	M	4

St. Andrews Channel (34 households)

Name	Age		Birthplace	Origin	Occupation		
John McNIEL	25	9	Scotland	Scotland	Farmer	S	
Donald McNIEL	22	9	Nova Scotia	Scotland	Farmer	S	
John McNIEL	17	9	Nova Scotia	Scotland	Farmer	S	
Murdoch McNIEL	35	1	Scotland	Scotland	Farmer	M	3
Robert McQUIN	28	1	Scotland	Scotland	Farmer	M	
Alexander McNIEL	25	13½	Scotland	Scotland	Farmer	S	
Colin CAMPBELL	28	1	Scotland	Scotland	Farmer	M	2
Roderick JOHNSON	42	1	Scotland	Scotland	Farmer	M	4
Niel McNIEL	40	8½	Scotland	Scotland	Farmer	M	
Duncan GILLIES	45	1	Scotland	Scotland	Farmer	M	4
Angus GILLIES	18	1	Scotland	Scotland	Farmer	S	
John GILLIES	27	1	Scotland	Scotland	Farmer	S	
John McEACHAN	21	1	P. E. Island	Scotland	Farmer	S	
Ronald McDONALD	23	1	P. E. Island	Scotland	Farmer	S	
Niel McDOUGALL	28	10½	Scotland	Scotland	Farmer	S	
Donald McNIEL	22	8	Nova Scotia	Scotland	Farmer	S	
Rory McNIEL	20	8	Nova Scotia	Scotland	Farmer	S	
Alexander McNIEL	24	8	Nova Scotia	Scotland	Farmer	S	
John McNIEL	32	8	Scotland	Scotland	Farmer	M	3
Donald McDONALD	38	4m.	Scotland	Scotland	Farmer	M	2
Dougall McDONALD	28	4m.	Scotland	Scotland	Farmer	M	1
Donald McDONALD	32	4m.	Scotland	Scotland	Farmer	M	1
Allen McDONALD	28	4m.	P. E. Island	Scotland	Farmer	M	3
John GILLIES	40	2	Scotland	Scotland	Farmer	M	5
Allen McDONALD	26	3½	P. E. Island	Scotland	Farmer	M	
Donald McDONALD	24	2	P. E. Island	Scotland	Farmer	S	
John McDONALD	19	2	P. E. Island	Scotland	Farmer	S	

William McDONALD	17	2	P. E. Island	Scotland	Farmer	S	
Donald GILLIES	24	16	Scotland	Scotland	Farmer	S	
Donald McLEAN	50	7	Scotland	Scotland	Farmer	M	8
Donald McEACHRAN	60	2	Scotland	Scotland	Farmer	M	3
Archibald CURRIE	36	4	Scotland	Scotland	Farmer	M	4
Donald McINNES	44	4	Scotland	Scotland	Farmer	M	5
Duncan CURRIE	45	4	Scotland	Scotland	Farmer	M	7

CENSUS OF SYDNEY COUNTY, NOVA SCOTIA, 1817: NATIVES OF SCOTLAND

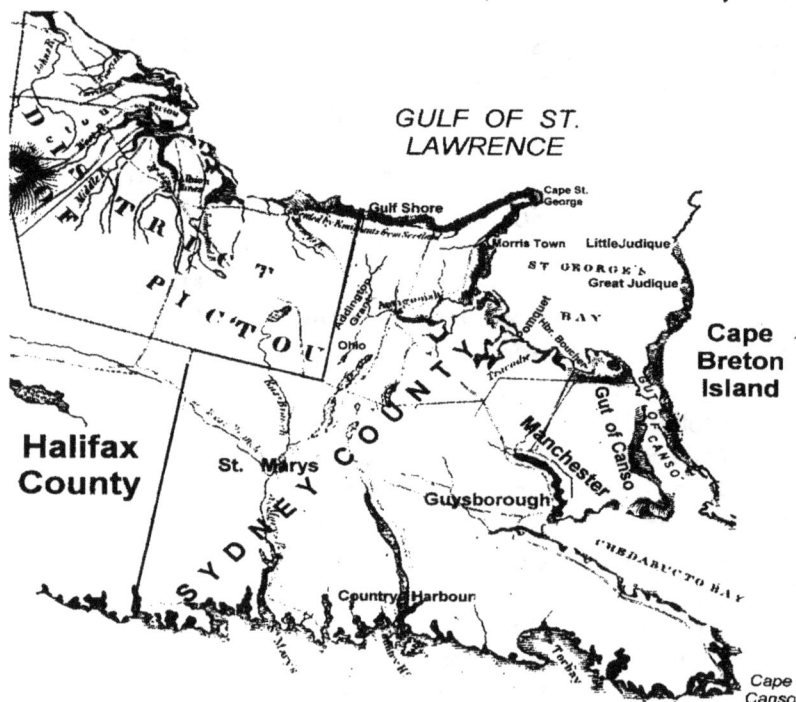

Sydney County was established in 1784 and was divided into an Upper and a Lower District. The Lower District was separated from Sydney County in 1836 to become Guysborough County. The remainder changed its name to Antigonish County in 1863. These counties constitute the easternmost extent of the Nova Scotia mainland, opposite to Cape Breton Island. Along with Pictou (top left on adjacent map) these areas, had the heaviest concentration of Scottish settlement in the mainland of Nova Scotia.

Map 6: Sydney County

DISTRICT	POPULATION		HOUSEHOLDS	
	Total	Scots-born	Total	Heads Scots-born
Addington Grant	85	28	13	12
Antigonish	1 409	473	202	162
Antigonish-Manchester Road	230	117	36	36
Cape St. George	379	97	60	51
Country Harbour	196	4	37	3
Gulf Shore	629	228	94	89
Gut of Canso	357	6	48	6

Guysborough	1 170	29	199	23
Harbour Boucher	299	20	42	10
Manchester	780	49	139	32
Morris Town	213	82	31	30
Ohio	180	74	29	28
Pomquet	195	2	31	1
St. Marys	330	49	56	18
Tracadie & Little River	453	21	75	12
Indians in the County	112	1	20	1
Blacks in Tracadie	174	0	37	0
TOTAL	**7 091**	**1 280**	**1 149**	**524**

The census used thirteen columns to present its data. The caption at the head of the following columns is keyed to the alphabetical order below. Thus if you read 3 under the heading D, it means that there were 3 boys (i.e., males below the age of 16) in the household. The headings are these:

Head of the Family.
A - Number of Men in the Household aged over 50.
B - Number of Men in the Household aged 16 to 49.
C - Number of Boys in the Household (i.e., males below 16).
D - Number of Women in the Household.
E - Number of Girls in the Household.
F -Total Number in the Household.
G - Born in England.
H - Born in Scotland [Bold print for emphasis].
I - Born in Ireland.
J - Born in America, including both United States and other part of British America.
K - Born in Germany or Other, i.e., Europe outside the British Isles.
L - "Acadian", meaning here anyone born in Nova Scotia regardless of ethnicity.

Head of the Family	A	B	C	D	E	F	G	H	I	J	K	L
ADDINGTON GRANT [now in Antigonish County]												
WILLIAMS, Zephariah	1	1	1	2	1	6		**1**		1		4
FRASER, Alexander, Sr.	1	1	3	4	1	10		**2**				8
MacLEAN, Angus	1		3	1	1	6		**2**				4
MacLEAN, John	1		3	1	1	6		**2**				4
WILLIAMS, Alexander		1				1		**1**				

BAXTER, Joseph		1	3	1	4	9		1				8
FRASER, Alexander, Jr.		1		1	3	5		1				4
MacGRA [MacRae], Murdoch	1	1	2	3	2	9		3				6
MacDONALD, Hugh		1		1	1	3		2				1
MacDONALD, John (Ban)		1	5	1	2	9		2				7
MacDONALD, John (Glenco)	1	1		1	3	6		3				3
CAMERON, John		2	2	1	3	8		8				
ANTIGONISH												
MacQUEEN, David, Sheriff		3	1	2		6		1	4			1
SYMONDS, Nathaniel, Esquire	1	5	1	3	3	13		3	3	3		4
MacDONALD, Alexander, Esquire		2		1	3	6		2	1			3
MacGILVERY, Widow		2	3	3	1	9		2				7
FRASER, Alexander		2		1	2	5		1				4
CLERK, John	1	2	3	2	4	12	1	1				10
MacNARE, Rodric		1	3	1	2	7		2				5
MacDONNELL, Alexander		1	1	1		3		1				2
MacDONNELL, Donald		2		1		3		2				1
THOMPSON, William	1	3	2	1	1	8		7				1
FERGUSSON, John		2	1	3	1	7		4				3
MUNRO, Rev. James	1					1		1				
MONRO, John		2	1	1		4		2		1		1
McDONALD, Alexander		2	1	2		5		2				3
CORBETT, John		4	1	1	2	8		1	5			2
CHISHOLM, Rev. [William]		1				1		1				
KELL, John[2]	1	5	3	2	5	16		2				14
MacDONALD, John	1			3		4		4				

[2] John **KELL** was a Loyalist. he received a grant of 250 acres at the Bay of St. Lewis [Cape St. George] in 1784.

Name												
GLASGOW, Walter[3]	1	2	1	1		5		**1**		1		3
McLELLEN, Donald	1	2	2	2	3	10		**3**				7
MacDONALD, Donald	1	3		3	1	8		**3**				5
HULBERT, Stephen		1	2	1		4		**1**		1		2
McDONALD, Donald	1	5	1	3		10		**4**				6
MacDONALD, James		1	1	1	1	4		**2**				2
SMITH, John	1	2	4	1	3	11		**2**				9
MacADAMS, Alexander		1	3	1	1	6		**1**				5
CHISHOLM, William		1		1	5	7		**2**				5
CHISHOLM, John		1	5	3	2	11		**2**				9
CHISHOLM, Kenneth	1	1	1	1	2	6		**2**				4
GORDON, John		1	2	1	2	6		**1**				5
KELLY, William		2	4	2	2	10		**2**				8
CAMERON, Widow		1		3		4		**4**				
MacARTHUR, Archibald		2	2	1	3	8		**3**				5
MacNEIL, John	1	3	5	2	1	12		**1**				11
MOORE, James H.		1		1	4	6		**2**				4
MARSHALL, Widow		1	1	1	1	4		**1**				3
CAMPBELL, Robert	1	3	2	2		8		**1**		6		1
MacPHERSON, John	1	3	1	2	1	8		**2**				6
MacKINNON, Dougald		1	4	1		6		**2**				4
CARTER, James		1		1	2	4		**1**		1		2
MacDONALD, John	1	3	2	3	1	10		**4**				6
CHISHOLM, Donald		2	2	1		5		**2**			1	2
DWYRE, Patrick		1	1	2	3	7		**2**	1			4
CAMERON, Duncan		1		2	1	4		**1**				3

---

[3] Walter "**GLASCO**" was a veteran of the Duke of Cumberland's Regiment, and served in the American Revolutionary War. He was granted 100 acres in Manchester Township in 1785.

Name												
CHISHOLM, John, Sr.	1	2		2		5		4	1			
CHISHOLM, John, Jr.		1	5	1	2	9		2				7
McLELLEN, Kenneth	1	1		2	1	5		2				3
MacDONELL, Allan		5	1	1	1	8		2				6
MacPHERSON, Donald		1	1	1	3	6		2				4
MacDONALD, Widow				2	3	5		3				2
MacGILVERY, Duncan	1	2	3	4	2	12		7				5
MacDONALD, Hugh		1	2	1	2	6		2				4
GILLES, Donald		1	3	1	5	10		2				8
SIPPLES, Michael		1	1	1	2	5		1	1			3
CAMERON, John		1	3	1	2	7		1				6
CAMERON, Widow			3	1	2	6		1				5
MacDONALD, Roderic		1	2	1	3	7		2				5
MacDONALD, Laughlin	1	3		2		6		4				2
MacDONALD, Donald		1	4	1	3	9		2				7
MacISAAC, Rannald		2	2	2	3	9		5				4
CHISHOLM, Alexander		1	2	2	2	7		3				4
CHISHOLM, Archibald		2	1	1	4	8		2				6
CHISHOLM, Roderic		1	4	1	2	8		2				6
GRANT, Roderic		1	4	2	2	9		4				5
CHISHOLM, Alexander	1	3	2	1	3	10		7				3
FRASER, John		1	3	1	4	9		7				2
MacKENZIE, Farquhar		1	1		2	4		1				3
MacKENZIE, William		2		1	1	4		3				1
MacINTOSH, John		2	2	3	2	9		5				4
CHISHOLM, Duncan		1	3	1	3	8		3				5
CHISHOLM, James		1	4	1	1	7		2				5
CHISHOLM, Donald	1	4	1	2	2	10		10				

Name												
CHISHOLM, Donald	1	4	1	2	2	10		**10**				
FRASER, Donald		1	4	1		6		**2**				4
MacKENZIE, John		1	3	1	3	8		**3**				5
MacHASKLE, Murdo		2		1		3		**2**				1
CAMPBELL, John		2	1	1	2	6		**4**				2
CHISHOLM, John		2	2	1	1	6		**4**				2
MacGILVERY, Allan		1		1	1	3		**2**				1
MacGILVERY, Angus		1		1	1	3		**2**				1
MacGILVERY, Angus		1	2	1	2	6		**2**				4
MacGILVERY, John	1	2	2	1	3	9		**4**				5
MacGILVERY, Widow			2	1	1	4		**1**				3
MacDONALD, John	1	2	2	1	3	9		**4**				5
MacISAAC, Archibald		1	5	1	3	10		**2**				8
MacISAAC, Duncan		1	3	1	3	8		**2**				6
MacISAAC, John		2		1	1	4		**2**				2
GILLES, Donald	1	2	3	1	4	11		**4**				7
MacISAAC, Archibald	1	1		2	2	6		**6**				
MacGILVERY, Angus	1	1	1	2		5		**5**				
MacEACHERN, John		1	1	1	1	4		**4**				
MacGILVERY, Donald		1	2	1	2	6		**2**				4
McDONALD, John		1	3	2	3	9		**3**				6
MacLEAN, Alexander		2	4	2	1	9		**4**				5
McLELLEN, Archibald		2	2	1	3	8		**3**				5
GILLES, Angus		2	4	2	4	12		**3**				9
MacDONALD, Hector		2	2	1	1	6		**3**				3
CHISHOLM, Donald (Oge)	1	3		3	1	8		**8**				
GRANT, Duncan		1		1	3	5		**4**				1
CHISHOLM, Donald (More)	1	2	2	3	3	11		**8**				3

Name												
MacMASTERS, John		2	1	3	1	7		5				2
DUNN, William	1	2	3	2	2	10	1	2				7
CAMPBELL, Robt. Mackintyre		1	1	1	2	5		2				3
MAHONEY, Samuel	1	1	3	2	4	11		1	1			9
MAHONEY, John		1	3	1		5		1				4
MacDONALD, John	1	4	2	2		9		2				7
CHISHOLM, Donald	1	2	4	4	2	13		8				5
MacNEIL, John		2				2		1				1
MacDONALD, Widow		1		1		2		1				1
CHISHOLM, Alexander		1	2	1	3	7		7				
MacGILVERY, Donald		1	1	1	1	4		2				2
MacNEIL, Donald		2	4	2		8		2				6
CHISHOLM, Collin		1	1	1	2	5		1				4
MacGILVERY, Rannald		1		1	2	4		1				3
MacEACHERN, Donald	1	1	3	3		8		8				
MacDONALD, Angus		3	3	1	3	10		4				6
MacDONALD, John	1			1		2		2				
CHISHOLM, Peter	1	3	2	2		8		8				
FRASER, Mary		2		1		3		3				
MacDONALD, Alexander		1	1	1		3		1				2
MacLELLEN, Donald		1	1	1	2	5		1				4
MacLELLEN, Angus		1	2	1	2	6		1				5
MacKENZIE, Donald		2	1	2		5		4				1
MacKINNON, John	1	3	2	2	1	9		3				6
MacDONALD, Angus	1		1	1	2	5		3				2
MacDONALD, Donald		1	4	1	4	10		2				8
MacDONALD, Donald		1	5	1	4	11		2				9
MacDONALD, John (Will'd Pt)		1	4	1	3	9		2				7

Name											
MacDONALD, Laughlin	1	2	2	2	2	9		**5**				4
MacDONALD, Roderic		1	2	1	4	8		**1**				7
BOYD, Angus		1	2	1	2	6		**2**				4
BOYD, Hugh	1	1	3	2	3	10		**4**				6
GILLES, Diamain		1		1	1	3		**2**				1
MacDONALD, Donald		1		1	1	3		**2**				1
MacDONALD, John		2	3	2	2	9		**4**				5
MacPHERSON, Donald	1		3	3	1	8		**4**				4
MacNEIL, Hugh		2		1		3		**3**				
MacNEIL, John		1	5	2	2	10		**3**				7
MacMILLEN, John		1	1	2		4		**3**				1
MacPHEE, Dougald	1		2	4	1	8		**8**				
MacMILLEN, John		1	1	2		4		**3**				1
MacMILLAN. Miles	1	4		4		9		**9**				
CUMMINGS, John		1	2	1		4		**2**				2
MacGREGOR, Duncan	1	2	3	2	3	11		**8**				3
MacPHERSON, Roderic	1	1	2	2	2	8		**6**				2
MacDONALD, Allan		1	2	1		4		**2**				2
MacDONALD, Donald		1	4	1	2	8		**2**				6
MacDONALD, Rannald		1	2	1	1	5		**2**				3
MacDONALD, Widow		3		1	3	7		**7**				
MacGILVERY, Hugh		1	1	1		3		**2**				1
MacDONALD, Angus	1			2		3		**3**				
CAMERON, Hugh		2	5	2	3	12		**4**				8
MacFARLANE, Archibald		1	3	1	5	10		**3**				7
MacDONALD, Widow			1	1	2	4		**1**				3
MacPHERSON, Widow			5	1	2	8		**1**				7
MacGILVERY, John		1	1	1	1	4		**2**				2

Name											
MacDONALD, Angus	1	2		2		5		**5**				
MacFARLANE, John		1	3	1	4	9		**2**				7
MacFARLANE, Peter		1	3	1	4	9		**1**				8
MacFARLANE, Angus	1	1	1	2		5		**4**				1
MacISAAC, Angus		1	4	1	3	9		**2**				7
MacISAAC, Hugh		1	2	1	1	5		**4**				1
MacGILVERY, John		1	2	1	1	5		**4**				1
ROAD FROM ANTIGONISH TO MANCHESTER												
CHISHOLM, Donald		1	3	1	3	8		**3**				5
CHISHOLM, Collin		1	2	2	4	9		**6**				3
CHISHOLM, Alexander	1	2	3	2	1	9		**6**				3
MacDONALD, Angus	1	1	3	2		7		**3**				4
MacDONALD, Alexander		1	1	1	2	5		**2**				3
MacDONALD, Donald		1	1	1	2	5		**2**				3
MacDONALD, John	1	1		1		3		**3**				
CHISHOLM, Archibald		1	1	1	3	6		**2**				4
CHISHOLM, Collin		1	5	1	2	9		**2**				7
CHISHOLM, John		1	2	1	1	5		**1**				4
CHISHOLM, Hugh		1	2	1	2	6		**2**				4
CHISHOLM, Archibald		1	4	2	3	10		**3**				7
CHISHOLM, Donald	1	1	1	1	3	7		**2**				5
CHISHOLM, Roderic	1			2		3		**3**				
MacDONALD, Donald		1		1	5	7		**2**				5
CHISHOLM, William	1	1	2	1	1	6		**3**				3
CHISHOLM, Christopher		1	3	1	1	6		**2**				4
CHISHOLM, Donald		2	4	1	1	8		**3**				5
CHISHOLM, Donald		1		1	6	8		**2**				6
MacDONALD, Alexander		1	2	1	2	6		**6**				

Name												
MacDONALD, Roderic	1		2	1	3	7		2				5
MacDONALD, Donald	1		1	1	2	5		2				3
MacDONALD, John	1	4	1	3		9		8				1
MacDONALD, John, Esquire		1	1	1		3		3				
MacDONALD, John		1	3	1	3	8		5				3
MacPHERSON, Donald		1	2	1	3	7		3				4
MacDONALD, Allan		1	1	1	2	5		2				3
MacDONALD, Angus		1	3	1	2	7		2				5
FRASER, Simon		1	2	1	4	8		3				5
CHISHOLM, Duncan		1	4	2	2	9		3				6
GRANT, John	1	3		2	2	8		8				
GRANT, James		1	1	1	1	4		2				2
MacDONALD, Nancy				1		1		1				
MacDONALD, Jenney				2		2		2				
MacDONALD, John	1	3	1	4		9		8				1
CAPE ST. GEORGE [now in Antigonish County]												
CHISHOLM, Alexander		3	2	3	2	10		1				9
MacDONALD, Dougald	1	2	2	2	2	9		2				7
MacDONALD, Dougald	1	2	4	1	4	12		2				10
CHISHOLM, Alexander	1	1	1	3	1	7		2				5
GILLES, John		1		3	1	5		2				3
MacNEIL, Malcom	1	2	2	1	1	7		2				5
MacINNES, John	1	2		1		4		2				2
MacKINNON, Neil	1			3		4		1				3
CHISHOLM, John	1	4	1	1	3	10		2				8
SMITH, Donald		1	1	3	3	8		2				6
MacINNES, Angus	1	3		2		6		2				4
MacNEIL, Malcolm		1	2	1	2	6		1				5

Name												
MacNEIL, John		1		1		2		**1**				1
MacDOUGALD, John	1	1		1		3		**3**				
MacDOUGALD, Donald		1		1		2		**2**				
MacLEAN, Donald	1	2	2	1	1	7		**2**				5
MacLEAN, Alexander		1	1	1	2	5		**1**				4
MacPHERSON, Alexander		1	5	1	4	11		**2**				9
MacDOUGALD, Angus		1	2	1	3	7		**2**				5
MacDONALD, Alexander	1	1	3	2		7		**2**				5
MacISAAC, Donald		2		3		5		**1**				4
MacNEIL, Donald		1	1	1	1	4		**2**				2
MacNEIL, Donald		1		1	1	3		**2**				1
MacDOUGALD, Angus		2		1	1	4		**1**				3
MacDOUGALD, Donald		1	1	1	3	6		**2**				4
MacDOUGALD, John		1		1	1	3		**1**				2
CAMPBELL, Archibald		1	2	5	4	12		**3**				9
CAMPBELL, Donald		1	2	1		4		**1**				3
LIVINGSTONE, Allan[4]		1	1	1	1	4		**1**				3
LIVINGSTONE, Duncan		2		1		3		**1**				2
MacMILLAN, John		1	3	1	2	7		**2**				5
MacDONALD, John		1	2	1	1	5		**2**				3
MacNEIL, John	1	1	6	1	2	11		**2**				9
MacEACHERN, Alexander		3	1	1		5		**1**				4
MacEACHERN, Archibald		4		2		6		**1**				5
GILLES, Angus		2	4	1	7	14		**2**				12
MacDONALD, Hugh		1	2	1	1	5		**2**				3
MacDONALD, John	1	3		2		6		**2**				4

[4] Allan was a son of Malcolm **LIVINGSTONE** from Argyllshire, Scotland.

Name												
MacISAAC, John		1	5	2	1	9		**9**				
MacDOUGALD, Donald		1	1	1	3	6		**2**				4
MacDOUGALD, John		1	1	1	1	4		**2**				2
MacISAAC, Allan	1	2			1		4		**2**				2
FOWLEY, Timothy	1	1		3		5		**1**	1			3
DUNN, John		1	1	1	5	8		**1**	1			6
MacDONALD, Duncan		1	4	1	5	11		**2**				9
MacINNIS, Donald		1	1	1	3	6		**2**				4
MacINNIS, Hugh		2	2	3	3	10		**5**				5
MacINNIS, Angus		1		1	2	4		**1**				3
HENDRICHAN, John		1	5	1	7	14		**1**	1			12
MacDOUGALD, Dougald	1		1	1	2	5		**2**				3
COUNTRY HARBOUR and LITTLE RIVER [now in Guysborough County]												
DAVISON, William		2		1		3		**1**				2
JACKSON, Edward	1		1	1	1	4		**1**				3
CAMERON, Archibald, Esquire[5]	1		1	2	3	7		**2**				5
GULF SHORE from MALIGNANT POINT to County Line [now in Antigonish County]												
MacDONALD, Angus	1	1		3	2	7		**2**				5
MacPHERSON, Angus	1	1		1		3		**2**				1
MacPHERSON, Donald		1	2	1		4		**2**				2
GILLES, John		1	2	1	2	6		**2**				4
MacDOUGALD, Archibald		1	2	1		4		**2**				2
MacDONALD, Allan	1	2	1	2	3	9		**2**				7
MacDOUGALD, Roderick	1		2	2	4	9		**2**				7
MacDONALD, John		1	2	1		4		**2**				2
MacDONALD, Donald	1	2	2	2	3	10		**2**				8

---

[5] Archibald **CAMERON** was a lieutenant in the King's Carolina Rangers and received a Loyalist grant of 650 acres at Country Harbour in 1784.

Name												
MacDONALD, Widow		3	1	2		6		**1**				5
MacGILVERY, Hugh	1	1		1		3		**1**				2
MacGILVERY, John		1	6	1	2	10		**2**				8
MacDONALD, John (Miller Cove)		2	3	3	1	9		**4**	1			4
MacGRA [MacRae], John	1		1	1	3	6		**4**				2
MacGILVERY, John	1	1		2		4		**4**				
MacGILVERY, Rannald		1	3	1	1	6		**2**				4
MacNEIL, Roderic[6]	1	2	2	3	2	10		**3**				7
MacNEIL, John	1	2	4	1	1	9		**2**				7
MacNEIL, Angus		1	1	1		3		**1**				2
MacNEIL, Widow		3	3	1	1	8		**1**	1			6
MacKENZIE, Donald	1	1		2	4	8		**4**				4
MacNEIL, Donald	1			1		2		**2**				
MacLEAN, Hector		1	1	1	1	4		**2**				2
MacKINNON, Donald		1	3	1	2	7		**2**				5
CAMPBELL, John	1	2		2		5		**2**				3
MacNEIL, Hector		2		2		4		**3**				1
MacISAAC, John		1	3	1	2	7		**2**				5
MacISAAC, Donald		1	1	3	1	6		**4**				2
MacDOUGALD, Hugh	1		6	1	1	9		**2**				7
McDONALD, Alexander	1	1	5	2	2	11		**2**				9
MacDONALD, Donald	1	1	2	3	5	12		**3**				9
MacVARRISH, Donald	1	1	4	2	3	11		**2**				9
MacDONALD, Donald	1	2	2	3	1	9		**3**				6
MacPHERSON, Alexander		2	1	3	1	7		**1**				6

---

[6] Roderick **McNEIL** and John McNEIL (following entry) were veterans of the 82nd Regiment. They settled in Malignant Cove in the 1780s.

Name	C1	C2	C3	C4	C5	C6	C7	C8	C9	C10	C11	C12
MacPHERSON, Angus		1	1	1	1	4		**1**				3
MacPHERSON, Angus	1		4	1	2	8		**2**				6
MacDONALD, Lewis	1	3	2	1	2	9		**2**				7
MacDONALD, William		1		2		3		**3**				
MacDONALD, Rev. Alexander		2				2		**2**				
MURRAY, Robert		2				2		**1**				1
MacDONNELL, Rannald		3		3	3	9		**5**				4
GILLES, Alexander	1		2	1	2	6		**1**				5
GILLES, Angus		1		2	1	4		**1**				3
GILLES, John		1		1	3	5		**2**				3
GILLES, John	1	1	2	3		7		**2**				5
McDONALD, John	1	1	2	1	1	6		**2**				4
MacDONALD, Donald		1	1	1		3		**1**				2
GILLES, Peter	1	2	3	3	2	11		**2**				9
MacDONALD, Donald		1	3	1	3	8		**1**				7
MacDONALD, Alexander	1	1		2		4		**1**				3
MacDOUGALD, Donald	1	2	1	1	2	7		**2**				5
MacDONALD, Alexander		1		2		3		**1**				2
MacDONALD, Angus	1	3	2	1	1	8		**2**				6
GILLES, Widow				2	1	3		**3**				
GILLES, William		1	1	1		3		**3**				
GILLES, Rannald		1	2	1	1	5		**2**				3
MacDONALD, Alexander		1	2	1	3	7		**6**				1
MacDONALD, Laughlin		1	1	1	2	5		**4**				1
CAMPBELL, Angus	1	1	2	4	2	10		**10**				
CAMPBELL, Angus	1		2	1	1	5		**5**				
MacDOUGALD, John		1		1	2	4		**4**				
MacDONALD, John	1			2		3		**2**				1

Name												
CAMPBELL, John	1	2	3	3	2	11		11				
MacDONALD, Donald		3	4	2	2	11		2				9
SMITH, Widow		2	1	2	3	8		1				7
SMITH, Alexander		1	1	1	1	4		1				3
MacADAM, Hugh	1	2	2	1	1	7		2				5
MacDONALD, Donald	1	1	2	1	3	8		4				4
MacPHERSON, Angus	1	1	4	2	2	10		2				8
MacDONALD, John	1	1	1	3		6		5				1
MacDONALD, Widow				2		2		2				
MacPHERSON, John		1	2	2	3	7		3				4
MacDONALD, Alexander	1	1	3	3	4	12		2				10
MacEACHERN, Angus		1	4	1	2	8		2				6
MacEACHERN, John		1	2	2		5		3				2
MacGILVERY, Alexander	1	2	3	2	3	11		2				9
MacGILVERY, Andrew	1	2	1	2		6		2				4
MacGILVERY, Angus	1	1	5	1	4	12		2				10
MacDONALD, Alexander	1	2	4	1	4	12		2				10
MacDONALD, Charles	1		5	1	5	12		2				10
MacLEOD, John	1		4	1	4	10		2				8
MacLEOD, Donald	1	1	4	1	3	10		2				8
GRANT, John		1	5	1	3	10		2				8
MacDONALD, Donald		1	2	1		4		1				3
MacLEOD, Hugh	1		5	1	2	9		2				7
MacDONALD, Allan		1	3	1		5		1				4
MacDONALD, Alexander	1	1	2	3		7		7				
MacDONALD, Martin	1	4	2	2		9		3				6
MacDONALD, Alexander		3	2	3		8		8				

GUT OF CANSO [Melford, Guysborough County]												
MacNARE [MacNair], Collin⁷	1	1	1	1	2	6		1	1			4
COWIE, James [ship carpenter]	1	1		1		3		1		1		1
MacPHERSON, David		1		1		2		1				1
MacGUIRE, Widow		3		2	1	6		1	3			2
DUNBAR, Alexander⁸	1		2	1	1	5		1			1	3
LOWRIE, Robert⁹	1	1	1	2		5		1				4
GUYSBOROUGH												
GAMMON, William, Sr.	1	3	1	2	2	9		1				8
MARSH, John		2		1	2	5	1	1				[3]
BEARS, James	1	2		1	1	5		2				3
PATTON, Widow¹⁰				1		1		1				
ROSS, Donald¹¹	1	2		1	4	8		1				7
CAMPBELL, Widow		2	1	2	3	8		1				7
GRESHINE [Gresheim], John		2	5	1	3	11		1				10
TAYLOR, Charles		2				2	1	1				
COGLE [Cogill], Widow		3		5	1	9		1	1			7
SHAW, Widow		2	1	2	1	6		1				5
WELLS, Michael		1	3	2	2	8		1	1			6
CAMPBELL, John		1	1	1	1	4		1				3

---

⁷ Colin **McNAIR**, a Loyalist, received a grant of 200 acres in Guysborough Township in 1785.

⁸ Alexander **DUNBAR** was a Loyalist and received a grant of 100 acres in Guysborough Township in 1785, and a town lot at Guysborough in 1790.

⁹ Robert **LAWRIE**, schoolmaster, a Loyalist from Albany, New York, received a grant of 200 acres in Guysborough Township in 1785. Robert **LOWRIE** was granted a town lot in Guysborough in 1790..

¹⁰ She was the widow of Patrick **PATON**, a Loyalist, who was granted 250 acres in Guysborough Township in 1785. Patrick **PATTON** had further grants of a water lot and town lot in Guysborough in 1790.

¹¹ Donald **ROSS**, a Loyalist, was granted 100 acres in Guysborough Township in 1785, and a town lot in Guysborough in 1790.

Name												
MORTIMER, Alexander	1			1	3	5		**1**				4
RATTRAY, Alexander		3		2	1	6		**1**	1			4
STEEL, John [trader]		2		2		4		**1**	1			2
MULLER, Christian, Esquire[12]	1	7		4		12		**2**	3		1	6
HUTCHESON, Matthew [cooper]		2	5	1	2	10		**1**				9
MacKENZIE, Alexander[13]	1	3	2	3	1	10	1	**1**				8
PORTER, Colin		1	2	1	1	5		**5**				
KING, Robert		1		1		2		**1**	1			
AITKINS, Donald [cooper]		1	1	1	1	4		**1**				3
WEEK[S], Henry	1	1		2		4		**1**				3
JAMIESON, John[14]	1	1	2	1	2	7		**1**				6
HARBOUR BOUCHER [now in Antigonish County]												
MacMILLAN, John		1	1	1		3		**2**				1
WRIGHT, Neil	2	1	1	2	5	11		**1**	3			7
MacDONALD, Donald		2	4	1	5	12		**2**				10
MacDONALD, John		3	4	1	2	10		**2**				8
MacDONALD, Duncan		1	1	1	4	7		**2**				5
O'BRIEN, John	1	1	3	1	4	10		**1**	1			8
MacDONALD, Angus		1	2	1	4	8		**2**				6
MacDONALD, John	1	5	1	1		8		**5**				3
MacDONALD, Angus		1	2	1		4		**1**				3
MacDONALD, Archibald		1	1	1	2	5		**2**				3

---

[12] Christopher **MILLER**, a German-born Loyalist, received 250 acres in Guysborough Township in 1785, and Christian MILLER was granted 500 acres at Chedabucto Bay in 1790 in lieu of the previous grant.

[13] Alexander **McKENZY**, a Loyalist, was granted 100 acres in Guysborough Township in 1785, and Alexander **McKENZIE** received a town lot in Guysborough in 1790.

[14] John **JAMESON**, a Loyalist, was granted 300 acres in Guysborough Township in 1785, and a town lot in Guysborough in 1790.

MANCHESTER [now in Guysborough County]												
MacKENZIE, Donald[15]	1	1	3	1	4	10		1		1		8
DAVISON, John	1		3	1	5	10		1				9
AIKINS, Samuel[16]	1	4				5	1	2				2
DAVISON, James	1	1	1	1	2	6		1				5
SELLERS, Donald[17]	1	1	2	2	3	9		1		1		7
KEY, James[18]	1	1	1	2		5		2				3
PERRY, James, Sr.	1			1		2		2				
MacKAY, James	1			3		4		2				2
DAVISON, William	1	1	4	3		9		2				7
GILLEY [Gillie], William, Sr.	1	2		1	1	5		2				3
MacDONALD, Donald	1	4		1	1	7		1		1		5
MacPHERSON, Paul[19]	1	2	2	2	1	8	1	1				6
HENDERSON, Alexander		3				3		1				2
MacMASTERS, George		1	1	1	1	4		1				3
MacMASTERS, John		1			1	2		2				
MONRO, John	1		1		1	3		1				2
MacDONALD, James	1		1	1		3		2				1
CAMPBELL, John, Clerk of Peace	1		1	1	1	4		1		1		2

---

[15] Donald **McKENZIE**, a Loyalist, was granted 100 acres in Guysborough Township in 1785. He was granted 5 acres and a town lot in Guysborough in 1790.

[16] Samuel **AICKINS**, a Loyalist, was granted 350 acres in Guysborough Township in 1785. Samuel **AIKIN** received a town lot and 5 acres in Guysborough in 1790.

[17] *Daniel* **SELLARS**, formerly in the Duke of Cumberland's Regt., was granted 100 acres in Guysborough Township in 1785, and a town lot in Guysborough in 1790.

[18] James **KEY**, a Loyalist, was granted 400 acres in Guysborough Township in 1785, and a town lot in Guysborough in 1790.

[19] Paul **McPHERSON**, a Loyalist, was granted 200 acres in Guysborough Township in 1785, and a town lot in Guysborough in 1790.

Name												
GRETNY [Gritney], Alexander		1	3	1	1	6		**1**				5
SIMPSON, William		2	3	2	3	10		**1**		1		8
JAMESON, Hugh	1	4		2	2	9		**4**				5
STEWART, John[20]	1	2	1	2	1	7		**5**				2
CUMMINGS, Alexander[21]	1	2	4	3		10		**2**				8
MacMASTERS, John	1	1		2	1	5		**2**				3
MacKAY, Alexander[22]	1	1	4	1	3	10	1	**1**				8
KERR [Carr], Robert[23]	1	3	1	1		6		**1**		1		4
GRANT, Alexander	1	1	3	1	3	9		**1**		1		7
KERR [Carr], Robert		4	3	4	1	12		**1**				11
MURDOCH, James	1		2	1	2	6		**2**				4
MILLER, Hugh	1		1	2		4		**1**		1		2
CONNER, Alexander		1	6	2		9		**1**				8
HARRAD [Harrid], James	1	3	1	5	1	11		**1**	2			8
MORRIS TOWN [now in Antigonish County]												
KENNEDY, Neil		6			1	7		**1**				6
MacISAAC, Angus		3	2	2	2	9		**3**				6
MacISAAC, John		2		2	2	6		**2**				4
MacGILVERY, Angus[24]	1		3	1	1	6		**2**				4

---

[20] John **STUART**, a Loyalist, was granted 550 acres in Guysborough Township in 1785, and John **STEWART** received 5 acres and a town lot in Guysborough in 1790.

[21] Alexander **CUMMING**, a Loyalist, was granted 250 acres in Guysborough Township in 1785, and Alexander **CUMMIN** received a water lot and a town lot in Guysborough in 1790.

[22] Alexander **McKAY**, a Loyalist, was granted 100 acres in Guysborough Township in 1785, and received 5 acres and a town lot in Guysborough in 1790.

[23] Robert **CARR** of the Royal North Carolina Regiment was granted 100 acres at Country Harbour East in 1784. Robert **KERR** received 200 acres in Guysborough Township in 1785.

[24] Angus **McGILLIVRAY** was a native of Arisaig, Scotland.

MacGILVERY, Hugh	1	3	2	1	2	9		2				7
CAMERON, Donald		2	2	1	3	8		4				4
MacPHERSON, John	1	1	1	2		5		3				2
MacDONALD, Angus	1		1	1	4	7		7				
MacDONALD, Archibald		1		2		3		2				1
MacDONALD, Donald		2	3	2	3	10		2	1			7
WALLACE, William	1	1		2		4		1	1			2
BOYD, Alexander		2	6	1	3	12		4				8
BOYD, John	1	1		2	2	6		3				3
MacGILVERY, William		1	1	1		3		2				1
MacDONALD, Donald		1	1	2	5	9		2				7
MacDONALD, John		2	2	1	1	6		3				3
MacDONALD, Alexander		1	1	1	2	5		1				4
MacDONALD, Angus		1	2	1	3	7		2				5
ANDERSON, James	1	4	1	2	3	11		2	1			8
LIVINGSTONE, John		1		1	3	5		1				4
MacLEAN, James		1	2	1	2	6		6				
LIVINGSTONE, Angus	1	3		2	1	7		6	1			
LIVINGSTONE, Allan		1	1	1	1	4		1				3
GRAHAM, Widow				2		2		1				1
MacPHERSON, Dougald		2		1	1	4		4				
MacDONALD, Hugh		1	3	2	2	8		3				5
HOGGAN, James		2	1	1	3	7		1	1	1		4
CAMPBELL, John		1	1	1	1	4		1				3
MacPHEE, Widow		2	2	3	1	8		7				1
BALLANTINE, David	2	3	3	3	2	13		3				10

OHIO on West River of Antigonish												
CHISHOLM, John	1	1	3	1	2	8		**3**				5
CHISHOLM, Thomas	1	2	3	1	3	10		**5**				5
MacDONALD, Kenneth		1		1	1	3		**2**				1
MacDONALD, Widow		1	1	3		5		**5**				
ROBERTSON, John	1	1		1		3		**3**				
McMILLAN, John, Sr.	1	3	1	2		7		**2**				5
MacINNIS, John [weaver]	1		5	1	5	12		**2**				10
MacMILLAN, John, Jr.		2		1		3		**2**	1			
McDONALD, Donald	1		3	1	3	8		**3**				5
MacNARE, Donald	1			2		3		**3**				
MacEACHERN, John	1	1	2	1	2	7		**7**				
MacDONALD, John		1	4	1	3	9		**2**				7
MacLEAN, Angus		1	4	1	3	9		**2**				7
MacLEAN, Donald		1	2	1	6	10		**2**				8
MacINNES, John, Sr.	1			2		3		**3**				
MacPHERSON, Donald, Jr.		1	2	1	3	7		**2**				5
MacINNES, Andrew[25]	1	2	1	1	5	10		**2**				8
MacDONALD, Alexander		1	3	1	2	7		**2**				5
MacPHERSON, Donald, Sr.[26]	1	1		2		4		**3**				1
MacPHERSON, Dougald		1	1	1	2	5		**1**				4
MacINNES, Donald	1	2		2		5		**5**				
MacINNES, Duncan		1	1	1	2	5		**1**				4
MacPHERSON, Angus		1	3	1		5		**2**				3

[25] Andrew **McINNES** was a native of Moidart, Scotland.

[26] Donald **McPHERSON** was a native of Moidart, Scotland.

Name												
MacGILVERY, Angus[27]	1	1	3	1	4	10		2				8
MacLEAN, Duncan		1	4	1	1	7		2				5
MacINNES, Angus [weaver]		1		1		2		2				
MacINNES, Angus, Sergeant		1	4	1	3	9		2				7
MacINNES, John, Sergt., brother		1		1		2		2				
POMQUET [now in Antigonish County]												
GRANT, William		1	2	1	2	6		2				4
ST. MARYS [Guysborough County]												
MacMILLAN, Malcolm		1	5	1	2	9		4				5
MacMILLAN, Hugh		1	2	1	2	6		2				4
CAMERON, John		1	2	3	6	12		8				4
CAMERON, Widow			3	1	3	7		2				5
STEWART, Alexander [cooper]		1	6	1	3	11		2				9
CAMERON, John	1		2	1	2	6		2				4
MacEACHERN, Archibald		1	3	1		5		2				
SINCLAIR, Alexander	1	1	3	3	1	9		9				
SINCLAIR, John		1				1		1				
CAMPBELL, James		2	1	2		5	1	4				
MacKENZIE, John A.		1	1	1	3	6		2				4
CAMPBELL, David		2				2		1	1			
KARTRUSS, Matthew		3				3		1	2			
MacDONALD, Hugh [trader]		1		1		2		1				1
MacINTOSH, John [carpenter]		3	1	1	1	6		2				4
INGOLS, John		1	1	1	1	4		1				3
MITCHELL, Daniel		3		1		4		3				1
SCOTT, John	1			1		2		2				

[27] Angus **McGILLIVRAY** was a native of Moidart, Scotland.

TRACADIE and LITTLE RIVER [now Afton River]												
MacKINNON, Angus		2	1	1	2	6	1	**1**				4
MacKINNON, Donald		1		1		2		**2**				
MacJESTNEYS [McChesney], Peter		1	1	1		3		**1**				2
O'BRIEN, Michael	1	1		1		3		**1**	1			1
GRAHAM, John		1	2	1	1	5		**1**				4
CHISHOLM, Archibald		1		1		2		**2**				
MacDONALD, Rannald		1	4	1	1	7		**2**				5
STEPHENS, Moses		1	2	1	3	7		**1**				6
MacKEOUGH, John	1	3	4	1	3	12		**1**	1			10
MacDONALD, Roderic		1		1	3	5		**2**				3
CHISHOLM, Kenneth	1	3		1		5		**5**				
CHISHOLM, Alexander		1	2	1	1	5		**2**				3
INDIANS in SYDNEY COUNTY												
MacPHERSON, Peter (Scotchman)	1		5		1	7		**1**				6

SCOTS-BORN, NOVA SCOTIA CENSUS OF 1770

Barely a few hundred natives of Scotland lived in the Maritime Provinces in 1770, if early census information is reliable. Unfortunately, much of the early population return has been lost. Since New Brunswick formed part of Nova Scotia until 1784 the loss is even more widespread. The surviving portions of this census record the presence of little more than 50 natives of Scotland in the mainland of the region.

Anyone who runs an eye down the following listings will observe that many families were made up of natives of Scotland as well as members born in North America. There is some anecdotal evidence to indicate that a good portion of the Scots who reached early Nova Scotia had emigrated first to New England and removed to Nova Scotia or the future New Brunswick as part of the greater immigration of New England Planters between 1759 and 1775.

Another characteristic which becomes apparent at once is that the Scots individuals in several of the families were not the party named as head of the household. A few were wives, as records in the several localities tell us, e.g., Janet **MONTGOMERY**, the wife of James **DOWNING** at Truro. Others were servants and farm hands employed by New England Planters. The presence of such people may be suspected when the number of "men" or "women" is greater than "1", although further evidence would be required to be certain. There was a group of twenty-one Scots in Falmouth Township on the properties of J. F. W. **DesBARRES**, but their names are not recorded, so we can only speculate that they were servants or tenants on his estates.

The 1770 census asked people whether they were Catholic or Protestant, but apart from thirty-nine Catholics (probably Acadian French) on the DesBarres property, the remaining 172 people were Protestant. I have omitted that column in the presentation that follows.

An asterisk (*) indicates that further information about that family is given at the end of each table.

AMHERST TOWNSHIP

Head of Household	Men	Boys	Women	Girls	Total	Born in Scotland	Born in America	Others
Patrick **CAMPBELL**	1		1		2	1		1 Irish
John **YOUNG**	1		1		2	2		
TOTALS	2		2		4	3		1 Irish

ANNAPOLIS TOWNSHIP

Head of Household	Men	Boys	Women	Girls	Total	Born in Scotland	Born in America	Others
*John **EASSON**	2				2	1		1 NS
Robert **WALKER	1	1	2	3	7	1	1 Eng	5 NS
TOTALS	3	1	2	3	9	2	1	6 NS

* Easson was commissioned as a master artificer by the Board of Ordnance in London, 1737, and was sent on service to the garrison at Annapolis Royal. He had a land grant in 1739 and married 27 Jan 1741, Avis **STEWART**, also Scottish-born, and died in Nov 1790, aged about 75. They had four children: John, Euphemia, David and William - W. A. Calnek, *History of the County of Annapolis*, p. 504.
** Walker came out to work for the garrison at Annapolis Royal. He married twice, and had five children: Robert, Andrew, Margaret, Anna and Sarah - W. A. Calnek, *History of the County of Annapolis*, p. 622.

CUMBERLAND TOWNSHIP

Head of Household	Men	Boys	Women	Girls	Total	Born in Scotland	Born in America	Others
*John **ALLAN**	1	1	1		3	1	1	1 Irish
William **ALLAN	1	3	1	3	8	1	7	
Anthony **BURKE**	1	1	2	4	8	2	5	1 Irish
Robert **SCHOTCH**	1				1	1		
TOTALS	4	5	4	7	20	5	13	2 Irish

* John was the eldest son of William **ALLEN**, and was born at Edinburgh, 3 Jan 1746, and died 7 Feb 1805 at Lubec, ME, where he settled following his involvement in the abortive Eddy Rebellion in which a group of sympathizers with the American Revolution attempt to seize Fort Cumberland at Chignecto Isthmus. John had been a member of the Nova Scotia House of Assembly. He married 10 Oct 1767, Mary, dau of Mark **PATTON**, an Irish settler in Cumberland. They had eight children: Isabella Maxwell, William, Elizabeth, Mark, George Washington, Winckworth Sergeant, Horatio Gates and John.

William **ALLEN was born at Edinburgh about 1718, and died in Nova Scotia, 19 May 1785. After serving as an officer in the Army, he settled in Nova Scotia. He married Isabella **MAXWELL** (died 30 Aug 1767) and had seven children: John (above), Elizabeth, George, Jane, Winckworth, Isabella and William.

FALMOUTH TOWNSHIP

*Jacob **MULLER**	3		2		5	1	1	1 Irish 1 Eng. 1 Ger.
George **STUART**	1	1	1	1	4	1	3	
J. F. W. **DesBARRES	42	5	13	33	93	21	17	24 Ire 14 Eng 17 Ger
TOTALS	46	6	16	34	102	23	21	58

* John Jacob Muller, or **Müller**, was a lieutenant in the 60th (Royal American) Regt. during the Seven Years' War, and was granted 1,000 acres in 1768. Undoubtedly he was the German in the household.

** Joseph Frederic *Vallet* DesBarres (1728 - 17 Oct 1824) was born in the Principality of Montbéliard, and had a long and distinguished career. His most notable achievement was the survey of much of the coastline of eastern North America (1764-1773), published as *The Atlantic Neptune*. His career is written up by R. J. Morgan in the *Dictionary of Canadian Biography*, VI, pp. 192-197.

LUNENBURG TOWNSHIP

*Edward **THOMAS**	1	2	1	2	6	1	3	1 Eng 1 Ger

* Thomas was a shoemaker at Lunenburg, who died 10 Mar 1775, age 45. He married, 16 Jan 1760 (St. John's Anglican, Lunenburg), Maria Gertrud (died 8 Aug 1778, age 62) from Hesse, the widow of Johann Conrad **WOLLENHAUPT** from Hesse-Hanau. One of the boys in the Thomas household in 1770 was John Caspar Wollenhaupt, his stepson.

GRANVILLE TOWNSHIP

Thomas **BROWN**	1	2	1		4	1	3	
*Ellexander **MacKENSEY**	2		1	1	4	1	2	1 Irish
Col. Henry **MUNROW	1	4	1	2	8	1	7	
Ellexander **ROBESON**	1		1		2	2		
George **RUDDOCK**	1	1	1		3	2	1	
TOTALS	6	7	5	3	21	7	13	1 Irish

* Alexander McKENZIE was born in Scotland ca. 1733 and died 14 July 1820. He married by licence dated 31 Dec 1763, Mary (1749-1843), dau of Walter **WILKINS**. They had eleven children: Sarah, Mary, Walter, William, Abba, Elizabeth, John, Nancy, Alexander, Susan and Mary - W. A. Calnek, *History of the County of Annapolis*, pp. 547-8.

** Henry MUNROE, Lt-Col. of Militia, J.P., and Member of the Assembly, 1765-68, was born in Argyllshire, and was a First Lt. in a Highland Regt. Disbanded in 1764, he was granted 2,000 acres the following year. He married in 1767, Sarah, dau of Thomas **HOOPER** and had seven children: George, Henry, John, Robert, David, Elizabeth and Sarah.

HILLSBOROUGH TOWNSHIP (now in New Brunswick)

John **BROWN**	1	2	1	2	6	1	5	

LONDONDERRY TOWNSHIP

*William **CORBETT**	1	5	2	1	9	1	8	

* Corbett was born in Scotland, but lived some years in the Thirteen Colonies. He served in the attack on Québec in 1759, and afterwards settled in Nova Scotia. He drowned in Oct 1784 when a boat in which he was traveling upstream in the Shubenacadie River upset. He married in 1748, Elizabeth **ROBINSON** of Plymouth, MA. They had ten children: Elizabeth, Agnes, Margaret, William, Robert, Eleanor, James, John, Joseph and Martha - Thomas Miller, *Historical and Genealogical Record of the First Settlers of Colchester County*, pp. 211-215.

NEW DUBLIN TOWNSHIP

William **JOHNSTON**	2				2	1		1 Irish

NEW DONEGALL, or PICTOU TOWNSHIP

Robert **PATTERSON**	2	5	1	2	10	1	6	1 Irish 1 Eng 1 Acad
Thomas **SHEED**	1				1	1		
TOTALS	3	5	1	2	11	2	6	3

SACKVILLE TOWNSHIP (now in New Brunswick)

Robert **SCOTT**	1	1	1		3	1	2	

TRURO TOWNSHIP

*James **DOWNING**	1	1	1	3	6	1	4	1 Irish
Widow Jane **GEMMLE		1	2		3	1	2	
***Alexander **NEILSON**	1	2	1	2	6	1	4	1 Irish
****James **YULE**, Esq.	2		2		4	3	1	
TOTALS	4	4	6	5	19	6	11	2 Irish

* Downing was born in Ireland, and died 28 Oct 1776, probably in his early 50s. He married in New England in 1749, Janet **MONTGOMERY** from Scotland, and had five children: Mary, Janet, James, Catherine and Nancy. Only the last was born in Nova Scotia. The others were born in New England - Thomas Miller, *Historical and Genealogical Record of the First Settlers of Colchester County*, pp. 338-340.

** Andrew **GAMMELL** died on 8 Mar 1769, when a tree fell on him while he was chopping in the woods. He married Elizabeth [*sic*] **THOMSON** from Scotland. They had four sons: John, Archibald, Andrew and Robert. John and Andrew seem to have died or gone away, as there is no further record of them here - Thomas Miller, *Historical and Genealogical Record of the First Settlers of Colchester County*, pp. 294-296.

*** Alexander **NELSON** (not Neilson) was born in Ireland. He married Margaret **ROBERTSON** from Scotland, and had five children: Elizabeth, William Montague, Agnes, Archibald and Charles - Thomas Miller, *Historical and Genealogical Record of the First Settlers of Colchester County*, pp. 135-142.

**** James **YUILL**, Esq., was born in 1717 in Clydesdale, Scotland, and died at Old Barns, NS, 4 Mar 1807. He married ca. 1742 in Clydesdale, Jane **BAILEY** (1721 - 11 Jan 1804) of the same place. They had a son James, also born in Clydesdale, where the father was a merchant before emigrating, first, to New England in 1753, and again in 1761 to Truro, Nova Scotia.

PROBATE RECORDS

The information in this section is derived from three sources. Those for Halifax County, Nova Scotia, are taken from the first six will books in the Probate Court which cover the period from 1749 to 1851. Those from New Brunswick are mainly based on R. Wallace Hale's *Early New Brunswick Probate Records 1785 - 1835* (1989). Of the few Newfoundland items, most come from the pages of the *Royal Gazette and Newfoundland Advertiser* between 1817 and 1839.

These are not complete abstracts of the wills, but contain the genealogically significant parts of the information. Whenever possible the date of death, either exact or approximate, has been added. The sole criterion for selection has been that Scotland or North Britain appears in the will itself or is mentioned in ancillary documents. The earliest date on a will herein is 1757 and the latest is dated 1851.

HALIFAX COUNTY, NOVA SCOTIA

ABERCROMBIE, Alexander, physician [died 31 Mar 1773, age 48]
Will dated 28 Mar 1767, proved 8 Apr 1773.
Siblings including eldest brother, John, a merchant in Aberdeen, Scotland.
(Vol.II, p. 81)

ADAMS, Ann, [died 3 May 1796, age 76] widow of Charles, innkeeper [died 15 June 1794]
Will dated 26 Jan 1796.
Her husband's son, James Adams, Dulnanvert [Dalnavert, Badenoch, Inverness], Scotland
(Vol. III, p. 142)

BREMNER, Ann, [died Jan 1810] widow of John [died 9 Dec 1806]
Will dated 20 Feb 1808, proved 16 Jan 1810.
John Bremner of Rothes, Morayshire, and *his* granddau Ann, dau of Alexander Bremner.
James and William, sons of Peter Bremner, Scotland.
(Vol. III, p. 358)

BROWN, Duncan, innholder, Halifax [buried 8 Aug 1802, age 50]
Will dated 10 Apr 1802, proved 10 Aug 1802.
Wife Elizabeth [**MILLER**, married 27 May 1797, St. Paul's Church, Halifax].
Adopted orphan child, George Brown.
Brother, David Brown of Glasgow, Scotland.
(Vol. III, p. 261)

DICKSON, James, surgeon, Agent for Sick & Hurt Seamen of HM's Squadron in Nova Scotia
[died 12 Jan 1782]
Will dated 10 Jan 1782.
Brother, Dr. George Dickson, Scotland.
Sister, Jane **NEWTON**.
Late sister, Mary **BLACKEY** [elsewhere called Mrs. **McINRAITH**].
£500 to Mary **BUTCHER** "who lives with me".
£1,000 each to their minor daus, Elizabeth and Isabella Dickson.
(Vol. II, p. 309)

DURIE, George, seaman, HMS *Sutherland* [off Louisbourg]
  Will dated 15 July 1758, proved 20 Dec 1758.
  Mother Janet and sister Catherine Durie, both of New Thornton, Maiden Shire, North
  Britain [perhaps Thornton in Fifeshire?]
  (Vol. I, p. 162)   [Died 1758, possibly during the siege of Louisbourg in July 1758]

FRASER, Hon. James, Esq., Halifax [died 14 Oct 1822, age 61]
  Will dated 13 Jan 1816, codicils of 8 and 12 Oct 1822, proved 19 Oct 1822.
  Oldest son, James DeWolf Fraser, and other children.
  Bequests to John Ogg Fraser; Hugh Fraser of Ruthven, Scotland; John Fraser of
  Halifax; Ann, wife of Thomas Fraser of Inverness, Scotland; and William **McDONALD** of
  Farnatine [?], Scotland.
  (Vol. IV, p. 101)

GORDON, Lt. James, commander of HM schooner *Vesta* [died 12 Mar 1808]
  Will dated 12 Mar 1808, proved 15 Mar 1808.
  Sisters, Margaret and Isabella.
  Executors: Capt. James **DUNBAR**, R.N., and his mother, Margaret Gordon of the Parish of
  Bellfair [?], Nairn, Scotland.
  (NSARM, mfm. 406)

GRANT, Donald, mason, Halifax [died 27 Apr 1848 in Ross-shire, Scotland]
  Will dated 8 May 1847, proved in 1848.
  Wife Elizabeth Amelia [**EARL**, married by licence dated 14 May 1835].
  Minor son, John George.
  Grant was a native of Miltown of Dellifour [?], Parish of Cromdale, Strathspey, Inverness-shire.
  Six sisters: Mary, Elspet, Catherine (dead), Margaret, Isabella and Janet.
  Executors: George Grant **GRAY**, shopkeeper, and John **SLAYTER**, notary, both of Halifax.
  (Vol. VI, p. 44)

GRANT, John, surgeon [died August 1757]
  Will dated 25 Aug 1757, proved 8 Sep 1757.
  Sister, Hellen Grant in Scotland.
  (Vol. I, p. 141)

HUME, Robert, M. D., Halifax [died 25 Apr 1853, age 78]
  Will dated 2 Mar 1851, proved in 1853.
  Son, James Compton Hume.
  Son-in-law, Oliver Thomas **MILLER**, [surgeon, R.N.]
  Two children of late son, Thomas Cochran Hume and his late wife [Isabella **SINCLAIR**]:
      William Sinclair and Isabella Barbara Hume.
  Codicil dated 20 Apr 1853 makes James McGill **RAE** of Nubactle [Newbattle], Midlothian,
      Scotland, factor to the Marquis of Lothian, guardian of the above two grandchildren.
  (Vol. VI, p. 169)

JACKSON, Alexander, carpenter, Ordnance Dept., Halifax [died 7 Apr 1828, age 79]
  Will dated 28 June 1819, proved 7 Apr 1828.
  Brother William Jackson, carpenter, Keith, Banffshire, Scotland.
  (Vol. IV, p. 244)

JAMESON, Jean, née **DENOON**, Church Street, Inverness, Scotland [died 10 May 1838 at Inverness], widow of Charles Jameson, goldsmith, Inverness.
Will dated 22 Dec 1837, proved in 1838.
Late brother, Hugh Denoon, Esq., Pictou, NS.
Four children: Elizabeth, wife of George **HEPBURN**, Greenock.
        Mary, wife of James **SMITH**, bookseller, Inverness.
        Catherine.
        Hugh Denoon, surgeon, R.N.
(Vol. V, p. 202)

KIDSTON, Richard, Esq., Halifax [died 17 June 1816, age 79]
Will dated 1 Aug 1815, proved 24 June 1816.
Eldest son, William, merchant at Anderston, near Aberdeen, Scotland, and his issue, including his eldest son Richard Kidston.
Son, James and wife Margaret and their youngest son, Richard William Kidston.
Youngest son Richard left *Bankhead Farm*, Halifax Peninsula, NS.
(Vol. III, p. 510)

LISWELL, Martha, [died 30 Oct 1847, age 65], widow, Halifax [of John, died 11 Apr 1821]
Will dated 24 Mar 1846, proved in 1847.
Children: John; Isabella **FLOHR**, widow, both of Halifax; and Bethia, wife of Peter **ANDERSON**, mariner, Glasgow, Scotland.
Executors: George **SMITHERS**, painter, and Archibald **SINCLAIR**, master saddler.
[Married by licence dated 3 Sep 1803: John Liswell and Martha **MITCHELL**]
(Vol. VI, p. 30)

LYON, Robert, Sr., dealer, Halifax [died 22 Apr 1816, age 67]
Will dated 14 June 1815, proved in 1816.
Brother, William (Executor) and his wife.
Son, Robert "at his education" in Glasgow.
Agnes **McLEAN**, "mother of my son . . . if she be alive".
(Vol. III, p. 485)

LYON, Robert, Jr., gentleman, Northwest Arm [died 1 Nov 1819, age 40]
Will dated 30 Aug 1818, proved 16 Nov 1819.
Mother, Agnes **LIGHTERNESS** of Erskine House, near Renfrew, Scotland.
Aunt Anne, Rothesay, Isle of Bute, Scotland, widow of uncle William **LYON**, merchant at Halifax [died 25 Sep 1806]
(Vol. IV, p. 51)

McCALLAN, James, merchant, Halifax [died 8 May 1815]
Will dated 24 Apr 1815, proved 12 May 1815.
Sister, Margaret, widow of Alexander **CASSIE**, ship master, Aberdeen.
Brother, Adam, a merchant at Miramichi, with children.
Nephews: Adam **VASS**, mariner, Halifax; James Vass, Aberdeen.
Ann, dau of nephew Nicholas Vass, cooper in Halifax.
(Vol. III, p. 483)

McDONALD, Charles, mariner, Halifax [died 5 Apr 1789, age 40]
  Will dated 17 Feb 1789, proved in 1789.
  Father: Donald, Inverness, Scotland.
  Brother John in North Carolina.
  (Vol. III, p. 64)

McDOWALL, Turnbull, shipwright, Halifax [died in March 1814]
  Will dated 2 Mar 1814, proved 7 Mar 1814.
  William McDowall, mariner, Dumbarton, Scotland.
  (Vol. III, p. 450)

McFARLANE, Duncan, grocer, Halifax [died 17 Apr 1842, age 60]
  Will dated 26 June 1841, proved 20 Apr 1842.
  Sister, Mrs. Christina McFarlane, Aberfoyle Park, Perthshire, Scotland, and her three sons,
      of whom Duncan is the eldest.
  Son of late sister Jannet.
  Mrs. **PATTERSON**, Glasgow, the child of late brother Parlen McFarlane.
  Two children of late brother John: John , 83rd Regt. of Foot, and a daughter.
  Executors: Thomas **WILLIAMSON**, Esq., and Charles W. **HILL**, butcher.
  (Vol. V, p. 213)

MATTHEWS, Thomas, gate porter, Careening Yard, Halifax [died 17 Sep 1840, age 72]
  Will dated 17 Dec 1833, proved 29 Sep 1840.
  He was a son of Andrew MATTHEWS, Greentrae, near Peterhead, Scotland.
  Sister Grizzle **GARNER**, widow, Peterhead, Aberdeenshire.
  Sister-in-law, Frances **WILSON**.
  Executor: William Alexander **ANDERSON**, gent.
  Witnesses: Anne Anderson, J. J. **SAWYER**, and Mary **WHIPPLE**.
  (Vol. V, p. 149)

MORRISON, Alexander, gent., Halifax [died 9 Jan 1814, age 67]
  Will dated 9 Nov 1813, proved 15 Feb 1814.
  Wife Anne.
  Sister, Margaret, widow of John **McCALLUM** of Glasgow, and her five children:
      William, Robert, Janet, Helen and Margaret.
  Mary, dau of late elder sister Mary, in Scotland.
  Martha, dau of wife's sister Martha and her husband William **BLACK**.
  (Vol. III, p. 430)

MORTIMER, Edward, merchant, Pictou, NS [died 10 Oct 1819, age 50][1]
  Will dated 25 Oct 1818, proved 10 Nov 1819.
  Wife Sarah.
  Brother, Alexander, in Guysborough, NS.
  Sister, Mary, wife of John **FORSYTH**, Keith, Scotland.
  (Vol. IV, p. 48)

---

[1] Edward **MORTIMER** was baptised 6 June 1768 at Keith, Banffshire, a son of Alexander and Mary (**KEITH**) Mortimer. He married about 1790, Sarah, dau of Robert **PATTERSON**. Mortimer was a member of the House of Assembly from 1799 until his death, and a magistrate.

ROSS, Alexander, trader, Windsor, NS [died in 1829]
Will dated 21 Feb 1828, proved 20 Nov 1829,
Four brothers: Angus, James, William and John.
Aunt, Augusta Ross.
Several stepbrothers.
Stepmother, Catherine Ross, Parish of Dornoch, Sutherlandshire, North Britain.
Stepsisters, Augusta and Ann Ross.
(Vol. IV, p. 275)

ROY, James, freeholder at Miramichi, NB [died 26 May 1823 at Newcastle, NB]
Will dated 6 Feb 1823, proved 5 Sep 1823.
Bequests to James Roy, Jr., James Roy, Sr., cousin, late of Longbrik [?]. and his dau
    Margaret; to cousin Elspit **DEAN** (Mrs. **BRANDER**, Aberdeen); and to James Dean and
    Isabel **SIMPSON**, children of late uncle Alexander Dean.
(Vol. IV, p. 341)

SHARP, James, mason, Halifax [died 27 Nov 1796, age 45]
Will dated 26 Nov 1796, proved Dec 1796.
Mother, Margaret **DONALD**, late of the Parish of Rothes, Morayshire, Scotland.
Siblings: John, William, Jean, Janet and Margaret Sharp.
(Vol. III, p. 149)

SLORACK, Adam, truckman, Halifax.
Will dated 20 Nov 1800, proved 26 Feb 1804.
Brother, George, Fockabus, Banffshire [Fochabers, Morayshire], Scotland.
John and Walter, sons of late brother Walter (Huntly, Aberdeenshire).
Niece, Jane, dau of brother James of Glass, Aberdeenshire, Scotland.
(Vol. III, p. 277)

STEWART, Archibald, merchant, Halifax [died 12 Jan 1835, age 66]
Will dated 11 Jan 1835, proved 19 Jan 1835.
Wife Susannah (Executrix).
Brother, Alexander **ANDERSON**.
Sister, Margaret Stewart, Queen's Ferry, Linlithgow, Scotland.
Cousin, Marion **STEELE**, Queen's Ferry.
(Vol. IV, p. 419)

SWAN, James, mason, Halifax [died 10 Apr 1842 age 37][2]
Will dated 6 Apr 1842, proved 2 June 1842.
Wife Elizabeth.
Mother, Margaret, widow, in Ayrshire, Scotland.
(Vol. V, p. 220)

---

[2] **SWAN** was the foreman of masons working on constructing the major fortifications on Citadel
Hill which still overlooks downtown Halifax City.

TAIT, Capt. David, Halifax, and late of Sydney, NS [died 4 Aug 1834, age 94]
Will dated 12 Jan 1832, proved 15 Aug 1834.
Late brother, Richard Tait.
Sister, Mrs. Alice **COLES**.
Nephews: James **KIRKWOOD**, and the two sons of Mrs. **SMITH**, Dunse, Berwick, Scotland.
(Vol. IV, p. 399)

THOMPSON, John, Halifax [died 24 Feb 1839, age 86]
Will dated in August 1827, proved 4 Mar 1839.
Niece, Miss Margaret **GENIE**, Halifax (Executrix).
Nieces and nephews in Scotland: James, Alexander, Marjery, John, Helen and
    George Thompson.
(Vol. V, p. 115)

WILLIAMSON, Thomas, Esq., Halifax [died 27 Mar 1848, age 57][3]
Will dated 23 Jan 1845, proved in 1848.
Wife Jane.
Brother, John (Executor).
Sister, Miss Margaret Ann Williamson, West Kilbride, Isle of Arran, Scotland.
George R. **YOUNG**, Esq. (Executor).
(Vol. VI, p. 40)

WILLS, Alexander, gardener, Halifax [died 24 Jan 1817, age 61][4]
Will dated 21 Jan 1817, proved 27 Jan 1817.
Siblings in North Britain: James, John, William and Amelia **WILLS**, and Jennett,
    wife of Thomas **GIBSON**,
(Vol. IV, p. 3)

Occasionally a genealogical gem is tucked away in a probate document. In the following case the document is not a will, but a power of attorney granted on 20 May 1822 to David **MUIRHEAD**, trader, Halifax, whose half brother, Samuel Muirhead died at Halifax, 12 Feb 1822, age 58, childless and intestate (Vol. IV, p. 275). David submitted a fairly detailed genealogical account of the immediate family and potential heirs of the decedent. In it [see p. 116] he lists all the offspring of their father, the late John Muirhead the elder, who died in August 1799 at Bankhead, Stirlingshire, Scotland. Four of the sons were Samuel, David, George and Thomas.[5]

---

[3] **WILLIAMSON** was mayor of Halifax in 1843. He had married, 4 Nov 1819 at St. Matthew's Presbyterian Church, Halifax, Jane Cassilis, dau of John and Agnes (**CASSILIS**) **BROWN**, Halifax.

[4] **WILLS** was gardener at Government House. He joined St. Andrew's Masonic Lodge in Halifax in 1793, and was master of the lodge in 1813.

[5] Samuel **MUIRHEAD** married 31 Oct 1802 at St. Matthew's Presbyterian, Halifax, Catherine **ROSE**, who died 20 Oct 1807, age 37. Their only child, John, baptised 17 Aug 1806, died in infancy. David Muirhead died 15 June 1825, age 51. He married 11 Dec 1808 at St. Matthew's, Halifax, Isabella Rose. They had several daughters: Catherine, Marion, Isabel, Ann and Jane. Isabella and her daughters were still living in Halifax at the time of the 1838 census. George Muirhead married Martha **MUNRO** who died 7 July 1818, age 34, by whom he had three children: Ann, Samuel and George. Thomas Muirhead died 13 Feb 1823, age 34, having married, 25 May 1822 at St. Paul's Anglican Church, Halifax, Catherine, dau of Christian and Catherine (**HARPER**) **SWINSBURG** of Shelburne, NS, but had no issue.

John Muirhead the elder was married three times and had issue from each marriage. By his first marriage to Ann **MILLER**, who died in Sep 1768, there were six children (those marked with an asterisk were alive in 1822):

1. *William, age 68, living at Balluno, Parish of Currie, Westlothian, Scotland.
2. Andrew, who died at sea, unmarried and childless.
3. Samuel, whose estate this was, died at Halifax in 1822, age 58.
4. Ann, who died at Bankhead, Scotland, unmarried.
5. *John, age 59, living at Bankhead, Parish of Denny, Stirlingshire, Scotland.
6. Robert, died as a child at Dand [?], Scotland.

John Muirhead married, secondly, Marian **ROBERTSON**, who died in Feb 1785, and had eight further children:

7. *James, age 52, a wright at Longcroft, Denny Parish.
8. Robert, died as a child at Bankhead.
9. *David, age 48, trader at Halifax, the applicant.
10. Iain, died at West Borland, Scotland, unmarried.
11. *Margaret, age 44, wife of William **AUCHINVALE**, weaver in the Parish of Kilsyth, Stirlingshire, Scotland.
12. *Catherine, age 42, wife of William **SCOTLAND**, shoemaker in the Parish of Kirkintilloch, Dumbartonshire, Scotland.
13. *George, age 40, living at Halifax.
14. Archibald, died at Bankhead, no issue.

John Muirhead married, thirdly, Jean **WITE** [*sic*] who died in Oct 1818. By her, John had five more children:

15. *Thomas, age 33, trader at Halifax.
16. *Christian, age 32, living at Haggs, Parish of Denny, Stirlingshire, Scotland.
17. *Agnes, age 31, of the same place.
18. *Elizabeth, age 29, of the same place.
19. *Marion, or Mary, age 24, of the same place.

NEW BRUNSWICK

Four of New Brunswick's fifteen counties are represented among the twenty-one probates that follow: Saint John 14, Charlotte 4, York 2, and Gloucester 1. By date, the earliest estate is from 1786 and the latest dated in 1834. In all cases Scotland is mentioned within the documents themselves.

ANDERSON, David, merchant, Fredericton.
Will dated 21 June 1794, proved 14 July 1794.
Estate to be liquidated and the proceeds sent to William **IRVIN**, merchant at Glasgow, Scotland for distribution as directed:
Father, David Anderson, "now or late of the Parish of Alves, Morayshire, North Britain".
Brothers, John and James, farmers, Morayshire.
Younger brother, Andrew, merchant in Glasgow.
Executors: Alexander **BLACK** and Peter **FRASER**, Fredericton, and Thomas **IRVIN**, Saint John, all merchants.
Witnesses: Duncan **BLAIR**, Frances **McBEATH**, and Allen **WILMOT**.
[Died in July 1794]

BLACK, Hon. John, merchant, Saint John, and later of Halifax, NS.
Will dated 28 Oct 1800, codicils, all proved 10 Nov 1823 at Halifax.
Daughter, Margaret, 15 months old, left £100 sterling for life.
Siblings: James, Andrew, William and Elizabeth, all of Aberdeen, Scotland, left £500 each.
Stepdau, Mary Stuart **McGEORGE**, £100 for herself.
John Black, Jr., about 12 years old, "son of Margaret **GIBB** of Aberdeen" £500 sterling for
    his maintenance and education and to set him up in "some respected business, trade or
      profession".
Isabella **KENNEDY** of Saint John £100.
Witnesses: Andrew **CROOKSHANK**, William **DONALDSON** and James **SMITH**.
[Died 4 Sep 1823 at Summer Hill, Aberdeenshire, age 60]

Codicil of 5 Mar 1807:
Has married Katherine, dau of Christopher **BILLOP**, Esq.
Wife, Katherine.
Daughter, Margaret.
Late mother, Margaret, wife of William **WEDDERBURN**, Aberdeen.
Witnesses: Andrew **CROOKSHANK**, Lauchlan and William **DONALDSON**

Codicil of 15 Nov 1816:
Has now another son and daughter.
Executors: Andrew **BLACK** of Forest Mill, Aberdeenshire, and Hon. James **STEWART**,
    a judge of the Nova Scotia Supreme Court.

BLAIR, Peter, merchant, Saint John.
Administration awarded, 18 Aug 1808, to William **DONALD** and Isabella, his wife.
Bondsmen: Andrew **CROOKSHANK** and James **GRIGOR**.
As of 23 March 1820 Blair's heirs were:
    William and John Blair, farmers, Gartmore, Abernethy Parish, Inverness-shire.
    Isabel, widow of Robert Blair, late forester, Rothiemurchus, Invernness-shire.
    Ann Blair, widow of Alexander **ROBERTSON**, farmer, Glackmore [?], Inverness-shire.
Discharge to William Donald before Francis **TAYLOR**, chief magistrate of the City of Elgin,
Scotland, witnessed by Peter Blair and John Robertson, both of Abernethy.
[Peter Blair died 16 Aug 1808, age 42]

CHALMERS, Bryce, innkeeper, St. David Parish, Charlotte County.
Will dated 30 July 1834, proved 20 Sep 1834.
Mother, Margaret, care of James **WEATHER** of Carriwell, Stonacher Parish, Galloway.
Wife Mary to be Executrix, with James **CARTER**
Children of his sister Margaret and her husband, William **McELVIE**.
Witnesses: Francis **AYMAR**, Jr., Alexander **CAMPBELL**, and William **WESCOTT**.
[Died August 1834 at Oak Bay, NB, age 38]

DONALDSON, William, merchant, Saint John.
Will dated 19 Nov 1794, proved 31 July 1797.
William (Executor) and John, both in New Brunswick, Robert and Margaret, issue of late
    brother Alexander Donaldson.
William and brothers, sons of my brother James Donaldson, factor to Hon. Thomas
    MANLE, Esq., near Dundee, Scotland.

William, law student, Edinburgh (Executor), or his next oldest brother, sons of John **INNES**, Esq., Blackhills, by my late sister Helen Innes.
Half brother, Robert, child of my father's second marriage, lately gone to Grenada, B. W. I.
Executors: Arthur **DINGWALL**, Esq., and Hugh **JOHNSTON**, Esq., merchants, Saint John, NB.
Witnesses: James **HAYT** and James **THOMAS.**
[Died in 1797]

DONALDSON, William, the Elder, merchant, Saint John.
Will dated 26 May 1808, proved 10 Apr 1810.
Sisters in Scotland: Margaret Donaldson and Jane **SIMPSON**.
Executors: James **HENDRICKS**, Hugh **JOHNSTON** and John **THOMPSON**, merchants at Saint John.
Witnesses: Arthur **DINGWALL**, Munson **JARVIS** and John **ROBINSON**.
[Died 20 Feb 1810]

EDMOND, Alexander, merchant, Saint John.
Will dated 20 Mar 1825, proved 26 Sep 1825 at Edinburgh, Scotland.
Brother, Francis, wright in Aberdeen (Executor), and his wife Katharine **PAUL**, and their children: Katharine, oldest dau, and Alexander, oldest son.
Sister, Jane, wife of George **RAE**, messenger at arms, Aberdeen, and their son, Alexander.
Nephews: Alexander, son of brother James, wright in Aberdeen
        Alexander, son of brother Charles, wright in Aberdeen.
        Alexander, son of brother John, Portland, ME.
Janet, Elizabeth and John, children of late sister Elizabeth, wife of James **WISHART**, Montrose, Scotland.
Executors: Andrew **BLACK**, Forrester Hills near Aberdeen, William **BLACK**, merchant at Saint John, and John Wishart, Saint John, my nephew and business partner.
Witnesses: Andrew **BURNETT**, Andrew **MORTON** and Alexander **STUART**, writers [lawyers] at Edinburgh, Scotland.

EWING, William, merchant at Glasgow, Scotland.
Intestate Administration granted, 4 Nov 1831, at Saint John, NB, to James **FRASER**, Jr., merchant at Saint John.
Ewing left a widow and next of kin in Scotland, but none in New Brunswick.
Bondsmen: Peter **BUSNARD**, merchant at Saint John, and Jedidiah **SLASON**, Fredericton.
Inventory made on 26 Nov 1831, valued the estate at £15,974.
[Died 19 Sep 1831 at Glasgow]

GILCHRIST, Sgt. William, 8th (King's) Regt., at Fredericton.
Will dated 13 Sep 1813, proved 20 Sep 1813.
Wife Agnes
Sons John and Andrew.
Executors: Aaron **WILEY**, Gallowgate St., Glasgow, and William **HUNTER**, Glasgow.
Acting Executor in New Brunswick: Capt. William **WALSH**, 8th Regt.
Witnesses: Lt. R. D. **TAYLOR** and Garret **CLOPPER**.
[Died in September 1813]

KNUTTON, Margaret, widow of John, Saint John [died 21 July 1827]
    Will dated 24 June 1829, codicil 18 Aug 1829, proved 8 Oct 1829.
    Nephews: John and Charles, sons of late brother, Charles **SOUTER**, Paisley, Scotland.
    Nieces, daus of late sister Mrs. Nancy **MALLARD**:
        Jane, widow of Thomas **PURDY**, and her children, Ann and Thomas PURDY.
        Nancy or Ann, wife of Mr. [William] **CLEVELAND**, Halifax.
        Jane, widow of Mr. **CORBETT**, Glasgow, Scotland.
    Executors: John **KERR**, auctioneer, Thomas **BARLOW**, merchant, and Samuel
        BAGSHAW, all of Saint John.
    Witnesses: Samuel BAGSHAW, W. B. **KINNEAR**, and Margaret G. **PURDIE**.
    Codicil adds a bequest to Margaret **BONSALL**.
    [Died 23 Aug 1829, age 72]

LORRAIN, William, lime burner, Portland Parish, Saint John, "about to depart on a voyage to the
    West Indies."
    Will dated 4 Jan 1803, proved 13 Jan 1804.
    Brothers: Walter, Andrew, John and James; sisters: Janet and Margrett, all of Annandale,
        Scotland.
    Executors: John **McLEOD**, Saint John, and John **WIGGINS,** Portland Parish, both merchants.
    Witnesses: Martha **HARDY**, John **KENNEY** and Charles **PETERS**.
    [Died 3 Jan 1804]

McFARLANE, John, farmer, St. Patrick Parish, Charlotte County, NB.
    Will dated 12 Aug 1805, proved 4 July 1807.
    Wife Elizabeth
    Eldest brother, Peter, in Scotland.
    Malcolm, son of brother, Duncan McFarlane.
    My apprentice, James **TAYLOR**.
    Executors: John **CAMPBELL**, merchant, and Hugh McFarlane.
    Witnesses: Hugh **CAMERON**, John **COCKBURN** and Walter McFarlane.
    [Died in 1807]

McGIBBON, John, carpenter, St. George, NB, but late of Trelawney, Jamaica,
    Will dated 22 Dec 1786, proved 7 May 1787.
    Uncle, Patrick McGibbon of Trelawney, Jamaica (Executor)
    Father, Duncan McGibbon of Glenquaich, Perthshire, North Britain.
    Sisters, Peggy and Ann in Scotland, under age, left the proceeds from sale of
        seven slaves in Jamaica.
    Uncle, James **CAMPBELL**'s daus: Mary Ann and Amy, of St. George, NB.
    Brothers: Duncan (with father), Joseph and Francis.
    Executor: "brother" Patrick **McNABB**.
    Witnesses: George **GUNN**, John **McKENZIE** and Alexander **MYLNE**.

McKAY, James, Saint John, formerly merchant in Glasgow, Scotland.
    Died intestate on 30 Jan 1828.
    Administration granted, 21 July 1828, to John **McLEAN**, gent., Robert **MacINTYRE**, merchant,
    and Elisha D. **RATCHFORD**, all of Saint John.
    Debts in Scotland and New Brunswick.
    Inventory, 7 Sep 1828.

MACKIE, Capt. John, mariner, Saint John, master of the brig *Ann*.
　　Will dated 20 Dec 1805, proved 12 Dec 1806.
　　Father at Dalry, Ayrshire, Scotland.
　　Brother, James, New York.
　　Wife Mary.
　　Sister's children.
　　No Executor named.
　　Witness: Henry **GILBERT**.
　　[Drowned in November 1806]

McMASTER, Daniel, Esq., St. Andrews, NB.
　　Will dated 2 Mar 1829, proved 17 July 1830.
　　A native of Galloway, [Kirkcudbrightshire] Scotland.
　　Children: Anne Elizabeth, Samuel James, George Patrick (Executor), Jane **HASLUCK**,
　　　　Edward Daniel, Thomas Edwin, Martha Lucy **STRACHAN** and Ann Elizabeth.
　　Executor: William **GARNETT**.
　　Witnesses: Alfred L. and George D. **STREET**, and J[ames] H. **WHITLOCK**.
　　[Died 16 June 1830]

MILLER, Capt. William T., mariner, Bathurst, NB, former master of brig *Margaret Ritchie*, and
　　formerly of Saltcoats, [Ayrshire], Scotland.
　　Will dated 7 Sep 1832, proved 1832.
　　Wife, Janet (**CRAWFORD**) Miller, Saltcoats, and only dau, Janet.
　　Executors: Andrew **BARBERIE**, Bathurst, and John **MONTGOMERY**, Dalhousie, NB.
　　Witnesses: Gavin **KERR**, James **MILLER**, and Samuel **WAITT**.
　　[Died 16 Sep 1832]

PAGAN, Misses Janet and Maxwell, Glasgow, Scotland, the only surviving daus of the late William
　　Pagan, sugar refiner, and his wife Margaret, née **MAXWELL**.
　　Settlement made at Edinburgh, 22 Apr 1823, registered at Saint John, NB, 16 Apr 1825.
　　Cites parents' marriage contract dated 2 June 1753.
　　Late sister, Agnes.
　　Late brothers, William, merchant at Saint John, and Robert, merchant, St. Andrews, NB.
　　George and Maria, children of late brother Thomas Pagan of New Brunswick.
　　Marian **PITT**, widow of Robert Pagan.
　　Miscellaneous bequests in Scotland.

PATTULO, Capt. Robert, mariner, Saint John.
　　Will dated 25 Aug 1794, codicil 10 Mar 1801, proved 23 Apr 1807.
　　Wife.
　　Brother George Pattulo's children in North Britain.
　　Executors: Peter **BLAIR** and Thatcher **SEARS**.
　　Witnesses: Isaac **CHURCH** and John **McNEALL**.
　　[Died 8 Apr 1807, age 58]

REID, James, storekeeper, Saint John.
    Will dated 9 May 1788, proved 9 Sep 1788.
    Parents: John and Margaret, Parish of Lanark, Clydesdale, North Britain.
    Executors: Arthur **DINGWALL** and John **THOMSON**.
    Witnesses: Thomas **ELMS,** vintner, and James **REED.**

WILLIAMSON, Archibald, shipwright, Saint John.
    Will dated 13 Aug 1827, proved 22 Sep 1827.
    Wife Lucy.
    Sister: Jane, wife of Dougald **McMILLAN**, near Campbeltown, Argyllshire, and
        Their son Archibald McMILLAN.
    Sisters at Greenock, Scotland: Catherine, Margaret and Barbara.
    Executors: Thomas **BARLOW**, merchant, and James **PETTINGALL**, shipwright,
        and his wife Lucy, all of Saint John, NB.
    Witnesses: Daniel **PETTINGALL**, James **REED** and Robert **ROBERTSON**.
    [Died 4 Sep 1827, age 45]

NEWFOUNDLAND

ALEXANDER, William, Campbeltown, Argyllshire, Scotland, and late of Bonavista, NL,
    merchant, administration of estate awarded to John **BLACK** and William **STEWART**
    - *RGNA*, 9 Sep 1828.

CHRISTIE, John, Glasgow, Scotland, and late of Brigus, Conception Bay, NL, administration of
    estate awarded to Neil **COCK** - *RGNA*, 23 Sep 1817.

CUTHBERT, John, of the Parish of Mary Kirk, County Meadaro [Kincardineshire], Scotland, and
    residing at St. John's, NL.
    Will dated 7 April 1825.
    Wife Hannah (Executrix) and son John.
    Executor: Hugh **HAMLIN**.
    Witnesses: Thomas Hamlin and William **PHIPARD**.
    (Will Book I, pp. 69-70]

McKINNON, John, baker, Kilmarnock, Scotland, late of St. John's, NL.
    Executors: John **BULLEY**, William **FREEMAN** and William **HADDON**
    - *RGNA*, 10 July 1832.

MORRISON, James, Edinburgh, Scotland, late of Ferryland, NL.
    Claims against the estate to be directed to **HUNTER** & Co., administrators
    - *RGNA*, 15 May 1832.

THOMSON, John, Glasgow, Scotland, formerly of St. John's, NL. Estate advertised in
    RGNA, 23 Apr 1839.

SCOTS IN LOCAL HISTORIES

Several county and community histories appeared in the late nineteenth century, extending, somewhat intermittently, into the twentieth. The authors ranged from the well-read Rev. A. W. H. Eaton (Kings County), to retired farmers such as Thomas Miller (Colchester County), to legal men such as George Patterson (Pictou County), and retired military officers like John V. Duncanson (Falmouth and Rawdon, Hants County). A variety of secondary sources was used, with the earlier authors being more dependent upon oral traditions and the memories of old timers than were the more recent writers. Without the documentary evidence to support their claims, some of the earlier accounts require verification. However, since some of this lore would not otherwise be available, it is included here more as a pointer to further research than as established fact.

Seventeen secondary sources (books or serialized columns) were examined. Most were published between 1873 and 1929, but one dates from 1954, one from 1962, and the three Duncanson books first appeared in the 1980s. Names were selected when it states definitely or with good probability that the people had been born in Scotland. When a family of immigrants is listed, names of children born in Scotland are included with their parent(s). The reader can often find more detail in the publication at the pages referenced here, but in some cases there is nothing to be added other than the context of the settlement of the area covered by the particular publication cited.

Brown, George S. *Yarmouth Nova Scotia Genealogies* (serialized in the *Yarmouth Herald* between 1896 and 1909), published as a book by Genealogical Publishing Co., Inc., Baltimore, 1993:
    MacCORMACK, John, d. 26 Feb 1869, age ca. 85, son of Alexander, of Ballantrae, Ayrshire (p. 348).
    MAGRAY, Capt. John, Scotland, to Chebogue, NS, 1770/1774 (p. 86).
    MURRAY, John (1791 - 1878), Banffshire, married Mary **RICHAN**, dau of next entry (p. 667).
    RICHAN, Capt. John (1756 - 1808), Orkney Islands, to Yarmouth, NS, 1788 (p. 665).

Calnek, W. A. *History of the County of Annapolis* (Toronto, 1897):
    McKENZIE, Alexander (1733 - 14 July 1820), from Scotland (p. 547).
    RUMSEY, Benjamin, from Scotland (p. 594).
    STARRATT, Peter, b. ca. 1720 probably in Scotland, came to NS via Fermanagh, Ireland, and Maine (p. 607).
    STRONACH, George, born in or near Glasgow (p. 609).

Crowell, Edwin. *A History of Barrington Township and Vicinity, Shelburne County, Nova Scotia 1604 - 1870* (Yarmouth, NS, 1923):
    CHRISTIE, Alexander, from Edinburgh (p. 445).
    CUNNINGHAM, John (1755 - 1845), son of Daniel and Mary, Inverary, [Argyllshire], Scotland. He settled in NS ca. 1784 following service in the 42nd (Black Watch) Regt. (p. 469).
    DIXON, Jacob, from Scotland, second mate in the *Loss*: bound for Saint John, New Brunswick, shipwrecked and settled at Cape Sable Island (p. 471).
    DUNCAN, Daniel, from Scotland (p. 479).
    FORBES, Alexander, Highlander (d. 1848, age 94), settled at Woods Harbour, and than at Forbes Point (p. 481).
    HOGG, Alexander, from Glasgow, arrived here in the 1780s and settled at Clyde River (p. 491).
    LYLE, John (4th Dragoons) and Gavin, sons of Thomas Alexander, tanner from Glasgow, settlers at Clyde River ca. 1784 (p. 602).

McCOY, James, from Scotland in the 1780s, settled at Birch Point, NS (p. 518).

ROBERTSON, William, b. 1765 at Renfrew, Scotland, came to Barrington Passage as part of a Loyalist family in the 1780s (p. 550).

WILSON, Archibald, from Edinburgh, emigrated to Boston, married Christiana WYLIE from Leith, Scotland. They came to NS as Loyalists (p. 594).

Duncanson, John V. *Falmouth; A New England Township in Nova Scotia* (Belleville, ON, 1983):

DUNCANSON, James, from Scotland, settled at Horton, NS, 1782 (p. 244).

MacDONALD, James, from Glencoe, [Argyllshire], Scotland, to NS about 1810 (p. 329).

Duncanson, John V. *Newport, Nova Scotia; A Rhode Island Township* (Belleville, ON, 1985):

HALIBURTON, Andrew, b. ca. 1700 in Berwickshire, d. 2 Sep 1745 at St. Andrews, Jamaica, whose son William, b. 16 Apr 1739 at Boston, d. 27 Feb 1817, having settled in NS in 1761 (p. 232).

HARVIE, James, miller from Dogartland, Dalry Parish, Ayrshire (ca. 1703 - 19 Dec 1792 at Newport, NS), emigrated to Rhode Island and thence in 1760 to NS; married 30 Apr 1735 at Dalry, Margaret BOYLE, and had five children born in Scotland: Margaret, bap. 23 Mar 1736; John, b. 6 Jan 1738 (remained in Scotland); Archibald, bap. 13 Mar 1743; James, bap. 16 May 1746; and Marion, b. 29 May 1752. With them came James' nephew, John, bap. May 1730 at Dalry, son of his brother Andrew Harvie (p. 242).

SMITH, James, d. 1797 at Newport, NS, probably born in Scotland; to NS in 1760 (p. 375).

STUART, Gilbert, b. ca. 1719 at Perth, d. autumn 1793 at Halifax, NS, emigrated to Rhode Island and came to NS in 1761. One of his sons was Gilbert Stuart, the noted portraitist, b. 3 Dec 1755 at North Kingstown, RI, d. September 1828 at Boston. Among his sitters were George Washington, Kings George III and IV, and King Louis XVI of France (p. 388).

Duncanson, John Victor. *Rawdon and Douglas; Two Loyalist Townships in Nova Scotia* (Belleville, ON, 1989):

BARRON, Alexander, from Scotland, came here after 1795, with children: William, b. ca. 1769; Isabella, b. 27 July 1771; Hugh, b. ca. 1773, and Lydia, b. 1775 (pp. 82-83).

BRYDEN, James, b. ca. 1798 at Roxburgh, Scotland, d. 1 Sep 1869 at Rawdon, NS (p. 116).

CAMERON, Alexander, 84th Regt., b. 23 Mar 1757 in Inverness-shire, d. 18 Oct 1835 at Douglas, NS (p. 119).

CAMERON, Donald, 84th Regt., b. ca. 1729 probably at Glen Urquhart, Inverness-shire, died after 1817 at East River, Pictou County; emigrated in the *Glasgow* in 1775, with wife Elizabeth, 4 sons and 2 daus, bound for New York, but intercepted by Royal Navy at the outbreak of the Revolutionary War. Enlisted in the 84th Regt. Came here afterwards with his son Duncan Cameron (b. ca. 1768 at Urquhart, Inverness-shire, d. after April 1834). Donald had brothers Finlay and Samuel Cameron who also came to NS (pp. 121-128).

CROW, Thomas Stewart, b. 1787 in Scotland, and came here by 11 July 1815 when he married Mary MUDIE, b. 1793 in Scotland (p. 159).

DEWEL, James (d. by June 1835), from Scotland before 1808, with wife Eleanor, and sons James and John (p. 173).

FERGUSON, John, b. 1731 probably in Scotland (p. 189).

FERGUSON, William, b. 1807 in Scotland, emigrated to NS in 1828 (p. 190).

FRASER, Alexander, Sgt.-Major, 4th Regt., native of Scotland, at Windsor in 1786 (p. 200).

FRASER, Hugh, b. ca. 1794 in Inverness; emigrated to Pictou in Dec 1818, and moved to Douglas to settle in 1819 (p. 201).

FRASER, James Mór, 4ᵗʰ Regt., from Strathglass, Scotland (p. 202).

FRASER, Neil, drummer, 84ᵗʰ Regt., b. 1772 in Scotland, d. 2 May 1812; married 18 Nov 1794 at Halifax, Nancy **McPHEE** (pp. 205-6).

GRANT, Donald, 84ᵗʰ Regt., b. 1755 in the Parish of Abernathy, Elginshire; married Aug 1773, Margaret Grant, b. 1752. Three older children born before they came to NS in 1785: Mary, b. 15 June 1777 at Strathspey; John, b. 6 May 1781 at Cordoba, Spain, where they were prisoners; and Donald, b. 5 May 1784 at Glasgow (p. 218).

GRANT, Capt. John, 42ⁿᵈ (Black Watch) Regt., b. Sep 1729 at Strathspey, d. 1790 at Summerville, Hants County, NS (p. 222).

GRANT, Peter, 84ᵗʰ Regt., b. Glen Urquhart, Inverness-shire, died at Port Hawkesbury, NS (p. 226).

McDONALD, Capt. Alexander, b. ca. 1725 in the Parish of Ardnamurchan, Isle of Mull (p. 303).

McDONALD, Sgt. Alexander, b. ca. 1720 in Scotland, d. before 1789 at St. Margarets Bay, NS; married Jannet, b. 1722 in Scotland, d. 3 June 1789 at St. Margarets Bay, NS. Son, Cpl. Hugh McDonald, 84ᵗʰ Regt., born in Scotland (p. 307).

McDONALD, Angus, b. 1745 in the Parish of Boleskine, Inverness-shire; Quartermaster of the 84ᵗʰ Regt.; married 26 Nov 1776 at Halifax, Amy **CHISHOLM** of Strathglas, Inverness-shire, and had seven children: Helen, Isabel, Christian, Allan, James, John, and Angus (p. 322).

McDONALD, Iain, 84ᵗʰ Regt., born in Inverness-shire; married (1ˢᵗ) Jannet, and had three children born in Inverness-shire: Duncan, Alexander and Mary. Iain married (2ⁿᵈ) Margaret **GRANT** of Glen Urquhart, Inverness-shire, and had children born in Scotland: Christy, Jane (b. ca. 1754), Ewen, Ann and Ellen. The family emigrated in the *Glasgow* in 1775, bound for New York, but the ship was intercepted by Royal Navy at the outbreak of the Revolutionary War (p. 334).

McDONALD, John, 84ᵗʰ Regt., b. 1754 at Strathspey, of Inverallan, Inverness-shire, d. 12 Apr 1827 in Hants County, NS (p. 345).

McDONALD, John, b. Glenmoriston, [Urquhart Parish], Inverness-shire (p. 347).

McDONALD, Patrick, 84ᵗʰ Regt., b. 17 Mar 1728 in N. District, Inverness-shire, d. 20 Jan 1802 in Douglas, NS (p. 359).

McDONALD, Peter, 84ᵗʰ Regt., b. 17 Mar 1744 in the Parish of Kilmonivaig, Inverness-shire; married 15 Apr 1768 in the Parish of Boleskine, Inverness-shire, Margaret **MacGUIRE** of that place, b. 20 Dec 1743. They came to NS in 1777, bringing two children born in Boleskine: Donald, b. 3 May 1769; and Alexander, b. 15 Sep 1771 (p. 360).

MacDOUGALL, Donald, b. ca. 1752 in the Parish of Urquhart, Inverness-shire, d. 1 Apr 1795 at Douglas, NS; m. 1778, Ann **REID** of Perth (p. 368).

McDOUGALL, Ewen, 84ᵗʰ Regt., b. 1734, d. by 1812 (p. 372).

McDOUGALL, William, 84ᵗʰ Regt., b, probably in Scotland, d. 1812 (p. 373).

McKAY, Evan, probably b. in Scotland, d. 1837/38 (p. 377).

McKENZIE, Adam, b. 7 Sep 1764 in Sutherlandshire, living in Douglas, NS, in 1813 (p. 379).

McKENZIE, Donald, b. 20 Mar 1747 at Brackacky, Kilmarnoch, Inverness-shire, d. 22 Apr 1836 at Salt Springs, Pictou County; came to NS in the *Hector* in 1773 (p. 379).

McKINNON, Ranald, b. ca. 1737 in the Isle of Skye, d, 4 Mar 1832 at Shelburne, NS. He was in NS by 1766 (p.383).

McLATCHY, John, blacksmith, b. Feb 1756 in Ayrshire, d. 4 Mar 1832 at Windsor, NS. He emigrated to NS in 1783 (p. 391).

McPHEE, Duncan, b. ca. 1800 in Scotland (p. 420).

MacPHEE, John, 84th Regt., b. 2 May 1725 at Easter Bunlait, Glen Urquhart, Inverness-shire; married Catherine, b. 1734. Their six children born in Scotland: James, b. ca. 1758; Evan, b. 2 May 1760; John, b. 17 Mar 1765; William, b. 1770; Ann, b. 1772. and Alexander, b. 20 July 1775. The family emigrated to Boston in 1775 (p. 421).

MacPHEE, William 'Tailor Billy', b. 1 Feb 1770 in Scotland, d. 9 Dec 1844 at Douglas, NS; emigrated to NS about 1776, son of the previous entry (p. 429).

MacPHEE, William, b. ca. 1760 in Inverness-shire, and married Janet **MacMILLAN** (1760 - 13 July 1832), and emigrated to NS in 1802 with four children: Alexander; William, b. ca. 1794; Donald, b. ca. 1799; and Duncan, b. ca. 1802 (p. 431).

MAIN, Andrew, b. 1740 at Dunfermline, Scotland, d. ca. 1823; married Jane **GIBSON** who d. 1773 in the ocean crossing in the *Hector* to Pictou; also a son Andrew, b. 1771/72, d. ca. 1856 at Noel, NS (pp. 436-7).

SCOTT, Alexander, J.P., b. 1758 at Crimond and Haddon, Aberdeenshire, living 1823; emigrated to NS in 1784 in the *Alexander*; married here, 1 July 1786, Ann **McROBERT**, b. 1755 in Morayshire (p. 529).

SCOTT, Archibald, b. 1730 in Scotland, d. 29 May 1823 at Nine Mile River, Hants County, NS; married and came to NS by 1790 with four children born at Glengarry, Scotland: Anne, b. 2 May 1772; Donald, b. 1772 [twin?]; Mary; and Daniel (pp. 532-3).

SIM, Alexander, b. 1790 in Morayshire, d. 1858 at Centre Gore, NS; emigrated to NS in 1820[1] with wife Annie **MILNE** and three children: William, b. 24 Apr 1815; Alexander, b. 16 Feb 1817; and Jean, b. 14 May 1820 on the voyage out from Scotland (p. 537).

STEVENS, James, b. 1764 at Glasgow, d. 4 July 1832, emigrated to NS in 1781 (p. 554).

THOMPSON, Donald, 84th Regt., b. Sep 1762 in Scotland, d. autumn 1827 (pp. 560-1).

WALLACE, William, d. 1813, from Inverness-shire, to NS in 1784 via Ireland (p. 566).

WARDROPE, James, b. Scotland, d. ca. 1816, emigrated to NS with his wife in 1785 (p. 571).

WEATHERHEAD, James, b. ca. 1800 in Berwickshire, d. 5 Feb 1867, son of William and Betty. He married in NS, 6 June 1830, Isabella **MELVILLE**, b. 9 Sep 1800 at Coldstream, Berwickshire (p. 572).

WOOD, John, of Berwickshire, came to NS in 1815, with sons: John, b. 20 June 1792, and James, b. 9 Aug 1799 (p. 591).

Eaton, Arthur Wentworth Hamilton. *The History of Kings County, Nova Scotia* (Salem, MA, 1910):

ANGUS, David, came from Scotland by 1771 (p. 546).

BRECHIN, James, from Aberdeen before 1788, and died in 1796 (p. 584).

CAMPBELL, William, from Scotland by 1788 (p. 598).

McKITTRICK, William, b. 1793 in Kirkcudbright, Scotland, d. 30 Oct 1886; emigrated in March 1817 to Saint John, NB, and removed to NS within a year. He married at Horton, NS, 26 Sep 1818, Agnes **KIRKPATRICK** from Dumfries (d. 9 Sep 1876) (pp. 747-8).

STEWART, John (deserted the Royal Navy) and Luke, sons of Archibald and Susan (**McNEIL**) Stewart (p. 835).

Jost, A. C. *Guysborough Sketches and Essays* (Kentville, NS, n.d.):

CUMMINGS, Alexander, came to NS in 1784 as a Loyalist, and died at Guysborough, 11 Dec 1818. He was of Scots descent (p. 350).

---

[1] Most probably in the *Isabella,* Capt. Thomson, which sailed from Aberdeen, 15 June 1820, for Pictou.

Miller, Thomas. *Historical and Genealogical Record of the First Settlers of Colchester County* (Halifax, 1873):

  BROWN, Rev. John, b. 1766 at Tossaway, Kinross, Scotland; married in Feb 1795 in Scotland, Margaret **BEVERIDGE** of Paisley, and came to NS later in 1795, via New York (pp. 262-3). [Rev. Mr. Brown died at Londonderry, NS, 7 Apr 1848.]

  CHRISTIE, John, b. 1739 in Roxburghshire, Scotland; came to NS in 1772, and died 28 May 1830 (p. 243).

  COCK, Rev. Daniel, b. in Clydesdale, Scotland, came to NS in 1770, returned to Scotland and brought out his wife and family in 1772. He married in Scotland, ca. 1754, Alison **JAMISON** and had six children who came to NS in 1772: Capt. William, b. ca. 1755; Patrick, b. 1757; Mary Ann, b. ca. 1759; Christian, b. ca. 1762; Robert, b. ca. 1765; Ebenezer, b. ca. 1769. Two others born in Truro, NS, afterwards (pp. 151-157). [Rev. Mr. Cock died 17 Mar 1805, aged about 88.]

  CORBETT, William, b. Scotland, came to NS via New England in 1760 (p. 211).

  DICKSON, John, b. Scotland; married there, 1 Feb 1757, Margaret **BURN**, and came to NS in 1773 with his wife and seven children: Jane, b. 7 Dec 1757; Margaret, b. 8 Jan 1760; John, b. 10 Jan 1763; Elizabeth, b. 6 Apr 1765; Janet, b. 21 Mar 1768; Myze Ann, b. 6 Mar 1771; and Magdalen, b. 22 Aug 1773. Three others born in NS afterwards (pp. 248-250).

  GRAHAM, Rev. Hugh, b. 1754 in Scotland, d. 5 Apr 1829 at Stewiacke, NS; came to NS in 1785 (pp. 239-241). [Born at West Calder, Scotland.]

  KENT, James, b. 1749 at Alloa, [Clackmannan], Scotland, died 31 Oct 1825 at Truro, NS; emigrated ca. 1770 (p. 349).

  ROSS, Rev. Duncan, b. Scotland, came out via New York in 1795 (p. 263). [Born at Tarbert, Ross-shire, ca. 1770, died at West River, Pictou County, 25 Oct 1834.]

  SMITH, Rev. David, b. 1732 in Scotland, died 25 Mar 1795 [at Londonderry, NS]; married 1756 Agnes **SPEAR** and came to NS in 1770 with his wife and two sons: James, b. ca. 1757; and David, b. 1759. Their youngest son, John, b. 1761, came out to NS later (p. 261).

  SMITH, John, white smith [tinsmith], b. 1742 at Colvin, Scotland; married 1764 Mary **McVICAR** and had two children born in Scotland: Mary, b. 1765; and William, b. 1767. The family emigrated to Prince Edward Island before moving to NS in 1774 (pp. 215-225).

  WADDELL, Rev. John, b. 10 Apr 1771 in the Glasgow area, Scotland, and came to Truro, NS, via New York in 1797 [Born at Kirk O'Shotts, Lanarkshire, died 13 Nov 1842.]

  YUILL, James, Esq., b. 1717 in Clydesdale, Scotland, died 4 Mar 1807; married ca. 1742 in Scotland, Jane **BAILEY** (1721 - 11 Jan 1804). With their son James, b. 1752. they emigrated to Boston in 1753, and thence to Nova Scotia in 1761 (p. 281).

More, James F. *The History of Queens County, Nova Scotia* (Halifax, 1873):

  FRASER, Simon, Scottish-born Loyalist from New York, came to Shelburne in 1783 and from there moved to Liverpool, NS (p. 182).

  JOHNSTONE, William, Esq., b. Scotland, d. 1795 age 82, settled in Queens County in 1772 (p. 158).

Patterson, Frank H. *History of Tatamagouche, Nova Scotia* (Halifax, 1917):

  BONNYMAN, John, son of William, of Rothmase, Aberdeenshire, to NS in 1828, and later moved to Illinois. Also his siblings: Edward, James and Susan, who came from Banffshire to Nova Scotia (p. 68).

  CLARK, John and James, from Aberdeen, came to NS in 1842/43 (p. 81).

  COOPER, Robert, from Aberdeenshire to NS ca. 1834 (p. 70).

  DONALDSON, David, (1807 - 1891) from Perthshire to Pictou, NS, in 1849 (p. 82).

GASS, Henderson (saddler) and Robert (shoemaker), sons of John GASS of Dumfries, came out to Pictou in 1816, along with their cousin, Robert, son of Joseph GASS (p. 79).

LOCKERBIE, John, from Castle Douglas, Kirkcudbrightshire in 1835. His brother-in-law, David **WILLIAMSON**, with his wife and two children emigrated via Halifax ca. 1838/40 in the ship *Burnhopeside* (p. 71).

McCULLY, William, came from Scotland ca. 1830 (p. 69).

MILLAR, John, son of Andrew, native of Edinburgh, emigrated to Pictou (p. 72).

ROSS, John, cartwright from Ross-shire, emigrated in 1832, followed by brothers: Alexander in 1833; George, William, Thomas and Hugh in 1841 (pp. 69-70).

Patterson, Rev. George. *A History of the County of Pictou, Nova Scotia* (Toronto, 1877): Passengers in the ship *Hector*, 1773, as listed by Patterson on pp. 450-456. There has been some difference of opinion as to the names of those crossing in this first shipload of Scottish Highlanders to reach Nova Scotia. The following is Patterson's reconstitution as found in his book. Where he indicates birthplaces and destinations, these are shown and presented here without comment on my part. The reconstituted passenger list of the *Hector* may be seen in J. M. Bumsted. *The People's Clearance 1770 - 1815* (Edinburgh, 1982), pp. 230-1, or in Lucille H. Campey. *After the Hector; The Scottish Pioneers of Nova Scotia and Cape Breton 1773 - 1852* (Toronto, 2004), pp. 193-6.

CAMERON, Alexander, d. 15 Aug 1831, age 103, from Loch Broom, Ross-shire, with children Alexander and Christiana, settled at Loch Broom, NS.

CAMERON, Donald and family, Inverness-shire, Roman Catholic, settled Antigonish County.

CHISHOLM, Archibald, Loch Broom, settled at East River of Pictou.

DOUGLASS, Colin and family, Inverness-shire, settled at Middle River of Pictou.

FALCONER, Alexander, Loch Broom, settled near Hopewell.

FRASER, Alexander and family (Alexander, Simon, Catherine, Isabella, Hugh), Inverness-shire, settled at Middle River of Pictou.

FRASER, Charles, settled at Fishers Grant.

FRASER, Hugh and family, Inverness-shire, settled at West River of Pictou.

FRASER, Kenneth and family, Sutherlandshire, settled at Middle River of Pictou.

FRASER, Thomas, Loch Broom, Ross-shire.

FRASER, William and family, Sutherlandshire.

GRAHAM, Donald, Sutherlandshire.

GRANT, Donald, Sutherlandshire.

GRANT, James and family, Inverness-shire, settled at East River of Pictou.

McCONNELL, George, settled at West River of Pictou.

McDONALD, Donald and family (Marion, 10; Nancy; and his niece Mary **FORBES**, from Inverness-shire, settled at Middle River of Pictou.

McGREGOR, John, Loch Broom, Ross-shire.

McKAY, Colin and family, Inverness-shire, settled at East River of Pictou.

McKAY, Donald the elder, Loch Broom, settled at East River of Pictou.

McKAY, Hugh and family (Donald, Jane and Mary), Parish of Kiltarlity, Inverness-shire, settled at East River of Pictou.

McKAY, John and family, Sutherlandshire.

McKAY, John, piper, Sutherlandshire.

McKAY, Roderick, blacksmith, and family, Beauly, Inverness-shire, settled at East River of Pictou.

McKAY, William, Sutherlandshire, settled at East River of Pictou, where he later drowned.

McKAY, William, d. 2 Mar 1827, age 97, and family (Donald, Alexander, James and Sarah), Inverness-shire, settled at East River of Pictou.

McKENZIE, Alexander, Loch Broom, Ross-shire.

McKENZIE, Alexander, Sutherlandshire.

McKENZIE, Angus, age 16, Sutherlandshire, settled at Green Hill, Pictou County.

McKENZIE, Colin and family (son Duncan, b. 1771), Loch Broom, settled at East River.

McKENZIE, Donald and family, Sutherlandshire, settled perhaps at Shubenacadie, NS.

McKENZIE, William, schoolmaster, from Loch Broom, settled at Loch Broom, NS.

McLEAN, Alexander, Loch Broom, settled at East River of Pictou.

McLELLAN, John, Loch Broom, settled at McLellans Brook

McLELLAN, William, Loch Broom, settled at West River of Pictou.

McLEOD, Alexander and family, Sutherlandshire, settled at West River of Pictou; he was drowned in the Shubenacadie River.

McLEOD, Hugh and family of 3 daus and son David, Sutherlandshire, settled at West River of Pictou.

McLEOD, James and family, Sutherlandshire, settled at Middle River of Pictou.

McLEOD, Philip and family, Sutherlandshire.

McRITCHIE, Kenneth and family, from Loch Broom.

MAIN, Andrew and family, Dunfermline, settled at Noel, NS.

MATHESON, Charles, Loch Broom, Ross-shire.

MATHESON, William and family (son John, 3), Sutherlandshire, settled at Rogers Hill.

MORRISON, George and family, Banff, settled at Barneys River.

MUNROE, Donald, Inverness-shire, settled at West Branch, East River of Pictou.

MUNROE, John and family, Loch Broom, Ross-shire.

MURRAY, James and family, Sutherlandshire, settled at Londonderry, NS.

MURRAY, Walter and family, Sutherlandshire, settled at Merigomish, NS.

PATTERSON, John [native of Paisley, Scotland; settled in Pictou Town].

ROSS, Alexander and family, Loch Broom, settled at Little River of Pictou.

SIM, Robert, Loch Broom, settled in New Brunswick.

STEWART, John.

SUTHERLAND, John, Sutherlandshire.

SUTHERLAND, John, Sutherlandshire, settled at Sutherlands River.

URQUHART, David and family, Sutherlandshire, settled at Londonderry, NS.

WESLEY, Andrew.

Dumfries Settlers, ca 1775/76. These were Scots Lowlanders brought first to Prince Edward Island in the *Lovely Nellie* in 1774 and 1775, and who moved about 1776 to Pictou County, NS. George Patterson, *A History of the County of Pictou*, p. 457, lists them:

BLAIKIE, Charles, settled at West River of Pictou.[1]

CLARK, William, settled at West River of Pictou.[2]

---

[1] Passengers in the *Lovely Nellie* in 1774: Charles **BLAIKIE**, farmer, 36, Parish of Southwick, Kirkcudbrightshire, with wife Jannet **HERRIES**, 36, and children: John, 6; William, 4; James, 3; and Ann, 10 months. This and notes 2-11 are derived from Bumsted, pp. 232-237.

[2] Passengers in the *Lovely Nellie* in 1775: William **CLARK**, 30, gardener from Carlowrick in Nithsdale [Dumfries-shire], wife Grizzle **KISSOCK**, and son John, 10 months.

McLEAN, John, settled at West River of Pictou.[3]
McLELLAN, Anthony, settled at West River of Pictou.[4]
RICHARD, Joseph, settled at West River of Pictou.
SMITH, William, settled at West River of Pictou.[5]
STEWART, David, settled at West River of Pictou.
BRYDEN, Robert, settled at Middle River of Pictou.[6]
CROCKET, John, settled at Middle River of Pictou.[7]
MARSHALL, Robert, settled at Middle River of Pictou.[8]
SMITH, John, settled at Middle River of Pictou.[9]
CULTON, Anthony, settled at McLennans Brook.[10]
TURNBULL, Thomas, settled at East River of Pictou.[11]

George Patterson lists military grantees at the end of the American Revolutionary War. Awarded 200 acres were non-commissioned officers in the 82nd Regt. (p. 459):
ARBUCKLES, Charles, from Falkirk.
CARMICHAEL, James, from Perthshire.
DUNN, Robert, from Glasgow.
FRASER, John, from Inverness.
ROBERTSON, Charles, from the estate of Lude [Blair-Atholl Parish, Perthshire].

Awarded 150 acres at Baillies Brook (p. 460):
BAILLIE, John, from Sutherlandshire.

---

[3] Passengers in the *Lovely Nellie* in 1775: John **McLEAN**, wife and son, sailed from Kirkcudbright.

[4] Passengers in the *Lovely Nellie* in 1775: Anthony **McLELLAN** and five children, sailed from Ballcarry, Port Kirkcudbright.

[5] Passenger in the *Lovely Nellie* in 1774: William **SMITH** from Corsack, Parish of Colvend, Kirkcudbrightshire.

[6] Passengers in the *Lovely Nellie* in 1775: Robert **BRYDEN**, 38, labourer from Dumfries, his wife Jean **KIRKPATRICK**, 26; children: James, 7; twins William and David, 4; Edward, 7 months.

[7] Passengers in the *Lovely Nellie* in 1774: John **CROCKET**, 31, farmer from Thornyhill, Parish of Colvend, Kirkcudbrightshire; wife Margaret **YOUNG**, 36; children: James, 6; William, 4; James, 1.

[8] Passengers in the *Lovely Nellie* in 1775: Robert **MARSHALL**, 37, weaver from Farquhar [Traquair] Parish; his wife Elizabeth, 32; children: John, 8; Andrew, 4; James, 4 months.

[9] Passengers in the *Lovely Nellie* in 1774: John **SMITH**, 45, mason from Preston, Kirkbeam Parish; his wife Janet **STURGEON**; children: Mary, 16; Janet, 9; Agnes, 5; Isabella, 3; and Nelly, 1.

[10] Passengers in the *Lovely Nellie* in 1775: Anthony **CULTON**, 30 [36?], labourer from Traquhar [Traquair] in Peebleshire; his wife Jannet **McCAUGHTER**, 36; children: Marrion, 12; Robert, 10; Grizel, 7; Jannet 5; John, 4; Ann, 7 months.

[11] Passengers in the *Lovely Nellie* in 1775: Thomas **TRUMBELL**, "Isleman"; wife Jean **MacKAY**, and three children. Shipped, i.e., taken aboard, at Douglas.

Awarded 100 acres were (p. 461):
ANDERSON, Andrew, from East Lothian, d. 3 Aug 1845; at Andersons Mountain.
COLLY, John, from Elginshire; at Middle River.
McKINNON, Charles, from the Isle of Barra; at Baillies Brook.
McNEIL, John, Donald, Matthew, Murdoch, John Jr., from the Isle of Barra; Antigonish County.
McPHERSON, John and James, from Badenoch [Kingussie, Inverness]; at Fishers Grant.
McQUEEN, Angus, from the Isle of Skye; at Little Harbour.
MUIRHEAD, Andrew, from the Lowlands; at Little Harbour [probate dated 26 Aug 1795].
ROBINSON, William, from Scotland; at Baillies Brook.

From the 84th Regt. were (pp. 462-3):
CAMERON, Donald, Finlay and Samuel, from the Parish of Urquhart [Morayshire]; settled on the East side of East River of Pictou.
CHISHOLM, John, and son John, from Strathglass; settled on the west side of East River.
FRASER, James (Big), from Strathglass; settled on the east side of East River of Pictou.

Grantees at the West Branch of the East River in 1797 (p. 463):
FRASER, John, Inverness; settled at Springville.
FRASER, Thomas, Inverness.
FRASER, William, Inverness; settled at Big Brook.
(also p. 464):
CHISHOLM, Donald, Inverness.
CHISHOLM, Donald, Strathglass [Kiltarlity, Inverness-shire].
DUNBAR, Alexander, Robert and William (brothers), Inverness.
FORBES, John, Strathglass [Kiltarlity, Inverness-shire].
McINTOSH, Alexander, Inverness.
McLEAN, Alexander and Hector (brothers), Strathglass [Kiltarlity, Inverness-shire].
McLELLAN, James, Strathglass [Kiltarlity, Inverness-shire].
McLELLAN, John, Inverness.
SHAW, Donald, Inverness.
(also p. 465):
FRASER, Alexander, Parish of Kilmorack, [Inverness-shire]; settled at McLellans Brook.
FRASER, Thomas, Parish of Kirkhill, [Inverness-shire]; settled at New Glasgow.

Others mentioned by Patterson, p. 283, included William **MacKENZIE**, Sutherlandshire, 1803; Donald **ROBERTSON**, Perthshire, 1801; Angus **MacKAY**, Clyne Parish, Sutherlandshire, ca. 1820; William **IRVING**, Dumfries-shire, 1820; and James **HAGGART**, Kenmore Parish, Perthshire, ca. 1810/15.

Rankin, D. J. *A History of the County of Antigonish, Nova Scotia* (Toronto, 1929). Father Rankin presented the families in Antigonish County in alphabetical order and gives miscellaneous information with no particular consistency of coverage, and a paucity of precise dates. His work is an example of research dependent largely upon memory and local lore, with the strengths and weaknesses attendant upon such a methodology. Several men had Gaelic nicknames. These, with their meanings, are: *ban* (white; fair), *breac* (spotted), *du* and *dubh* (black, dark), *mor* (large, big), *og* (young), and *ruadh* (red).
BALLENTYNE, Daniel, from Scotland; settled at Ballentynes Cove (p. 78).
BOYLE, Angus, from Scotland; settled at Beauly (p. 82).
BROWN, Thomas, mason from Scotland (p. 84).

CAMERON, Dougald, d. 1770 at Sron Na Li, Lochaber, Scotland, had two sons who came to NS in 1791: Hugh and John "Red" (p. 85).

CAMPBELL, Alexander, from Glengarry, Scotland (p. 91).

CAMPBELL, Donald, b. ca. 1795 in Scotland; settled at Doctors Brook (p. 90).

CHISHOLM, Alexander, from Strathglass; settled at Long Point, Inverness County. His brother Archibald settled at Lismore, NS. Their sister Ann also came to NS (p. 98).

CHISHOLM, Alexander, from Scotland; settled at Salt Springs, NS (p. 108).

CHISHOLM, Donald "Og" and Donald "Mor", from Strathglass in the *Aurora* (1803), sailing from Fort William, Scotland, to Pictou, NS, and settled at Antigonish Harbour (p. 97).

CHISHOLM, Donald, from Strathglass in 1780; settled at South River, NS (p. 112).

CHISHOLM, Duncan, from Strathglass in 1801; settled at Monks Head, NS (p. 114).

CHISHOLM, Duncan, from Strathglass; settled at Little Harbour, Pictou County (p. 98).

CHISHOLM brothers from Strathglass, Inverness-shire: Finlay, Alexander, Donald (soldier) and Rev. William, d. 3 Aug 1819, age 46 (p. 99).

FRASER, John and his sister Janet, from Strathglass; settled at James River, NS (p. 136).

FRASER, Ronald, from Isle of Eigg in 1823; settled at Arisaig, NS (p. 134).

GILLIS, Angus, from Morar [see map, page 16]; settled at Morar, NS (p. 139).

GILLIS, Duncan, from Morar; settled at South River, NS (p. 139).

GILLIS, Hugh, from [Inverness-shire], Scotland; settled at Arisaig, NS (p. 141).

GILLIS, John, from Morar; settled at Miramichi, NB, and later at Merigomish, NS (p. 141).

GILLIS, Peter, from Scotland; settled at Doctors Brook, NS (p. 145).

GRAHAM, John, from Scotland; settled at Cape George, NS (p. 149).

KENNEDY brothers: Angus (teacher), Alexander, Donald and John, and their cousin John Kennedy "Red", from Lochaber; settled at Broad Cove, Cape Breton (p. 158).

LIVINGSTONE, Malcolm, from Lochaber; settled at Livingstones Cove, NS (p. 161).

MacADAM, Ewan, or Hugh, from Airinsdale, Scotland, in 1790; settled at Moidart, NS (p. 162).

MacARTHUR, Archibald, from Lochaber; settled at Fraser Mountain, NS (p. 165).

MacDONALD, Alexander "Breac", b. 1777 near Fort William, Inverness-shire, married Katherine **KENNEDY**, and came to NS in the brigantine *Good Intent* in 1816, with sons Angus, 5, and Donald, 2½; settled at Arisaig, NS (p. 187).

MacDONALD, Alexander "Mor", son of Donald "Ruadh" of Lochaber, Scotland, came to NS in 1832 with his wife Isabel **MacDONALD**, and four sons (Ronald, Angus, Allan and Alexander) in 1832; settled at South East Mabou River, NS. His eldest son Donald came out in the *Dunlop* in 1824 to Miramichi, NB, then joined his family at Mabou (p. 187).

MacDONALD, Alexander and Ronald, sons of Donald, son of John (p. 227).

MacDONALD, Alexander, son of Donald, son of Dougald, of Moidart, settled at Baileys Brook (p. 248)

MacDONALD, Allan "the ridge", son of Alexander (Alasdair Ruadh an Ridge), son of Alexander, son of Alexander Mor, son of Angus, son of Angus Mor, son of Alexander, son of John Dubh, son of Ronald Mor, 7th Chief of Keppoch. Allan, b. 1794 in the Braes of Lochaber. Emigrated to NS in 1816, settled at South West Mabou until 1847, and then lived at Upper South River until his death in 1868 (pp. 202-3).

MacDONALD, Angus "Red", from Bornish, Scotland; settled in Antigonish County (p. 170).

MacDONALD, Angus, son of Allan, of Knoydart; settled at Lakevale, NS (p. 180).

MacDONALD, Angus, from Isle of Eigg; settled at Fox Brook, Pictou County (p. 185).

MacDONALD, Angus and Donald, from Arisaig, settled at Cape George, NS (p. 247).

MacDONALD, Daniel and John from Scotland (p. 232).

MacDONALD, Donald and John, from Ard na Furan (Spring Hill), sons of Angus, son of Donald, settled at MacAras Brook, NS (p. 235).

MacDONALD, Donald, tailor formerly with the Army, from Isle of Eigg, ca. 1800 (p. 246).

MacDONALD, Dougald "Mor", son of Hugh, son of Donald, Moidart, Scotland. Also Donald, settled at Antigonish Harbour; Hugh "Ban"; and John, at Inverness (p. 259).

MacDONALD, John, Allan, Ronald and Annie, from Moidart in 1827; settled at Monkshead, NS (p. 182).

MacDONALD, Lauchlin, son of Ronald of Moidart; settled at Browns Mountain, NS (pp. 171-2).

MacDONALD, Lauchlin and his son John "Ban" from Moidart to NS (p. 174).

MacDONALD, Martin, from Knoydart in 1786/7; settled at Maryvale, NS (p. 176).

MacDONALD, Rory, of Clanranald (Keppoch), from Moidart, had son John, who emigrated to Pictou, then lived at Arisaig and at last at the south side, Antigonish Harbour (p. 245).

MacDONALD brothers from Moidart in 1802: Hector, who settled at Antigonish Harbour; John, who settled at Malignant Cove, NS; and Donald (p. 173).

MacDONALD, brothers Allan "Du", Angus "Red" and Donald "Breac", from Lochaber, Scotland (p. 201).

MacDONALD, brothers from Arisaig, Scotland: Alexander, settled at Browns Mountain; Lauchlin, settled at East Bay, NS; and Angus, settled at Glebe Road, NS (p. 208).

MacDONALD, brothers from Castle of Mingary, Arisaig: Alexander, Angus "Ban", Hugh and Donald (p. 234).

MacDONALD, brothers from Moidart in the *Dove* of Aberdeen in 1801: Donald, Angus and Dougald (p. 244).

MacDONALD, siblings from Glen Roy, Lochaber, [Kilmonivaig Parish, Inverness-shire], Scotland: Donald, Alexander, Mary, and Donald "Og" (pp. 206-7).

MacDONELL, Angus, from Glengarry [Kilmonivaig Parish], settled at South River (p. 264).

MacDOUGALL, Donald, and three sons (Angus, Donald and James) from Arisaig, settled at rear of Arisaig, NS (p. 268).

MacDOUGALL, Hugh, from Arisaig, settled at Highfield, NS (p. 269).

MacDOUGALL, Neil "Ban", from Moidart, Scotland (p. 267).

MacEACHERN, Archibald, from Lochaber, Scotland, settled at Lochaber Lake, NS (p. 270).

MacEACHERN, John, from Dunmaglass, Scotland, in 1792, settled at Arisaig, NS (p. 271).

MacFARLANE, Dougald, b. 1801 at Druimnaliaghart, Glennachaidh, Argyllshire, married Margaret **MacDONALD** from Knoydart. Emigrated to Pictou, then settled at South River (p. 273).

MacGILLIVRAY, brothers from Dunmaglass, Scotland: Duncan, John, William (settled in Cape Breton), and Hugh (p. 279).

MacGREGOR, Donald, b. 1802 at Aulich, Rannach, Perthshire; came to NS in July 1825 (p. 282).

MacINNIS, sons of John "Ban" (John, Donald and Angus "Ban"), emigrated from Scotland and settled at Cape George (p. 287).

MacINTOSH, siblings from Lochaber, Scotland: John "Og" and Alexander, settled at South River, NS; Flora; and Donald B., settled at Lismore, NS (p. 289).

MacINTYRE, John, and wife Eunice **MacPHERSON**; Donald and wife Nancy **FRASER**, from Lismore, Scotland, settled in Antigonish County, NS (p. 291).

MacISAAC, Ronald, widower, from Rudha Na Foachaig, Moidart, emigrated ca. 1790, with his children: John, Mary, Sara, Margaret and Donald, settled at Arisaig, NS (p. 296).

MacISAAC, brothers John, Malcolm and Lauchlin, sons of Rory MacIsaac of the Isle of Eigg, settled at Eigg Mountain, NS (p. 298).

MacKAY, Allan, from the Isle of Mull, emigrated in 1840, settled at Keppoch, NS (p. 301).

MacKENZIE, Donald and John, from Strathglass in 1799. Donald settled at Malignant Cove, NS, and John at St. Andrews, NS (p. 301).

MacKINNON, Donald and John, brothers from Isle of Eigg, settled at Baileys Brook (p. 304).

MacLEAN, Angus, Donald and Ronald, sons of Angus MacLean of Moidart, settled at Ohio, NS (p. 310).

MacLEAN, Donald, from Isle of Barra, settled at Arisaig, NS, in the late 1700s (p. 312).

MacLEAN, John, from Argyllshire, settled at Beaver Meadow, NS (p. 311).

MacLEAN, John, from Arisaig, settled at Fairmount, NS (p. 313).

MacLEAN, Lauchlin "Lachain Saor" [Lauchlin the mason or builder], from the Isle of Coll, settled at Keppoch, NS (p. 309).

MacLELLAN, Archibald and Angus, sons of Archie, son of Niel MacLellan of Morar, came to NS in 1804. Archibald settled at South River, and Angus in Inverness County, NS (p. 314).

MacLELLAN, Archie, from Eigg, emigrated in 1825 and settled at Eigg Mountain, NS (p. 316).

MacLELLAN, Mary, Archibald, Angus and Donald, from Arisaig, settled at Fairmount, NS (p. 315).

MacLEOD, Neil, from the Isle of Eigg, his wife Mary **CAMPBELL** from the Isle of Skye, and children emigrated to Parrsboro, NS, and later settled in Antigonish County: John, at Arisaig; Donald (became a Member of the Legislature); Neil; Hugh, settled at North Grant, NS; Eunice; and Ann (pp. 317-9).

MacMASTER, Angus, Ann and Margaret, from Lochaber, Scotland (p. 321).

MacMILLAN, Donald, son of Angus, Isle of Eigg, and wife Ann **MacEACHERN**, lived at Judique, then at Mulgrave, and settled at Maple Ridge, NS (p. 322).

MacNEIL, Donald "Fiddler", from Moidart, emigrated in 1803 and settled at Upper South River, NS (p. 328).

MacNEIL, John "Breac"", from Knoydart, emigrated in 1788 and settled at Gulf Shore, NS (p. 329).

MacNEIL brothers from Moidart: John, Alexander and Donald, settled in Cape Breton; and Hugh, who settled in Antigonish (p. 328).

MacPHEE, Dougall, from Lochaber, emigrated to New Brunswick in 1803, and settled at Upper South River, NS, in 1808 (p. 337).

MacPHEE, Hugh, from Lochaber, emigrated to New Brunswick in 1808, and settled at Avondale, NS (p. 337).

MacPHERSON, Dougald, from Moidart, emigrated in 1792 in the ship *Aurora*, with children: Rory, John, Donald and Mary, settled at Moidart, NS (p. 338).

MacPHERSON, John, and wife Mary **MacDONALD** of the Isle of Eigg, had a son Alexander "Big" married to Catherine **GILLIS** of Knoydart. Alexander and Catherine emigrated in 1810 with children: Ann; James and Alexander (settlers at Cape George, NS); Martin and John (settlers at Broad Cove, Cape Breton); and Mary (p. 343).

MacPHERSON brothers from Scotland: Angus and Dougald, settled at Ohio, NS, and Donald, settled at Broad Cove, Inverness County, NS (p. 345).

MacPHERSON siblings emigrated from Scotland ca. 1801: Mary, lived at South River, NS; Dougald, settled in Cape Breton; Donald, settled at Rear Judique; and John, settled at Hallowell Grant, NS (p. 342).

MacRAE, John, from Strathglass [Parish of Kiltarlity, Inverness-shire], settled at Malignant Cove, NS (p. 349).

MANSON, Alexander, from Wick, [Caithness], emigrated to Halifax, thence to Sherbrooke, thence to Stillwater, and settled at Goshen, NS (p. 349).

WILKIE, brothers James, George and John, from Banff, Scotland (p. 374).

Rutledge, James E. *Sheet Harbour: A Local History* (Halifax, 1954):

CRUICKSHANKS, Peter, from Strathspey, emigrated via Pictou in 1789 (p. 50).

CURRIE, Sgt. Neil, 42nd (Black Watch) Regt., from Clydesdale, settled in NS in 1783 (p. 35).

FRASER, Alexander (1735 - 1830) from Scotland (p. 31).

RUTLEDGE, Simon (1739/40 - 1827), from Dumfries-shire (p. 33).

SUTHERLAND, Lt. James (1739 - 26 Apr 1815), born in Caithness-shire, and died at Sheet Harbour, Halifax County, NS (p. 28).

[no author]. *Stewiacke 1780 -1900* (Truro, NS, 1902):

BRENTON, Thomas, d. 1833, native of Scotland (p. 94).

CROCKETT, James, native of Scotland, to NS by 1802 (p. 98).

DEYARMOND, Robert, native of Scotland, to NS in 1790 (p. 99).

GRAHAM, Rev. Hugh, native of Scotland, to NS in 1785 (p. 102).

GRAHAM, William, native of Scotland, to NS by 1820 (p. 102).

McCULLOCH, Gilbert, native of Scotland (p. 106).

YOUNG, James, Laurance and Andrew, with their mother emigrated from Scotland ca. 1840 (p. 110).

Trueman, Howard. *The Chignecto Isthmus and its first settlers* (Toronto, 1902):

ALLAN, Benjamin, Scottish-born Loyalist (p. 259).

BLACK, William, b. 1727 at Paisley, Scotland, settled in NS in 1774 (p. 170).

DAVIDSON, William, from Dumfries, and James **AMOS**, moved to Charlottetown, PE, in 1820 (p. 255).

FULLERTON, James, from the Scots Highlands, came to NS in 1790 (p. 199).

MAIN, David, with sons John and James, from Dumfries, settled at Richibucto, NB, in 1821 (pp. 208-9).

MONRO, Alexander, from Banffshire, son of John who emigrated from Aberdeen to Miramichi, NB, in 1815 (p. 222).

SCOTT, Adam, from Langholm, Dumfries-shire, emigrated to NB via Québec in 1834 (p. 210).

The only one dealing with New Brunswick is W. M. Burns, *A History and Story of Botsford* [in Albert County, NB] (Sackville, NB, 1962):

ALLEN, Benjamin, born in Scotland 1735, family emigrated to Connecticut; served under Wolfe in the Seven Years War; later settled in Botsford Parish, NB (p. 51). [Died 14 Apr 1823 - headstone.]

BLACKLOCK, Thomas, born in 1778 at Ecclefechan [Dumfries-shire], Scotland; married Jennie **HALL**, went to Prince Edward Island in 1821 and taught school, moved to New Brunswick in 1827. They settled in Little Shemogue, NB, in June 1833 (p. 61).

GRANT, John and James, natives of Dollas, Aberdeenshire, emigrated first to Prince Edward Island , then in 1809 to Little Shemogue, NB (p. 70).

HASTINGS, James, born at Thorne Hill [Dumfries-shire], Scotland, 1815, died 1902; emigrated to NB in 1841. His wife was Isabel **MURRAY**, who died in 1887 (p. 72).

LAMB, James, stonecutter, and his sister Elizabeth, natives of Glasgow, Scotland, arrived in Halifax in 1828, and later removed to Botsford Parish, NB (pp. 74-74).

McGLASHING, John, born Scotland in 1791, emigrated in 1810 and settled at Cape Tormentine (p. 85).

McKAY, Alexander, born Scotland, emigrated in 1810 and settled at Cape Tormentine (p. 85).

MAIN, David, native of Langholm, Dumfries-shire, settled at Murray Road, NB, in 1821. He had two sons: James, born in 1801, and John, born in 1803 (p. 78).

MURRAY, John, native of Dumfries-shire, emigrated to Miramichi in 1823, and removed to Botsford Parish by 1829. He had a wife and several children who emigrated with him from Dumfries-shire, Scotland. One was William, born 1819 (p. 80).

SCOTT, Adam, native of Langholm, Dumfries-shire, emigrated to Prince Edward Island in 1834, and later removed to New Brunswick[12] (pp. 96-97).

SIMPSON, Thomas, Scots Lowlander, married about 1793, Margaret McLEAN, Highlander, and removed from Prince Edward Island to Cape Tormentine, NB, in 1799 (p. 97).

SMITH, James, native of Aberdeenshire, and his wife, Isabelle BRUCE from Scotland were early settlers in Botsford Parish[13] (p. 97).

HEADSTONES OF SCOTTISH IMMIGRANTS

The people remembered by these gravestones were born in Scotland, or married to people who were. Although some death dates fall as late as the early twentieth century, all the people in this section had reached the Maritimes by 1850.

NEW BRUNSWICK

BUDGE, Thomas, d. 14 Jan 1862, age 41, native of Halkirk, Caithness (Old Church of England Burying Ground, East Saint John).

BUIST, James, d. 10 June 1847, age 78, and his wife Helen, d. 8 Jan 1883, age 91, natives of Scotland (Old Cedar Hill Cemetery, Saint John West).

MacKAY, Colin, b. 1772 at Beauly [Kilmorack Parish, Inverness-shire], d. 1850 at Pictou, NS (Loyalist Burying Ground, Saint John).

McKENZIE, Isabella, d. 22 Oct 1825, age 24, and Elizabeth, d. 20 June 1841, age 53, daus of John McKenzie and Ann MUNRO, natives of North Britain (Old Church of England Burying Ground, East Saint John).

MOWAT, Robert, d. 28 Oct 1867, age 77, native of Aberdeen, and his wife Sarah, d. 20 May 1880, age 77, native of Durham, England (Old Church of England Burying Ground, East Saint John).

WALLACE, Thomas, died 28 Dec 1839, age 24, native of Fleurs, Ayrshire, Scotland (Old Church of England Burying Ground, East Saint John).

---

[12] Adam SCOTT was born about 1795. He married Janet AMOS, and had children born in Scotland: Adam, Janet, James, Ellen, Robert and Agnes.

[13] James SMITH was born at MacDuff, Aberdeenshire, 18 Mar 1793, died 16 Aug 1865, and married Isabella BRUCE of Banffshire, who died 17 June 1842, age 48. Their oldest children, Isabella and John, were born in Scotland.

NOVA SCOTIA

ANDERSON, Hanna L., b. 1837 at Aberdeen, d. 1928 (Palmerston Cemetery, Pugwash, Cumberland County).

ANDERSON, John, d. 15 Sep 1858, age 89; his wife Ann, d. 15 Jan 1859, age 90; their dau, Jobina, d. 9 Oct 1861, age 50 [from Morayshire] (Riverside Cemetery, Musquodoboit Harbour, Halifax County).

ANDERSON, James, d. 6 Dec 1874, age 80, native of Rothes, Morayshire; his wife Mary Ann, d. 15 June 1883, age 78, born in Nova Scotia (Riverside Cemetery, Musquodoboit Harbour, Halifax County).

ANDERSON, Peter, d. 18 Dec 1874, age 83, native of Rothes, Morayshire; his wife Sarah F., d. 13 July 1885, age 96, native of Portsoy [Fordyce Parish], Banffshire (Riverside Cemetery, Musquodoboit Harbour, Halifax County).

ARCHIBALD, James; his wife, Martha **SMITH**, d. 13 Oct 1854, age 37, native of Lochlee Parish, Forfarshire (St. John the Evangelist Anglican Cemetery, Sackville, Halifax County).

BAILLIE, Donald, d. 13 Sep 1875, age 81, native of Sutherlandshire; his wife Elspie, d. 29 Nov 1910, age 94 (Baillie Cemetery, Lovat, Pictou County).

BAILLIE, George, d. 27 Dec 1855, age 71; his wife Catherine, d. 1 June 1826, age 46, natives of Clyne Parish, Sutherlandshire (Stewart Cemetery, West River Station, Pictou County).

BAILLIE, John, d. 7 Dec 1881, age 76, native of Clyne, Sutherlandshire; his wife Margaret, d. 3 Sep 1869, age 73, native of Sutherlandshire (Baillie Cemetery, Lovat, Pictou County).

BAILLIE, Robert, d. 19 Aug 1832, age 75, native of Clyne, Sutherlandshire; came to NS in 1814 (Baillie Cemetery, Lovat, Pictou County).

BAILLIE, William, d. 14 Sep 1875, age 74; his wife Janet, d. 5 Oct 1881, age 72, natives of Clyne [Sutherlandshire] (Baillie Cemetery, Lovat, Pictou County).

BALFOUR, William, d. 25 Apr 1823, age 61; his wife Elizabeth **FERGUSON**, d. 5 Aug 1839, age 78, natives of Perthshire; came to America in 1801 (Millbrook Cemetery, Pictou County).

BEATON, Alexander "Lex" R., d. 4 July 1831, age 34, native of Lochaber, Inverness-shire, and son of Finlay Beaton (West Mabou Pioneer [Catholic] Cemetery, Inverness County).

BELL, James, d. 12 Aug 1892, age 70, native of Hadden, Dumfries-shire; his wife Mary Jane **RODDICK**, d. 21 Oct 1911, age 89 (Stillman Cemetery, Pictou County).

BETHUNE, Donald; his wife Ann **ANDERSON**, natives of Sutherlandshire; came to NS in 1822 (Lansdowne Cemetery, Pictou County).

BOYD, John, b. 1829, d. 8 Dec 1906; his wife, Christie **McKEIGAN**, b. 20 Dec 1834, d. 15 July 1922, natives of North Uist (Brookside Cemetery, Sydney Mines, Cape Breton County).

BROWN, John, d. 27 Apr 1898, age 93, native of Banffshire; his wife Nancy **CAMERON**, d. 9 Feb 1901, age 87 (Stillman Cemetery, Pictou County).

BROWN, John, b. 9 Apr 1830, d. 31 Mar 1902; his wife Elizabeth, b. 7 Apr 1830, d. 27 Sep 1893, natives of Fifeshire (Brookside Cemetery, Sydney Mines, Cape Breton County).

BROWN, Robert, d. 4 July 1861, age 58, native of Caithness (Caledonia, Pictou County).

BROWN, Thomas, d. 19 Feb 1839, age 87; his wife Ann, d. 31 Aug 1841, age 70, natives of Scotland (Caledonia Cemetery, Pictou County).

CAMERON, Alexander, d. 31 Oct 1889, age 80, native of Lochaber [Inverness-shire] (North Lochaber Cemetery, Antigonish County).

CAMERON, Donald "Achosnich", River Denys 1804 - 1884, native of Camsuine [?], Scotland; his wife Margaret, 1818 - 1908, native of Lochaber, Scotland (Newtown Road Cemetery, Port Hastings, Inverness County).

CAMERON, Dougald, d. 23 July 1870, age 60, native of Lochaber, Inverness-shire; his wife Mary **MacEACHERN**, d. 3 May 1894, age 72 (North Lochaber Cemetery, Antigonish County).

CAMERON, John, d. 6 June 1892, age 82, native of Scotland (Church Point Cemetery, Sheet Harbour, Halifax County).

CAMERON, Samuel's wife Mary, b. 1780 at Lochaber [Inverness-shire] , d. 3 Mar 1884 at Lochaber, NS (North Lochaber Cemetery, Antigonish County).

CAMPBELL, Alexander, C. E., b. 15 Oct 1810 at Aberdeen, d. 26 Feb 1899 at Galt, Ontario (Stewart Cemetery, West River Station, Pictou County).

CAMPBELL, Alexander R., d. 15 Oct 1879, age 70, native of Inverness-shire; his wife Catherine, d. 25 Dec 1901, age 89 (Hill Cemetery, West River Station, Pictou County).

CAMPBELL, Angus, d. 18 Feb 1846, age 60, native of Lochaber, Inverness-shire; his wife Catherine (West Mabou Pioneer [Catholic] Cemetery, Inverness County).

CAMPBELL, Angus, d. 15 Oct 1856, age 73, native of the Isle of Skye, came to NS in 1833; his wife, Mary **McDONALD**, 1807 - 4 Mar 1888, Native of North Uist (Stewartdale Cemetery, Inverness County).

CAMPBELL, Anne, d. 11 Oct 1894, age 77, native of the Isle of Tiree, came to NS in 1831 (Stewartdale Cemetery, Inverness County).

CAMPBELL, Donald, d. 24 Dec 1835, age 58, native of Clyne [Sutherlandshire]; his wife, Jane **McKAY**, d. 25 Jan 1894, age 91 (Stewart Cemetery, West River Station, Pictou County).

CAMPBELL, Donald, d. 27 Jan 1869, age 63, native of the Isle of Tiree, came to Cape Breton in 1831 (Stewartdale Cemetery, Inverness County).

CAMPBELL, Murdoch, d. 16 Sep 1878, age 73, native of Uist, came to Cape Breton in 1831; his wife, Mary **MacKINNON**, 20 Aug 1812 - 11 Apr 1874, native of the Isle of M . . .(Stewartdale Cemetery, Inverness County).

CAMPBELL, Murdock, d. 1819, age 37, native of "Rothshire" [Ross and Cromarty]; came to NS in 1803 (Caledonia Cemetery, Pictou County).

CAMPBELL, William H., d. 30 Aug 1852, age 30, native of Paisley; his wife Elizabeth **MURRAY**, d. 29 July 1863, age 43 (Pioneer Cemetery, Union Centre, Pictou County).

CANTWELL, Annie, 1788 -1850, native of Crannich, Weem Parish, Perthshire, wife of Michael (Presbyterian Cemetery, Wallace, Cumberland County).

CARMICHAEL, John, d. Apr 1874, age 66; his wife, Catherine **MacCALLUM**, d. 24 Dec 1897, age 87, natives of the Isle of Tiree (Little Narrows, Victoria County).

CHISHOLM, Colin, 5 June 1800 - 26 Feb 1890, native of Strathglass, Inverness-shire (Judique RC Cemetery, Inverness County).

CHISHOLM, Donald, d. 14 Feb 1854, age 86; his wife Mary, d. 17 Nov 1846, age 70, natives of Strathglass, Inverness-shire (Marydale, Antigonish County).

CHISHOLM, John, 1792 - 4 Jan 1860, native of Strathglass, Inverness-shire (Judique RC Cemetery, Inverness County).

CHISHOLM, Rev. William, d. 31 Aug 1819, native of Inverness-shire (St. Mary's RC Cemetery, Town of Antigonish).

CLARK, Alexander, Sr., b. 11 Nov 1796, d. 19 Nov 1888; his first wife, Helen **THOMSON**, b. 11 Mar 1790, d. 5 Mar 1839, natives of Aberdeenshire (Presbyterian Cemetery, Middle Musquodoboit, Halifax County).

COLLIE, Anthony, d. 9 May 1878, age 79; his wife, Barbara **HUGHEN**, d. 17 Apr 1884, age 84, native of Dumfries-shire (Pioneer Cemetery, Union Centre, Pictou County).

CONN, William 1789 - 1863, native of Ayrshire; his wife Mary 1798 - 1876 (Conns Mills Cemetery, Cumberland County).

CORDINER, Arthur, 1785 - 13 May 1869, native of Scotland (St. Andrew's RC Cemetery, Little Bras d'Or, Cape Breton County).

CUMMINGS, Alexander, d. 20 Nov 1847, age 85, native of Inverness (St. Peter's Anglican Cemetery, Eastern Passage, Halifax County).

DAVIDSON, Kenneth, d. 24 Nov 1874, age 100, native of Ross-shire; his wife, Isabella **FRASER**, d. 5 Nov 1881, age 75, native of Inverness-shire (Hill Cemetery, West River Station, Pictou County).

DONALDSON, John, d. 10 Oct 1877, age 57, native of the Shetland Islands; his wife Sarah, b. 12 Oct 1831, d. 30 Jan 1873 (St. Peter's Anglican Cemetery, Eastern Passage, Halifax County).

DOUGALL, Donald, d. 10 Apr 1795, age 45, native of Scotland, left a widow and five children (McDonald Cemetery, Riverside Corner, Hants County).

DOUGLAS, Donald, d. 21 May 1818, age 45; his wife, Margaret **GRANT**, d. 26 Jan 1838, age 63, natives of Sutherlandshire who came to NS in 1803 (Millbrook Cemetery, Pictou County).

FARQUHAR, John, d. 25 Oct 1846, age 52, native of Elgin, Morayshire (Woodlawn United Cemetery, Dartmouth, Halifax County).

FERGUSON, Alexander, d. 29 Dec 1817, age 52; his wife, Eleanor **GRANT**, d. 14 Oct 1818, age 46, natives of Glenmoriston [Inverness-shire] (Nine Mile River Churchyard, Hants County).

FERGUSON, David, d. 27 Apr 1854, age 85, native of Inverness-shire; his wife, Isabella **McLEOD**, d. 8 May 1872, age 87 (Millbrook Cemetery, Pictou County).

FIFE, William's wife, Mary **STRACHAN**, 1784 - 23 Mar 1865, native of Aberdeen (St. Andrew's RC Cemetery, Little Bras d'Or, Cape Breton County).

FINLAYSON, Duncan, d. 1875, age 75; his wife, Christy **MacAULAY**, 1808 - 1901, native of Loch Alsh, Ross-shire, came to NS in the brig *Pallas*, 28 Aug 1821 (Grand River Presbyterian Cemetery, Richmond County).

FLEMING, Alexander, b. 28 Apr 1835, d. 14 Sep 1903, native of Stirlingshire; his wife, Mary **SMITH**, b. 22 Jan 1837, d. 20 Feb 1932, native of Ayrshire (St. John the Evangelist Anglican Cemetery, Sackville, Halifax County).

FORBES, William, d. 4 Mar 1838, age 80, native of Kilmoraig, Scotland, came to NS in 1801 (Caledonia Cemetery, Pictou County).

FRASER, Alexander, d. 8 Sep 1828, age 73, church elder, native of Paud of Kilmorack, Inverness-shire, came to NS in 1775; his wife, Mary **McDONALD**, d. 1 Apr 1849, age 86 (Pioneer Cemetery, Union Centre, Pictou County).

FRASER, Alexander R., West River, d. 1832, age 35. native of Inverness-shire, came to NS in 1818; his wife, Annabella **MUNRO**, d. 1 May 1829, age 30, native of Gairloch [Ross-shire] (Caledonia Cemetery, Pictou County).

FRASER, Alexander, d. 11 Jan 1846, age 45, native of Kiltarlity, Inverness-shire, came to NS in 1801; his wife, Mary **GORDON**, d. 6 Jan 1872, age 71, native of Inverness-shire (Hill Cemetery, West River Station, Pictou County).

FRASER, Donald, West River, d. 21 Jan 1859, age 77, native of Inverness-shire, came to NS in 1803; his wife Elizabeth, d. 29 Nov 1864, age 88 (Oak Grove Cemetery, Lime Rock, Pictou County).

FRASER, Donald, d. 26 Feb 1868, age 87, native of Inverness-shire, came to NS in 1820 (Hill Cemetery, West River Station, Pictou County).

FRASER, Hugh, Mount Thom, d. 7 Dec 1860, age 72, native of Inverness-shire; his wife, Mary **STUART**, d. 14 Dec 1861, age 69, native of Ross-shire (Caledonia Cemetery, Pictou County).

FRASER, John, d. 23 Feb 1842, age 77, native of Kiltarlity, Inverness-shire (Hill Cemetery, West River Station, Pictou County).

FRASER, John, d. 30 Apr 1861, age 72; his wife, Christina **SUTHERLAND**, d. 18 Dec 1857, age 63, natives of Sutherlandshire who came to Pictou in 1818 (Lansdowne Cemetery, Pictou County).

FRASER, John, d. 26 Apr 1874, age 82, native of Ross-shire (Knox Presbyterian Cemetery, Bay Road, Baddeck, Victoria County).

GILLIS, Lawrence, d. 13 Feb 1912, age 89, native of the Isle of Barra, came to NS in 1833 (St. Andrew's RC Cemetery, Boisdale, Cape Breton County).

GORDON, Christian, native of Culmaillie, Golspie Parish, Sutherlandshire, d. 20 Mar 1832, age 77, wife of John **McKAY** (Millbrook Cemetery, Pictou County).

GORDON, George, d. 15 Sep 1849, age 70; his wife, Catherine **GRANT**, d. 28 May 1873, age 80, natives of Sutherlandshire (Gunn Cemetery, Six Mile Brook, Pictou County).

GORDON, William, d. 28 Mar 1892, age 97, native of Sutherlandshire; his wife Isabella, d. 12 Mar 1880, age 64 years, 1 month (Lansdowne Cemetery, Pictou County)

GRAHAM, Alexander, Six Mile Brook, d. 23 Sep 1862, age 75, native of Sutherlandshire; his wife, Christy **MUNRO**, d. 18 Nov 1883, age 90, native of Ross-shire (Caledonia Cemetery, Pictou County).

GRAHAM, John, 1791 - 1864; his wife, Ellen **SUTHERLAND**, d. Sep 1849, age 58, native of Sutherlandshire (Hill Cemetery, West River Station, Pictou County).

GRAHAM, William, d. 16 May 1871, age 68; his wife Ann, d. 9 Dec 1877, age 72, natives of Sutherlandshire (Caledonia Cemetery, Pictou County).

GRANT, Alexander, d. 18 Apr 1810, age 76; his wife, Margaret **MITCHELL**, d. 7 June 1812, age 69, natives of Glenmoriston, Inverness-shire (Nine Mile River Churchyard, Hants County).

GUNN, John, Esq., d. 29 Jan 1841, age 47, native of Caithness (Caledonia Cemetery, Pictou County).

GUNN, Robert, West River, d. 8 June 1843, age 70, native of Kildonnan, Sutherlandshire, came to NS in 1836; his wife, Sarah **DUNN**, Eight Mile Brook, d. 17 Dec 1867, age 85 (Millbrook Cemetery, Pictou County).

HOWATSON, Robert, 8 July 1822 - 29 Mar 1910, native of Ayrshire, came to Cape Breton in 1842 (St. Andrew's RC Cemetery, Little Bras d'Or, Cape Breton County).

INNES, Kenneth, d. 13 Apr 1864, age 67, native of Loch Broom [Ross-shire], came to NS in 1803 (Caledonia Cemetery, Pictou County).

JOHNSTON, John, d. 18 Nov 1841, age 40; his wife Mary, d. 10 Nov 1900, age 80, natives of Scotland (St. Andrew's RC Cemetery, Little Bras d'Or, Cape Breton County).

KISSOCK, Alexander, d. 7 Nov 1863, age 56, native of Dumfries-shire (St. John the Evangelist Anglican Cemetery, Sackville, Halifax County).

LAWSON, George, PhD, LLD, FRS, professor at Dalhousie and Queens (Kingston, Ontario), born 12 Oct 1827 at Newport [on-Tay], Fifeshire, died 10 Nov 1895 at Halifax, NS; his wife, Lucy **STAPLEY**, native of Tunbridge Wells, Kent, England, d. 2 Jan 1871. Their children born at Edinburgh: Alexander Stapley, died age 18 months; Jessie, b. 4 June 1854, d. July 1934 at Brighton, England, wife of W. F. **MacCOY**, KC. (St. John the Evangelist Anglican Cemetery, Sackville, Halifax County).

LIVINGSTONE, Allan, d. 20 Aug 1854, age 73, elder in the Presbyterian church, native of Lochaber, [Inverness-shire] (St. David's Presbyterian Cemetery, Antigonish County).

McARTHUR, Allan, 1767 - 1840, native of the Isle of Canna; his wife, Catherine **McDONALD**, 1792 - 18 May 1869, native of the Isle of Arran; their children: Mary, b. 1817 in [Canna], d. 20 Apr 1913; and Archibald, b. 18 Dec 1821 in Canna, d. 1907, all came to NS in 1827 . Also Annie, d. 16 Apr 1878, age 42, wife of Archibald (Pond Road Cemetery, Sydney Mines, Cape Breton County).

McAULAY, Donald, d. 28 .... 1884, age 87, native of the Isle of Lewis (Little Narrows, Victoria County).

McAULAY, Murdoch, 1791 - 20 Aug 1872, native of the Isle of Lewis; his wife, Mary **SMITH**, d. 24 May 1890, age 91 (Little Narrows, Victoria County).

McAULAY, Norman, a church elder, d. 19 Nov 1899, age 87, native of the Isle of Lewis, came to NS in 1827 with his parents; his wife, Ann **SMITH**, d. 24 Dec 1893, age 75, came to NS in 1825 from Scotland with her parents (Little Narrows, Victoria County).

McBEATH, Neil's wife, Catherine **McKAY**, d. 22 Aug 1863, age 67, native of Gairloch, Sutherlandshire. She left four sons and three daughters (Gairloch Cemetery, Pictou County).

McDONALD, Angus, d. 16 Dec 1857, age 76, native of North Uist, came to Cape Breton in August 1828; his wife Margaret, d. 16 Dec 1888, age 102 (McCuish Cemetery, Richmond County).

McDONALD, Charles, 3 Jan 1808 - 12 Jan 1856, native of the Isle of Tiree; his wife, Catherine **CAMERON**, 13 Jan 1808 - 24 Sep 1897, native of Fort William, Inverness-shire (Little Narrows, Victoria County).

McDONALD, Donald, b. 1793, d. 4 July 1893, a Waterloo veteran; his wife, Catherine **ROSS**, d. 22 Apr 1863, age 55, natives of Sutherlandshire (Lansdowne Cemetery, Pictou County).

MacDONALD, Donald, church elder, 1829 - 21 Mar 1894, came to Cape Breton in 1838; his wife Annie, d. 9 May 1916, age 82 (Little Narrows, Victoria County).

MacDONALD, Duncan, 1815 - 1888, native of Lairg, Sutherlandshire (MacNab's Hll Cemetery, South Shore, Malagash, Cumberland County).

MacDONALD, Hugh, Lime Rock, West River, d. 16 Nov 1866, native of Perthshire; his wife Margaret, d. 16 Apr 1897, age 88 (Caledonia Cemetery, Pictou County).

McDONALD, Hugh, d. 4 Apr 1881, age 85, native of Lairg, [Sutherlandshire], came to NS in 1812; his wife, Catherine **FRASER**, d. 18 Oct 1880, age 75, native of Dornoch, [Sutherlandshire], came to NS in 1810 (Lansdowne Cemetery, Pictou County).

MacDONALD, James, died 11 Oct 1850, age 46, native of Lochaber, [Inverness-shire], Scotland; also his wife Mary, died 19 May 1850 (Mabou Catholic Cemetery, Inverness County)

McDONALD, John, d. 12 Aug 1841, age 73, native of Moidart, Inverness-shire (Long Point Pioneer Cemetery, Inverness County).

MacDONALD, John, 1791 - 1858, native of Milton, Inverness-shire; his wife Mary, 1793 - 1857, native of East River, NS (Presbyterian Church Cemetery, Wallace, Cumberland County).

MacDONALD, Morrison, 1792 - 14 Jan 1868, native of Caithness; his wife Christy A. J., 8 Jan 1804 - 19 May 1892 (Knox Presbyterian Cemetery, Bay Road, Baddeck, Victoria County).

McDONALD, Murdoch, d. 22 July 1887, age 78; his wife, Catherine **ROSS**, d. 8 Feb 1903, age 90, natives of Scotland (St. Andrew's RC Cemetery, Little Bras d'Or, Cape Breton County).

McDONALD, Neil, d. 23 July 1851, age 101, native of Sutherlandshire, came to NS in 1801; his wife, Catherine **CAMPBELL**, died age 80 (Caledonia Cemetery, Antigonish County).

MacDONALD, Norman; his wife, Margaret **MORRISON**, d. 26 Apr 1841, age 22, native of "north of Inverness-shire" (Oban Cemetery, Richmond County).

MacDONALD, Philip, d. 18 Oct 1836, age 77; his wife Ann, d. 10 Oct 1852, age 87, natives of Gairloch, Sutherlandshire (Millbrook Cemetery, Pictou County).

McDONALD, Robert, teacher, d. 23 Nov 1835, age 49, native of Sutherlandshire, came to America in 1802. He left a widow and nine children (Lansdowne Cemetery, Pictou County).

MacDONALD, Thomas, d. 23 June 1846, age 58, native of Dornoch, [Sutherlandshire], leaving widow and children; his wife Nancy, d. 17 Jan 1888, age 91 (Millbrook Cemetery, Pictou County).

MacDONALD, William, d. 23 Mar 1867, age 85, native of Rogart, [Sutherlandshire]; his wife, Maria **ROSS**, West River, d. June 1834, age 48, native of Sutherlandshire, came to NS in 1819 (Baillie Cemetery, Lovat, Pictou County).

McDONELL, Rev. Alexander, died 19 Sep 1841, age 59, native of Scotland (St. Andrew's Cemetery, Judique, Inverness County)

McDONALD, William, Elder, d. 13 Nov 1879, age 82, native of Sutherlandshire; his wife, Isabella **ROSS**, d. 6 May 1845, age 41, native of Lairg, [Sutherlandshire] (Lansdowne Cemetery, Pictou County).

McDONELL, Alexander, d. 23 Dec 1878, age 65, native of Dornie, Kintail, Ross-shire (Long Point Pioneer Cemetery, Inverness County).

McDOUGALL, Neil, d. 27 Feb 1813, age 74, native of the Isle of Eigg, came to America in 1791 (Judique RC Cemetery, Inverness County).

McFADYEN, Allen, d. 14 July 1878, age 65; his wife Jane, d. 17 Feb 1899, age 90, natives of the Isle of Tiree (Little Narrows, Victoria County).

McFADYEN, Archie, d. 10 Jan 1874, age 92; his wife Mary, d. 10 July 1869, age 80, natives of the Isle of Tiree (Little Narrows, Victoria County).

MacFARLANE, Daniel, magistrate and legislator, 1784 - 13 Nov 1849, native of Glendochart, [Perthshire], came to NS in 1806; his wife, Helen **MacNAB**, 1795 - 1849 (Presbyterian Cemetery, Wallace, Cumberland County).

MacFARLANE, John, 1793 - 1876, native of Scotland (MacNabs Hill Cemetery, South Shore, Malagash, Cumberland County).

MacGILLIVRAY, Alexander, d. 26 Nov 1874, age 86; his wife, Nancy **McLEOD**, natives of Inverness-shire (Caledonia Cemetery, Pictou County).

McGREGOR, Alexander, d. 10 Dec 1874, age 87, native of Loch Alsh [Ross and Cromarty]; his wife, Mary **MacKINNON**, d. 24 Mar 1878, age 82, native of the Isle of Coll (Malagawatch Cemetery, Inverness County).

MIGRIGOR [McGregor], John's wife Ann, d. 12 Jan 1839, age 45, native of Perthshire (St. John the Evangelist Anglican Cemetery, Sackville, Halifax County).

McINNIS, John, 1810 - 1889, native of Argyllshire (Community Cemetery, Wallace, Cumberland County).

McINTOSH, Donald, d. 2 May 1842, age 62, native of Bannach [Badenoch?], Atholshire [i.e., Perthshire]; his wife, Christie **FRASER**, d. 7 July 1897, age 93 (Hill Cemetery, West River Station, Pictou County).

MacINTOSH, Hugh, 1815 - 1883, native of Scotland; his wife Catherine, 1811 - 1852 (Presbyterian Cemetery, Wallace, Cumberland County).

McINTYRE, John, d. 18 Nov 1857, age 74; his wife Catherine, d. 13 July 1857, age 72, natives of South Uist (St. Andrew's RC Cemetery, Boisdale, Cape Breton County).

McINTYRE, Roderick, d. 18 Apr 1883, age 62, native of South Uist (St. Andrew's RC Cemetery, Boisdale, Cape Breton County).

MacIVER, Malcolm, d. 21 Sep 1868, age 68, native of the Isle of Lewis (Little Narrows Cemetery, Victoria County).

MacIVOR, John, 1794 - 1877, native of Stornoway [Isle of Lewis] (United Church Cemetery, Fox Harbour, Cumberland County).

McKAY, Andrew, d. 29 Apr 1869, age 83, native of Sutherlandshire (Millbrook Cemetery, Pictou County).

142   SOME EARLY SCOTS IN MARITIME CANADA - 1

McKAY, Angus, West River, d. 8 July 1840, age 73, native of Sutherlandshire, came to NS in 1803 (Caledonia Cemetery, Pictou County).

McKAY, David, 1790 - 1880; his wife, Christy **MUNRO**, d. 1 Apr 1872, age 72, natives of Embo [village], Dornoch, Sutherlandshire, came to NS in 1820 (Millbrook Cemetery, Pictou County).

McKAY, Donald, d. 28 July 1861, age 73, native of Lairg Parish [Sutherlandshire], came to NS in 1818 (Lansdowne Cemetery, Pictou County).

MacKAY, Donald, d. 27 Sep 1866, age 86, native of Rogart Parish, Sutherlandshire; his wife, Sarah **MacKENZIE**, d. 4 Nov 1869, age 80 (Millbrook Cemetery, Pictou County).

McKAY, George, d. 9 July 1867, age 72, native of Sutherlandshire, came to NS in 1803 as a child (MacKay Cemetery, Mount Thom, Pictou County).

McKAY, George, d. 12 Jan 1882, age 76; his wife, Elizabeth, d. 13 Feb 1864, age 63, dau of Hector **McLANE** of King[ai]rloch, [Lismore Parish], Argyllshire (MacLean Cemetery, Port Hastings, Inverness County).

McKAY, Hugh, New Lairg, d. 20 June 1867, age 59, native of Sutherlandshire, came to NS in 1831 (Lansdowne Cemetery, Pictou County).

McKAY, Hugh, d. 10 June 1892, age 96, native of Criech Parish, Sutherlandshire; his wife, Marion **SUTHERLAND**, d. 7 June 1893, age 83 (Millbrook Cemetery, Pictou County).

McKAY, Hugh G., d. 26 Jan 1907, age 88, native of Rothshire [Ross and Cromarty] (MacKay Cemetery, Mount Thom, Pictou County).

McKAY, James, d. 1 Nov 1833, age 68; his wife Augusta, d. 1 Jan 1844, age 78, natives of Sutherlandshire (Millbrook Cemetery, Pictou County).

McKAY, James, d. 17 Apr 1878, age 73, native of Sutherlandshire; his wife, Janet **GRAHAM**, d. 27 Jan 1895, age 72 (Lansdowne Cemetery, Pictou County).

McKAY, John, d. 15 Feb 1832, age 76; his wife, Jean **MURRAY**, d. 19 June 1843, age 96, natives of Criech Parish, Sutherlandshire (Millbrook Cemetery, Pictou County).

McKAY, John, West River, d. 24 June 1847, age 56, native of Rogart Parish, Sutherlandshire; his wife Margaret, d. 30 Aug 1861, age 66 (Millbrook Cemetery, Pictou County).

MacKAY, John, d. 31 Dec 1856, age 76, native of Dornoch, Sutherlandshire; his wife, Christy **MATHESON**, d. 9 Mar 1883, age 87 (Millbrook Cemetery, Pictou County).

McKAY, Malcolm, d. 30 Dec 1887, age 84; his wife Margaret, natives of Uig, Isle of Lewis, came to Cape Breton in 1825 (Little Narrows, Victoria County).

McKAY, Murdoch, d. 6 Sep 1850, age 80, native of Sutherlandshire; his wife, Christian **MATHESON**, d. 18 Apr 1844, age 65, native of Shinness, Lairg Parish, Sutherlandshire. They came to NS in 1819 (Lansdowne Cemetery, Pictou County).

McKAY, Neil, d. 1869, age 69; his wife Margaret, d. 1858, age 57, natives of Inverness-shire (Little Narrows, Victoria County).

McKAY, Robert, d. 24 Oct 1853, age 61; his wife Catherine, d. 17 Nov 1882, age 86, natives of Sutherlandshire (St. Luke's Cemetery, Salt Springs, Pictou County).

McKAY, Robert, d. 28 June 1874, age 90, native of Sutherlandshire, came to NS in 1812 (Millbrook Cemetery, Pictou County).

MacKAY, William, 1811 - 1881, native of Dornoch, Sutherlandshire; his wife Annie, 1818 - 1854 (Presbyterian Cemetery, Wallace, Cumberland County).

McKENZIE, Alexander, d. 15 Oct 1819, age 50, native of Ross-shire (Caledonia Cemetery, Pictou County).

McKENZIE, Alexander, d. 29 Mar 1845, age 60, native of Sutherlandshire; his wife, Catherine **McPHERSON**, d. 29 Nov 1862, age 72 (Caledonia Cemetery, Pictou County).

MacKENZIE, Alexander, 1784 - 1851; his wife Barbara, 1795 - 1869, native of the Isle of Lewis (MacKenzie Cemetery, North Shore, Malagash, Cumberland County).

MacKENZIE, Alexander, 1797 - 1859, native of the Isle of Lewis (United Church Cemetery, Malagash, Cumberland County).

McKENZIE, Alexander, Waterville, West River, d. 28 Dec 1874, age 79, native of Loch Broom, Ross-shire, came to NS in 1803; his wife, Helen **McCULLOCH**, d. 20 Mar 1859, age 52 (Caledonia Cemetery, Pictou County).

MacKENZIE, Allan, 1786 - 1850, native of Lochs Parish, Isle of Lewis (MacKenzie Cemetery, North Shore, Malagash, Cumberland County).

McKENZIE, Catherine, d. 11 Jan 1837, age 64, native of Loch Broom [Ross-shire] (Caledonia Cemetery, Pictou County).

McKENZIE, Donald, West River, d. 22 Apr 1836, age 87, native of Brackachy [?], Inverness-shire, came to NS in 1812; his wife Mary, d. 19 Oct 1834, age 77 (MacKenzie Cemetery, Lovat, Pictou County).

MacKENZIE, Donald, d. 1859, age 77; served in the Battle of The Nile and at Trafalgar, native of Scotland; his wife, Ann Margaret **McKINNON**, d. 1884, age 84 (Malagawatch Cemetery, Inverness County).

McKENZIE, Donald, d. 12 Dec 1868, age 76, native of Drough-hills [?], Scotland; his wife Charlotte, d. 8 Dec 1874, age 84 (Hillcrest Cemetery, Upper Musquodoboit, Halifax County).

MacKENZIE, George, 1800 - 1875; his wife Ellen, 1820 - 1890, natives of the Isle of Lewis (MacKenzie Cemetery, North Shore, Malagash, Cumberland County).

McKENZIE, Hector, d. 12 Mar 1888, age 80; his wife, Annie 'Nancy' **FERGUSON**, d. 21 Jan 1878, age 68, natives of Inverness-shire (Millbrook Cemetery, Pictou County).

MacKENZIE, John, 1762 - 1849, native of the Isle of Lewis, came to NS in 1811 (MacKenzie Cemetery, North Shore, Malagash, Cumberland County).

MacKENZIE, John, 1791 - 1863, native of the Isle of Lewis (MacKenzie Cemetery, North Shore, Malagash, Cumberland County).

McKENZIE, Murdoch, d. 6 Feb 1853, age 96; his wife Janet, d. 27 Aug 1846, age 76; their dau, Ellen, d. 27 Nov 1879, age 87, natives of Loch Broom, Ross-shire, came to NS in 1803 (Caledonia Cemetery, Pictou County).

McKENZIE, Roderick, d. 24 Mar 1865, age 64, native of Ross-shire; his wife, Marion **STEWART**, native of Mount Thom, NS, d. 28 June 1887, age 84, at Rogers Hill (Caledonia Cemetery, Pictou County).

McKENZIE, Roderick, d. 21 Apr 1868, age 90, at Mount Pleasant, West River, a native of Inverness-shire, came to NS in 1801 [in the *Dove*]; his wife Ann, d. 14 Apr 1867, age 81 (MacKenzie Cemetery, Lovat, Pictou County).

McKENZIE, Roderick, d. 18 Sep 1894, age 84, native of Applecross, Ross-shire; his wife, Annie **McKAY**, d. 3 Feb 1887, age 60 (Grand River Presbyterian Cemetery, Richmond County).

McKENZIE, William, d. 29 Apr 1822, age 65; his wife Nancy, d. 9 Mar 1835, age 80, natives of Ross-shire, both of whom came to NS in 1803 (Caledonia Cemetery, Pictou County).

MacKINNON, Alexander, d. 29 Sep 1860, age 62; his wife Elizabeth, d. 4 Dec 1875, age 80, natives of Argyllshire (North Lochaber Cemetery, Antigonish County).

McLEAN, Donald, d. 27 June 1818, age 58, native of Loch Broom, Ross-shire (Millbrook Cemetery, Pictou County).

McLEAN, Donald, d. 4 Dec 1898, age 99, native of Glenelg, [Inverness-shire]; his wife, Mary S. **SYMONDS**, d. 28 Aug 1871, age 67, native of Boyndie, Banffshire (McLean Family Cemetery, Boularderie Island, Cape Breton County).

McLEAN, Hector, d. 13 Mar 1862, age 83; his wife Elizabeth, d. 8 June 1867, age 56, natives of Ross-shire (Knox Presbyterian Cemetery, Bay Road, Baddeck, Victoria County).

McLEAN, Isabella, d. 9 Apr 1865, age 55, native of Inverness-shire, dau of Alexander and Catherine **McVARISH** (Judique RC Cemetery, Inverness County).

McLEAN, John, Gairloch, d. 20 Oct 1860, age 78, native of Rothshire [Ross and Cromarty]; his wife Elizabeth, d. 29 Apr 1867, age 67, native of Clyne, Sutherlandshire (Stewart Cemetery, West River Station, Pictou County).

MacLEAN, Laughlin, d. 27 May 1849, native of Argyllshire; his wife, Margaret **MacDONALD**, from Inverness-shire (Grand Anse, Richmond County).

McLEAN, Murdoch, d. 3 Nov 1852, age 70, native of Loch Broom, [Ross-shire]; his first wife, Mary **FRASER**, d. Nov 1831, age 31, native of Inverness-shire; his second wife, Catherine **FRASER**, d. 12 Oct 1888, age 84, native of Inverness-shire (Stewart Cemetery, West River Station, Pictou County).

McLEAN, Nancy, d. 17 Apr 1906, age 85, native of Loch Broom, [Ross-shire] (Stewart Cemetery, West River Station, Pictou County).

McLENNAN, Alexander, d. July 1865, age 47, native of the Isle of Lewis, came to NS in 1830; his wife, Catherine **ROSS**, d. Jan 1854, age 44 (Little Narrows, Victoria County).

McLEOD, Donald, New Lairg, d. 11 May 1855, age 75, native of Lairg, Sutherlandshire (Millbrook Cemetery, Pictou County).

McLEOD, Donald, New Lairg, d. 11 Feb 1869, age 80, native of Lairg Parish, [Sutherlandshire], came to NS in 1819; his wife, Christy **MATHESON**, d. 11 Nov 1854, age 67, native of Sutherlandshire (Lansdowne Cemetery, Pictou County).

McLEOD, George, d. 1 Jan 1847, age 49; his wife Elizabeth, d. 16 Dec 1882, age 88, natives of Sutherlandshire (Lansdowne Cemetery, Pictou County).

McLEOD, Hector, 1793 - 28 June 1867, native of Sutherlandshire (St. James Anglican Cemetery, Port Dufferin, Halifax County).

McLEOD, James, d. 5 May 1829, age 80, native of Sutherlandshire; his wife Christy, d. 1 Mar 1830, age 95 (Millbrook Cemetery, Pictou County).

McLEOD, James, d. 13 Jan 1857, age 71, native of Lairg [Parish, Sutherlandshire] (Millbrook Cemetery, Pictou County).

McLEOD, John, d. 5 Jan 1827, age 55, native of Assynt Parish, Sutherlandshire, came to NS in 1803 (Millbrook Cemetery, Pictou County).

McLEOD, John, New Lairg, d. 21 July 1843, age 75, native of Lairg Parish, Sutherlandshire, came to America in 1803; his wife, Barbara **McKAY**, d. 9 Feb 1871, age 77, native of Criech Parish Sutherlandshire (Millbrook Cemetery, Pictou County).

McLEOD, John, d. 25 May 1895, age 81, native of Lairg, Sutherlandshire; his wife, Christy **McLEAN**, d. 19 Aug 1909, age 82 (Gairloch Cemetery, Pictou County).

McLEOD, Joseph, Mount Thom, d. 9 Sep 1879, age 92; his wife, Ellen **GRANT**, d. 23 Feb 1876, age 102, natives of Sutherlandshire (Caledonia Cemetery, Pictou County).

McLEOD, Mary, d. 1864, age 23, native of Ross-shire (Stewart Cemetery, West River Station, Pictou County).

McLEOD, Thomas, d. 21 Mar 1866, age 71, native of Inverness-shire; his wife Nancy, d. 22 Aug 1868, age 71 (Pioneer Cemetery, Union Centre, Pictou County).

McLEOD, William, d. 27 Aug 1832, age 61; his wife, Jane **McDONALD**, d. 18 Jan 1849, age 58, natives of Sutherlandshire, they came to America in 1819 (Millbrook Cemetery, Pictou County).

McLEOD, William, d. 10 Apr 1874, age 79; his wife Isabella, d. 2 Feb 1874, age 76, natives of the Isle of Lewis (Little Narrows, Victoria County).

MacNAB, Alexander, 1762 - 11 May 1824, native of Glendochart [Parish of Killin], Perthshire (MacNab's Hill Cemetery, South Shore, Malagash, Cumberland County).

MacNAIR, Roderick, d. 22 Oct 1856, age 77, native of Inverness-shire (St. Mary's Catholic Cemetery, Town of Antigonish).

McNEIL, James, d. 10 Oct 1869, age 71, native of Glasgow (St. Andrew's RC Cemetery, Boisdale, Cape Breton County).

McNEIL, James, d. 9 Sep 1878, age 84, native of the Isle of Barra (St. Andrew's RC Cemetery, Boisdale, Cape Breton County).

McPHERSON, Alexander, "one of the first settlers of Gairloch, killed at Millbrook about the year 1811." (Millbrook Cemetery, Pictou County).

McPHERSON, Andrew, d. 28 Mar 1870, age 83; native of Inverness-shire; his wife, Lucy **McDAIRMAID** d. 2 Feb 1878, age 81 (Lower Middle River Cemetery, Pictou County).

MacPHERSON, Donald, d. 10 Jan 1814, age 75, native of Gairloch, Ross-shire; his wife, Christina **MacDONALD**, d. 13 Jan 1843, age 97 [native of Ross-shire] (Millbrook Cemetery, Pictou County).

McPHERSON, Hugh, West River, d. 12 Oct 1843, age 64, native of Golspie, Sutherlandshire; his wife, Anne **SUTHERLAND**, d. 8 Sep 1857, age 74 (Baillie Cemetery, Lovat, Pictou County).

McPHERSON, Murdoch, d. 29 Dec 1840, age 54, native of Gairloch, Ross-shire; his wife, Jane **McLELLAN**, d. 18 Mar 1894, age 94 (Millbrook Cemetery, Pictou County).

McRITCHIE, Kenneth, d. 17 Feb 1885, age 81; his wife Catherine, d. 14 Sep 1863, age 56, natives of the Isle of Lewis (Little Narrows, Victoria County).

McRITCHIE, Malcolm, d. 13 Aug 1883, age 88, native of the Isle of Lewis (Little Narrows, Victoria County).

MacVICAR, John, 1813 - 1891, native of Greenock (Newtown Road Cemetery, Port Hastings, Inverness County).

McWILLIAM, Alexander, d. 31 Aug 1864, age 64, native of Keith Parish, Banffshire (St. Andrew's United Church Cemetery, Elderbank, Halifax County).

MATHESON, Angus, d. 7 June 1875, age 85; his wife Margaret, d. 1858, age 57, natives of Inverness-shire (Little Narrows, Victoria County).

MATHESON, Catherine, d. 16 Dec 1843, age 78, native of Lairg Parish, Sutherlandshire (Lansdowne Cemetery, Pictou County).

MATHESON, Donald, d. 30 May 1866, age 73; his wife, Isabella **SUTHERLAND**, d. 29 Sep 1850, age 64, natives of Sutherlandshire (Lansdowne Cemetery, Pictou County).

MATHESON, Donald, d. 8 Apr 1869, age 75; his wife Ellen, d. 16 Apr 1869, age 65, natives of the Isle of Lewis (Little Narrows, Victoria County).

MATHESON, Duncan, d. 30 Apr 1879, age 82, came to Pictou in 1819; his wife Jane, d. 20 Jan 1874, age 76, came to Pictou in 1818; natives of Sutherlandshire (Lansdowne Cemetery, Pictou County).

MATHESON, John, 1787 - 1860, native of Loch Alsh, Ross-shire; his wife Elizabeth, 1789 - 1872, native of Scotland (Grand River Presbyterian Cemetery, Richmond County).

MATHESON, John; his wife Mary, d. 20 Dec 1874, age 74, native of the Isle of Lewis (Little Narrows, Victoria County).

MATHESON, Neil, d. 10 May 1866, age 76; his wife Catherine, d. 27 Aug 1866, age 69, natives of Lairg Parish, Sutherlandshire (Lansdowne Cemetery, Pictou County).

MATHESON, Neil, d. 29 Feb 1880, age 66; his wife, Isabella **McINTOSH**, d. 2 Jan 1880, age 70, natives of Redcastle, Ross-shire (Gunn Cemetery, Six Mile Brook, Pictou County).

MATHESON, Walter, d. 6 June 1861, age 91; his wife Margaret, d. 8 Feb 1855, age 76, natives of Sutherlandshire (Millbrook Cemetery, Pictou County).

MAXWELL, Duncan, b. 20 July 1810, d. 20 Apr 1869, native of Loch Broom, [Ross-shire], came to NS in 1838 (Ebenezer Cemetery, Salt Springs, Pictou County).

MAXWELL, William Dunbar, d. 6 Oct 1852, age 63, native of Dumfries-shire; his wife, Jane **McCALLUM**, d. 2 Apr 1854, age 62, native of Argyllshire (Ebenezer Cemetery, Salt Springs, Pictou County).

MERCHINSON, Alexander F.'s wife, Jane **URQUHART**, d. 9 June 1870, age 72, native of Loch Alsh, Ross-shire (Grand River Presbyterian Cemetery, Richmond County).

MICHIE, John, 1789 - 1861, native of Banffshire, came to NS in 1818 (Linden Cemetery, Cumberland County).

MORRISON, Alexander, d. 2 Dec 1843, age 76; his wife Christiana, d. 7 Oct 1856, age 64, natives of the Isle of Lewis (MacLeod Pioneer Cemetery, Richmond County).

MORRISON, John, 1799 - 17 Sep 1868; his wife Sarah, 1807 - 14 Mar 1889, natives of North Uist (Morrison Cemetery, Cape Breton County).

MORRISON, John, 24 Dec 1804 - 22 Nov 1900; his wife Catherine, d. 23 Oct 1877, age 62, natives of the Isle of Lewis (Little Narrows, Victoria County).

MUNRO, Donald, d. 13 Apr 1863, age 81, native of Ross-shire, came to NS in 1831 (Caledonia Cemetery, Pictou County).

MUNRO, John, d. 10 Mar 1872, age 80, native of Embo [a fishing village], Dornoch, Sutherlandshire, came to NS in 1815; his wife, Mary Ann **McKENZIE**, d. 5 May 1881, age 80 (Millbrook Cemetery, Pictou County).

MUNRO, Kenneth, d. 20 May 1872, age 82, native of Keltarn [?], Ross-shire; his wife Ann, d. 6 May 1876, age 78 (Caledonia Cemetery, Pictou County).

MUNRO, Marion, d. 12 June 1871, age 67, native of Sutherlandshire, wife of John (Millbrook Cemetery, Pictou County).

MUNRO, Murdoch, d. 30 Apr 1838, age 80; his wife, Catherine **McLENNON**; their son, George, d. 27 Mar 1872, age 84, natives of Scotland, came to NS in 1803 (Caledonia Cemetery, Pictou County).

MUNRO, William, d. 2 Sep 18..., age 46, native of Ross-shire (Caledonia Cemetery, Pictou County).

MUNROE, Donald's wife, Elizabeth **SMITH**, d. 15 Sep 1856, age 58, native of Perthshire (Creighton Cemetery, Upper Mount Thom, Pictou County).

MURRAY, Angus, Mount Thom, d. 16 Dec 1844, age 64, native of Golspie, Sutherlandshire; his wife, Elizabeth **MacDONALD**, d. 25 Nov 1840, age 54, native of Sutherlandshire (Baillie Cemetery, Lovat, Pictou County).

MURRAY, Donald, New Lairg, d. 15 Feb 1848, age 80, native of Lairg Parish, Sutherlandshire, came to NS in 1802; his wife, Mary **McLEAN**, d. 6 July 1843, age 60, native of Inverness-shire, came to NS in 1801 (Lansdowne Cemetery, Pictou County).

MURRAY, John, d. 17 Oct 1849, age 89, native of Sutherlandshire, came to NS in 1803; his wife, Mary **FRASER**, b. 13 May 1789, d. 25 July 1878 (Millbrook Cemetery, Pictou County).

NICOLSON, Murdoch, Sr., 1785 - 1850, native of Uig Parish, [Ross and Cromarty] (Presbyterian Church Cemetery, Wallace, Cumberland County).

NICOLSON, William, d. 1862, native of the Isle of Lewis (United Church Cemetery, Fox Harbour, Cumberland County).

NOBLE, John, surgeon, no dates; his wife, Julia **McNIVEN**, d. 1 June 1843, age 38, native of the Isle of Tiree, Argyllshire (Stewartdale Cemetery, Inverness County).

PORTEOUS, James, "father", d. 2 Mar 1856, age 36; and Jane, "mother", d. 26 Nov 1854, age 30, natives of Scotland (St. John the Evangelist Anglican Cemetery, Sackville, Halifax County).

REID, James, d. 21 Oct 1870, age 74, native of Aberdeenshire, came to NS in 1815; Jane D., his wife, d. 8 Mar 1890, age 92 (Presbyterian Cemetery, Middle Musquodoboit, Halifax County).

RETTIE, John, d. 16 May 1875, age 82, native of Banffshire; his wife, Christina **CALLIE**, d. 30 June 1869, age 73, native of Dornoch [Parish, Sutherlandshire] (Caledonia Cemetery, Pictou County).

ROBERTSON, James, Eight Mile Brook, d. 22 Feb 1867, age 83, native of Banffshire; his wife, Abigail **STEWART**, d. 2 Dec 1887, age 88 (Caledonia Cemetery, Pictou County).

ROBERTSON, John Sutherland, b. 26 Mar 1783, d. 27 Dec 1812, native of Dornoch Parish, Sutherlandshire, came to NS in 1809 (Millbrook Cemetery, Pictou County).

ROSS, Alexander, d. 26 Dec 1838, age 84; his wife Catherine, d. 11 Oct 1836, age 72; their son John, d. 3 Sep 1868, age 76, natives of Rogart, [Sutherlandshire], came to NS in 1802 (Millbrook Cemetery, Pictou County).

ROSS, Alexander R., 1771 - 30 June 1840, native of Tarbetness, Ross-shire, came to NS in 1833; his wife Elizabeth, 1780 - 1849 (Presbyterian Church Cemetery, Wallace, Cumberland County).

ROSS, Alexander, d. 27 July 1887, age 61; his wife Jane, b. 22 July 1826, d. 27 Feb 1916, native of Ross-shire (MacKay Cemetery, Mount Thom, Pictou County).

ROSS, Andrew, 1784 - 1870, native of Dornoch, [Sutherlandshire], came to NS in 1815; his wife, Sarah **MacKENZIE** (Stillman Cemetery, Pictou County).

ROSS, Catherine, d. 7 Aug 1836, age 68, native of Tain, Ross-shire; mother of Alexander ROSS, d. 27 Oct 1860, age 64 (Millbrook Cemetery, Pictou County).

ROSS, Rev. James, d. 12 July 1877, age 66, native of Redcastle, Ross-shire (Grand River Presbyterian Cemetery, Richmond County).

ROSS, Janet, d. 5 Oct 1883, age 83, native of Ross-shire, wife of Alexander (Millbrook Cemetery, Pictou County).

ROSS, John, d. 4 Sep 1841, age 74; his wife, Catherine **McKAY**, d. 8 Jan 1847, age 66; their children: Hugh, d. 26 Aug 1834, age 24, and Jane, d. 20 Apr 1834, age 18; came to NS in 1832 (Lansdowne Cemetery, Pictou County).

ROSS, John, d. 24 Nov 1874, age 84; his wife Mary, d. 18 Dec 1858, age 68, natives of Criech Parish, Sutherlandshire (Caledonia Cemetery, Pictou County).

ROSS, Walter, Millbrook, d. 11 July 1841, age 78; his wife Christy, d. 3 Feb 1846, age 79, natives of Tain, Ross-shire, came to NS in 1803 (Millbrook Cemetery, Pictou County).

ROSS, William, d. 8 Feb 1884, age 92, native of Rogart, [Sutherlandshire]; his wife, Catherine **FRASER**, d. 3 Mar 1841, age 38 (Millbrook Cemetery, Pictou County).

SCOTT, Mary J. Porteous, d. 4 Oct 1876, age 75, native of Dumfries-shire, mother of Rev. James Scott (William Black United Church Cemetery, Glen Margaret, Halifax County).

SCOTT, Robert, 1784 - 1866, native of Irament [?], Scotland; his wife Jane, 1793 - 1867, native of London, England (Knox Cemetery, Wallace, Cumberland County).

SEDGEWICK, Rev. Robert, 48 years a Presbyterian minister, d. April 1885, age 82, native of Paisley; his wife, Jessie **MIDDLETON**, d. Sep 1878, age 62; their son George, d. Oct 1858, age 4 (United Church Cemetery, Middle Musquodoboit, Halifax County).

SHIELS, Andrew, b. 12 Mar 1793 in the Parish of Oxnam, Roxburghshire, d. 5 Nov 1879 at Dartmouth, NS; his first wife, Ellen, d. 19 Aug 1846, age 52 (Woodlawn United Church Cemetery, Dartmouth, Halifax County). [Verse from his epitaph quoted on page 149.]

SHORT, Robert, d. 7 Jan 1860, age 78; his wife Isabella, d. 1 Jan 1841, age 67, native of Berwickshire (Short Cemetery, West River Station, Pictou County).

SHORTT, John, d. 18 July 1853, age 50, native of Scotland, came to NS in 1817; his wife, Catherine **CHISHOLM**, d. 17 Mar 1882, native of Inverness-shire (Caledonia Cemetery, Pictou County).

SMITH, Donald, native of Dumfries, no dates (Creighton Cemetery, Upper Mount Thom, Pictou County).

SMITH, Donald, d. 9 June 1843, age 81, native of Perthshire; his wife, Jennet **McINTOSH**, d. 5 Sep 1852, age 79 (Creighton Cemetery, Upper Mount Thom, Pictou County).

STEELE, John, d. 5 Oct 1865, age 63, native of South Uist (St. Andrew's RC Cemetery, Boisdale, Cape Breton County).

STEVENSON, John, 1799 - 1890, native of Aberdeen; his wife, Margaret **NAVIN**, 1805 - 1890, native of Cornwall [?], Lanarkshire (Community Cemetery, Wallace, Cumberland County).

STEWART, Alexander's wife, Margaret **McFARLAN**, d. 7 Mar 1833, age 70, native of Perthshire (North Lochaber Cemetery, Antigonish County).

STEWART, Alexander, d. 21 Feb 1830, age 69, native of Ross-shire, came to America in 1801; his wife, Merrin **McLEAN**, d. 12 Jan 1830, age 68 (Caledonia Cemetery, Pictou County).

STEWART, Donald, d. 3 Apr 1855, age 62, native of Perthshire (North Lochaber Cemetery, Antigonish County).

STEWART, James, d. 17 June 1874, age 72, native of Perthshire (North Lochaber Cemetery, Antigonish County).

STEWART, Peter, d. 21 Apr 1832, age 45, native of Perthshire, came to NS in 1804; his wife Isabella, d. 21 Apr 1866, age 77, native of Inverness-shire, came to NS in 1801 (Creighton Cemetery, Upper Mount Thom, Pictou County).

STUART, James, d. 16 Nov 1857, age 61, native of Perthshire; his wife, Janet STEWART, d. 17 June 1875, age 75 (North Lochaber Cemetery, Antigonish County).

SUTHERLAND, Alexander, d. 20 Dec 1838, age 49, native of Clyne Parish, Sutherlandshire; his wife Margaret, d. 4 May 1882, age 84, native of Kildonan Parish, Sutherlandshire (Pioneer Cemetery, Union Centre, Pictou County).

SUTHERLAND, Alexander, d. 23 Aug 1870, age 88; his wife, Margaret **MUNRO**, d. 12 June 1862, age 85, natives of Clyne Parish, Sutherlandshire (Caledonia Cemetery, Pictou County).

SUTHERLAND, David, Elder, d. 12 Apr 1871, age 72, native of Sutherlandshire; his wife Christy, d. 2 July 1861, age 60 (Millbrook Cemetery, Pictou County).

SUTHERLAND, Donald, Wilkins Grant, d. 5 Jan 1841, age 74, native of Creich Parish, Sutherlandshire, came to NS in 1818 (Lansdowne Cemetery, Pictou County).

SUTHERLAND, Donald, New Lairg, d. 18 May 1848, age 66, native of Lairg Parish, Sutherlandshire, came to NS in 1802; his wife, Isabella **GORDON**, d. 19 Nov 1853, age 66, native of Clyne Parish, Sutherlandshire (Lansdowne Cemetery, Pictou County).

SUTHERLAND, Hugh, Gairloch, d. 28 Mar 1855, age 61, native of Sutherlandshire; his wife Nancy, d. 5 May 1877, age 75 (Millbrook Cemetery, Pictou County).

SUTHERLAND, James, d. 27 Nov 1854, age 78; his wife Jane, d. 4 Apr 1869, age 82, natives of Sutherlandshire (Millbrook Cemetery, Pictou County).

SUTHERLAND, John, d. 1 Sep 1838, age 48, native of Sutherlandshire, came to America in 1833 (Lansdowne Cemetery, Pictou County).

SUTHERLAND, John, d. 29 Sep 1877, age 92, native of Clyne Parish, Sutherlandshire; his wife, Elizabeth **McKAY**, d. 25 Jan 1894, age 91 (Stewart Cemetery, Pictou County).

SUTHERLAND, John's wife, Jane **MacKINTOSH**, d. 3 Jan 1885, age 69, native of Redcastle, Ross-shire (Millbrook Cemetery, Pictou County).

SUTHERLAND, Robert, d. 26 Apr 1843, age 78; his wife, Christy **McDONALD**, d. 27 June 1842, age 72 (Lansdowne Cemetery, Pictou County).

SUTHERLAND, William, d. 21 Nov 1874, age 83, native of Sutherlandshire; his wife, Ann **McDONALD**, d. 13 Mar 1895, age 84, native of Rogart Parish, Sutherlandshire (Lower Middle River Cemetery, Pictou County).

SUTHERLAND, William, d. 30 Nov 1874, age 71, native of Lairg Parish, Sutherlandshire; his wife, Mary **McDONALD**, d. 22 July 1888, age 71 (Lansdowne Cemetery, Pictou County).

SUTHERLAND, William G., M.D, Waterville, d. 30 May 1895, age 83, native of Wich [probably Wick, Caithness]; his wife Eliza Ann, d. 6 Apr 1857, age 31 (Caledonia Cemetery, Pictou County).

TAYLOR, Henry, Esq., d. 15 Jan 1853, age 73, native of Ayrshire (Calvin Presbyterian Church Cemetery, Margaree Harbour, Inverness County).

THOMPSON, Andrew, d. 24 May 1873, age 78, native of Kirkcudbrightshire; his wife Elizabeth, d. 13 May 1870, age 74, native of Caithness (Caledonia Cemetery, Pictou County).

THOMPSON, David, 1781 - 1841; and James Thompson, 1816 - 1856, natives of Dumfries (Presbyterian Church Cemetery, Wallace, Cumberland County).

THOMSON, Robert, d. 12 Oct 1858, age 96; his daughter Marion, d. 11 Nov 1869, age 75, wife of . . . **MAXWELL**. They were natives of Kirkcudbrightshire (Caledonia Cemetery, Pictou County).

URQUHART, Alexander, d. 26 June 1837, age 77; his wife, Catherine Ann **MacKENZIE**, died 16 May 1846, age 83, natives of Ross-shire (Grand River Presbyterian Cemetery, Richmond County)

URQUHART, George, d. 17 Oct 1852, age 50, native of Redcastle, [Ross-shire]; his wife, Marion **FRASER**, d. 2 Jan 1879, age 75 (Pioneer Cemetery, Union Centre, Pictou County).

Verse from headstone of Ellen **SHIELS**, Woodlawn, Halifax County, NS:

> *And here when aged twenty years/ my firstborn's grave was seen;*
> *Next my Euphemia bathed in tears/ was laid at seventeen.*
> *Two Margarets infants side by side/ in Halifax are left,*
> *And John my hope and James my pride/ I'm of them both bereft;*
> *For one a grave, the strangers' hands/ in Demerara made.*
> *The other in Australian lands/ his comrades weeping laid.*

Her husband, Andrew Shiels, erected the stone sometime between 1854 and 1879. He wrote verse under the pseudonym, *Albion*. This inscription is attributed to him. Shiels remarried, by licence dated 15 Aug 1847, Isabella **BLAIR**. The children commemorated on the stone were "the firstborn", Ellen, who died 13 Apr 1837, age 20 (*AR*, 15 Apr 1837); Euphemia, who died 8 Nov 1846 (*NS*, 9 Nov 1846); Margaret Partis, died 13 Nov 1821, age 2 years and 4 months (*FP*, 13 Nov 1821); Margaret, died 1 Jan 1825 (AR, 8 Jan 1825); John, died in Demerara [Guyana] in Oct 1838, age 18 (*AR*, 1 Dec 1838); and James N., died 29 Aug 1853 at Melbourne, Australia, age 21 (*AR*, 7 Jan 1854). Shiels had other children.

SOME PICTOU COUNTY SCOTS SETTLERS IN 1809

Six documents among the Nova Scotia land papers (NSARM, RG 20, Series 'A') offer what amounts to a mini-census of parts of Pictou County in 1809. The communities are the Middle River of Pictou, Rogers Hill in the Scotsburn area, Caribou, McLellans Mountain, New Lairg, Bailey Brook and Knoydart. The earliest extant census of the area dates from 1817, eight years later. I estimate that the 929 people here account for about one-eighth of the population of Pictou County at the time.

MIDDLE RIVER OF PICTOU

Here were 41 Scotsmen, 32 wives, and 150 children, 223 in all. The first figure below is the number of years the man had been in Nova Scotia, while the second figure is the number of dependent children he had. I have not assumed the existence of a wife for those men shown with no children. Doubtless a few had a wife but no children, whilst a few of the men with children may have been widowers. These factors would tend to cancel one another out statistically in so small a listing. Three sons of Robert and Jean (Kirkpatrick) Braiden of Dumfries who came out in the *Lovely Nellie* in 1775 are indicated by an asterisk (*).

B[E]ATEN, John 7/3
*BRA[Y]DEN, David 34/7
*BRA[Y]DEN, James 34/5
*BRA[Y[DEN, William 34/4
CAMERON, William 8/7
COLLY, John 24/6
CROCKET, William 34/4
FERGUSON, David 8/1
FRASER, Alexander 8/9
FRASER, William 8/2
GORDEN, Robert 6/7
GRANT, Catherine 8/2
HORN, Alexander 8/4
KIRK, William 25/5
McBANE, Mary 4/5
McDONALD, John 4/1
McDONALD, Paul 7/0
McDONALD, Philip 4/6
McDONALD, Robert 7/0
McGILVERY, Malcolm 3/8
McKAY, George 35/5

McKAY, John 3/5
McKAY, William 7/0
McKENZIE, Alexander 6/4
McKENZIE, Alexander, 2nd, 4/0
McKENZIE, Alexander 4/0
McKENZIE, John 4/3
McKENZIE, Kenneth 4/3
McKENZIE, Murdoch 4/0
MacLEAN, Alexander 25/4
McLEAN, Roderick 6/0
McLEOD, George 6/0
McLEOD, John 6/4
McLEOD, Kenneth 8/0
McPHERSON, Donald 4/6
MATTHEWSON, Findley 7/0
MATTHEWSON, Robert 8/3
MILLER, Lawrence 34/7
MURRAY, Alexander 6/0
REID, George 8/2
ROSS, Donald 35/11
ROSS, Walter 6/5
SUTHERLAND, John 7/2.

ROGERS HILL, WEST RIVER

There were 23 Scotsmen, 18 wives, and 61 children at Rogers Hill, 102 in total. The first figure below is the number of years the man had been in Nova Scotia, while the second figure is the number of his dependent children. For present purposes, I have not assumed the existence of a wife for those men shown with no children. Doubtless some men had a wife but no children, whilst a few of the men with children may have been widowers. These factors would tend to balance one another out statistically in such a small listing. All 23 families were present in the census of 1817. Four men marked with an asterisk (*) came out in August 1803.

CAMPBELL, Donald 6/0	McINTOSH, Hugh 2nd 6/unm.	McLOUD, John 3/4
CAMPBELL, Hugh 6/1	McINTOSH, Robert 6/8	*MONROW, Andrew 6/2
CAMPBELL, John 6/5	McINTOSH, William 7/7	MURRAY, Alexander 6/3
*GORDEN, Alexander 6/0	McKAY, Alexander 7/4	MURRAY, Alexander 7/unm.
GORDEN, John 6/4	McKENZIE, Roderick 6/7	MURRAY, Donald 6/unm
*GUNN, William 6/2	McLOUD, Donald 3/1	MURRAY, Donald 6/3
McINTOSH, Hugh 1st 7/unm.	McLOUD, Hugh 3/unm.	MURRAY, John 6/5
*STEWART, Murdock 6/3	SUTHERLAND, Alexander 6/2	

CARIBOU

These 36 Scottish Protestant men at Caribou, Pictou County, came out a few years before. There were 34 wives and 106 children, making a total of 176 persons. The total number in each family shown after the name. The last man listed was probably Edward STEWART.

BONE, Robert 6	McDONALD, Finlay 5	McLEOD, Kenneth 7
CAMERON, Donald 1	McDONALD, John 9	McLEOD, William 5
CAMERON, Ewen 2	McDONALD, Norman 5	McLISE, Angus 7
CAMPBELL, John 6	McFARLAN, John 8	McPHEE, John 2
GRAHAM, William 5	McINTOSH, Donald 8	MATHIESON, William 2
LOGAN, James 2	McKENZIE, John 3	MORRISON, Angus 7
LOGAN, John 1	McKENZIE, Murdoch 4	MORRISON, Donald 4
LOGAN, Robert 5	McKENZIE, Roderick 3	MORRISON, Murdoch 8
McANGUS, Henry 7	McLEOD, Finlay 3	MUNRO, Duncan 8
McCONICKLE, James 8	McLEOD, John 6	MURDOCH, David 8
McDONALD, Donald 6	McLEOD, John 4	MURRAY, Donald 4
McDONALD, Ewen 2	McLEOD, John 3	STUDWARD, Edward 2

McLELLANS MOUNTAIN, EAST RIVER

In this list, 42 Scotsmen, 2 Scotswomen, 1 Irishman (Delaney), 38 wives, and 185 children, 268 souls altogether, appear. The first figure below is the number of years the man had been in Nova Scotia, while the second figure is the number of dependent children he had. For present purposes, I have not presumed the existence of a wife for those men shown with no children. Doubtless a few had a wife but no children, whilst a few of the men with children may have been widowers. These factors would tend to balance one another out statistically in so small a listing.

CAMERON, Alexander 8/6	FRASER, Hugh 8/0	McDONALD, Finlay, Jr. 8/5
CAMERON, Donald 8/5	FRASER, James 6/8	McGRATH, John 7/5
CAMERON, Hugh 8/5	FRASER, James 8/7	McGREGOR, George 8/8
CAMERON, James 8/3	FRASER, John 8/6	McINTOSH, Andrew 7/0
CAMERON, Thomas 8/7	FRASER, John 8/5	McINTOSH, Donald 8/3
CAMPBELL, Alexander 4/4	FRASER, Mary 7/0	McKAY, John (piper) 4/7
DELANEY, John 15/3	FRASER, Sophiah 7/5	McKENZIE, Donald 8/6
FRASER, Alexander 6/7	FRASER, William Og 25/1	McLEAN, Donald 8/1
FRASER Alexander, 8/3	GRANT, Hugh 6/2	McLEAN, William 8/1
FRASER, Alexander 25/0	McBANE, John 8/6	McLELLAN, John 8/4
FRASER, Alexander 8/8	McDONALD, Alexander 7/0	McLELLAN, Murdoch 8/4
FRASER, Alexander 8/5	McDONALD, Donald 7/6	McPHERSON, Donald 7/6

FRASER, Angus 7/3	McDONALD, Donald, Jr. 4/1	MATTHEWSON, John 8/5
FRASER, Donald 8/7	McDONALD, Duncan 6/4	STEWART, Donald 7/0
FRASER, Donald 8/1	McDONALD, Findlay 8/6	STEWART, Peter 7/6

NEW LAIRG, MIDDLE RIVER, ON STEWIACKE ROAD

Some 131 people – 27 Scotsmen, 23 women and 81 children – make up this list. The first figure below is the number of years the man had been in Nova Scotia, while the second figure is the number of dependent children he had. For present purposes, I have not presumed the existence of a wife for those men shown with no children. A few were indicated as being unmarried. Doubtless others were newly married and had a wife but not yet a child, whilst a few of the men with children may have been widowers. These factors would tend to balance one another out statistically in so small a listing.

BALFOUR, Duncan, 8/unm.	McKINZIE, Donald 6/6	MUR[RA]Y, Donald 6/2
BALFOUR, William 8/3	McKINZIE, John 6/3	MUR[RA]Y, George 6/3
CAMPBELL, Robert 7/4	McLEAN, Donald 6/6	ROSS, Donald 7/3
DOUGLASS, Donald 6/6	McLEAN, heirs of Donald 0/1	SUTHERLAND, Alexander 7/2
FRASER, Alexander 34/8	McLOUD, Angus 6/4	SUTHERLAND, Angus, 7/unm.
GARDEN, James 7/3	McLOUD, John 6/1	SUTHERLAND, Donald 7/1
GUN[N], Alexander 7/5	MATTHEWSON, Isabella, widow 1/7	
McDONALD, Duncan 4/unm.	MATTHEWSON, John, 7/unm.	SUTHERLAND, Donald 1½/1
McDONALD, Robert 7/0	MATTHEWSON, Walter 6/6	SUTHERLAND, Donald 7/0
McKINZIE, Alexander 6/2	MUNROW, Donald 6/1	SUTHERLAND, George 6/3

KNOYDART and BAILEY BROOK

Rory McDonald's name heads a list of Scots who had settled in Pictou, at either Knoydart or at Bailey Brook, on the Gulf Shore, between 1784 and 1802. Although this list does not give the numbers in the families, it does state where in Scotland people had come from, and the year in which they had emigrated, two useful pieces of information for the genealogist.

Settled at **Knoydart**, now in Antigonish County:

GILLIES, William, from Arisaig, emigrated in 1791

McACHRAN, Mary, widow of John, from Arisaig, emigrated in 1791

McDONALD, Allan, from Knoydart, emigrated in 1784 when he was 7 yrs. old, with his father who died 1794

McDONALD, Archibald, from Moidart, emigrated in 1791

McDONALD, Rory, Angus, Jr., Lachlan and Ronald, from Arisaig, emigrated in 1791

McGILLIVRAY, Angus, Alexander, Jr., and Andrew, from Arisaig, emigrated in 1791

Settled at **Bailey Brook**, Pictou County:

McDONALD, Angus, Sr. and Alexander, from Moidart, emigrated in 1791

McDONALD, John and Evan (John's son), from Arisaig, emigrated in 1791

McDONALD, Katherine (widow of John) and Roderick Jr., from Moidart, emigrated in 1791

McDONALD, Roderick Sr., from Knoydart, emigrated in 1790

McDOUGALD, Evan, from Ardnamurchan, emigrated in 1802

McGILLIVRAY, Angus Jr., from Ardnamurchan, emigrated in 1802

McGILLIVRAY, Donald, from Ardnamurchan, emigrated in 1791

McGILLIVRAY, John Sr., from Arisaig, emigrated in 1790

McGILLIVRAY, John, Sr., and Jr., Alexander, Jr., and Evan, from Ardnamurchan, emigrated in 1790

McGILLIVRAY, Katherine, widow of William, emigrated in 1791

McKINNON, Angus Sr. and Jr., from Cannich, emigrated in 1791

McLEAN, Donald, from Moidart, emigrated in 1791

McLELLAN, Archibald, from Uist, emigrated in 1802

SMITH, Alexander, from Moidart, emigrated in 1791

Geography Note: Knoydart, Moidart, Ardnamurchan and Arisaig are the names of peninsulas in western Scotland. Cannich is both a town and a glen. There is also a town of Arisaig on the peninsula of the same name.

Ardnamurchan (*Àird-na-mòir-chinn*) = height over the great headland; (*chinn* from *caenn*); this is a peninsula in Argyllshire, southwest of Moidart, facing the Isle of Coll.

Arisaig (*Aros + aig*) = bay of the house. (*aig* from *aik,* from Norse *-vik*); a town on Morar Peninsula.

Badenoch; an area near Kingussie in the headwaters of the River Spey in Inverness-shire.

Glen Garry; valley of the River Garry in northern Perthshire and Inverness-shire.

Kintyre; a peninsula in south-western Argyllshire between the Isles of Arran and Islay in the Irish Sea.

Knapdale; the northern part of the long peninsula that becomes Kintyre south of Tarbert.

Knoydart (*Cnut + ort*) = Canute's fjord; a peninsula between Loch Houen and Loch Nevis, facing the Isle of Skye across the Sound of Sleat.

Lairg (*learg*) = a plain, or a beaten path; a place in Sutherlandshire.

Lochaber; area near Ben Nevis, north-east of Loch Linnhe; parish of Kilmonivaig (see map, p. 16).

Moidart/Moydart (*modd + ort*) = muddy fjord (not *magh + dairt* = field of the heifer); a district in Inverness-shire between Loch Shiel and the Sound of Arisaig.

Morar; a peninsula surrounding Loch Morar, and facing the isles of Rhum and Eigg.

Strathspey; the valley of the River Spey in the Highlands.

Uist (*i-vist*) = in-dwelling, or abode; north and south Uist form part of the Hebrides chain.

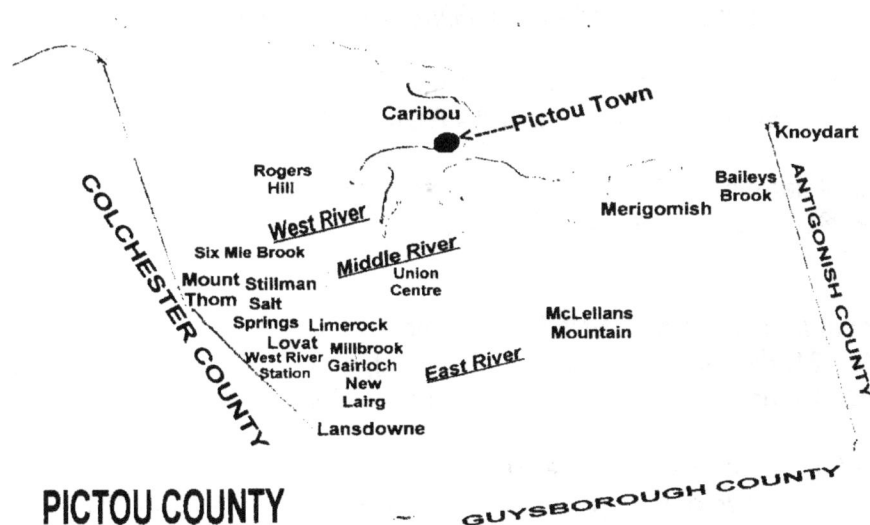

PICTOU COUNTY

SCOTS DESERTERS FROM SHIPS, 1812-1813

By the summer of 1812, the British had been at war with France, with brief respite, since February 1793. Whatever the sentiments of their rulers, many of Britannia's subjects were war weary. The outbreak of war with the United States in mid-June 1812 added to the feeling that peace would remain elusive. As morale fell, the number of desertions rose. In St. John's, Newfoundland, the Royal Navy was the largest loser in that regard. The following newspaper notices were placed by authorities or employers seeking to recapture deserters of one kind or another. Men born in Scotland were not immune to the wish to escape their engagements. In a region where many families had an ancestor who "jumped ship", these men and others like them married and had families, perhaps among them some reader's ancestor.

Lt-Col. **HALY**, Nova Scotia Regt., offered a reward for the apprehension of a deserter named
John **HOWARD**, 19, a weaver by trade, native of Perth, Scotland. He had a fresh complexion, hazel eyes and brown hair - *RGNA*, 9 July 1812.

Deserted the sloop *Muros*, J. **ABERDOUR**, Commander, two men born in Scotland:
Lauchlan **McQUARRIE**, 30, carpenter, and Peter **MONNOW** [Monro?], 26, carpenter - *RGNA*, 26 Nov 1812.

Deserted HMS *Hazard,* John **COOKESLEY**, Commander, on 27 Dec 1812:
John **McKENNAN**, quarter gunner, native of Campbeltown [Argyllshire], Scotland - *RGNA*, 4 Feb 1813.

Deserted HMS *Hazard,* John **COOKESLEY**, Commander, on 5 March 1813:
James **STOBIE**, 24, native of Scotland, brought up at sea - *RGNA*, 11 Mar 1813.

Deserted the service of **STUART & RENNIE** a few days before:
Donald **McCLEVER**, 23, and Dougald **MATHIESON**, 23, natives of Scotland, and seamen in the brig *Cossack* - *RGNA*, 9 June 1813.

Deserted HMS *Dryad*, Capt. Edward **GALWAY**:
William **CREAGGY**, 39, native of Scotland - *RGNA*, 10 June 1813.

Deserted HM schooner *Pike*, Lt. D. **BUCHAN**, Commander, on 9 June 1813:
John **WILEY**, able seaman, native of Scotland - *RGNA*, 16 June 1813.

Deserted the service of James **JOHNSTONE**, cabinetmaker:
Thomas **ROBERTSON**, 22, native of Scotland; "seen lurking about Torbey on Sunday, the 6th" - *RGNA*, 10 Aug 1813.

Deserted HMS *Crescent*, Lt. Thomas **BENNETT**, Commander:
Alexander **SMITH**, 21, native of Port Patrick, Scotland, and
John **FLEMMING**, 19, native of Greenock, Scotland - *RGNA*, 19 Aug 1813.

Deserted HMS *Talbot* at St. John's, NL, 26 Aug 1813:
Douglas **WILKIE**, 20, native of Campbeltown, Scotland - *RGNA*, 23 Sep 1813.

THE NORTH BRITISH SOCIETY, HALIFAX, NOVA SCOTIA, 1768 - 1782

Out of concern for their fellow-countrymen who might fall on hard times in the new world, a small group of men, natives of Scotland, formed the North British Society of Halifax on 26 March 1768. Where possible, I have added a death or burial date from contemporary sources such as church registers, newspapers and headstones. For more information, you are referred to James S. MacDonald's *Annals of the North British Society of Halifax, Nova Scotia, 1768 - 1893* (Halifax, 1894).

Founding Group in 1768

CLARK, James [died 2 Feb 1777, age 46]   McCRAE, John [John MacCRA died in 1788]
FRASER, John   McLENNAN, Thomas
GEDDES, John   McLENNAN, William
GILLESPIE, John [died 19 June 1772, age 52] MORRISON, Daniel
HARKNESS, Walter   SCOTT, William
KILLO, Robert [died 29 Dec 1797, age 67]   TAYLOR, John [buried 19 Apr 1776]
LUKE, William   THOMSON, James

Adhered 1769 - 1773

1769: George ELLIOTT   James SUTHERLAND
1770: Peter McNAB [died 3 Nov 1799, age 64]
1771: John PATTERSON [died 5 Aug 1772]
1773: Robert GILLESPIE [a doctor, buried 11 Dec 1788, age 45]

Adhered 1774

ALLAN, William [died 19 May 1785, age 67]   CAMPBELL, Robert [died 31 Jan 1775, age 57]
McDONALD, Major A., 59th Regt.   McGOWAN, Robert [died 12 Nov 1779 at Truro]
ROSS, Alexander [died 27 Mar 1791, age 62]   THOMPSON, Alexander [returned to Scotland]

Adhered 1777

BLACK, James   BOWIE, William
BRYMER, Alexander, from Glasgow   DICKSON, James
HOWATT, John   MILLER, John
RATRIE, John

Adhered 1778

HYNDMAN, Lt. M., HMS *Revenge*   HOGG, William

Adhered 1779

NISBET, Robert [died 23 Jan 1783, age 60]

Adhered 1780

ADAMS, Charles [died 15 June 1794, age 64]   McGILL, Andrew
McMASTER, Patrick [died 23 Dec 1797, drowned in the Bay of Fundy]
THOMPSON, Andrew [dead by 11 Aug 1795]   WALLACE, Michael [died 8 Oct 1831, age 84]

Adhered 1782

ANDERSON, Alexander [died 2 Feb 1833]   BREMNER, John [died 9 Dec 1806, age 53]
BURNS, Robert   CATER, William [dead by 12 Aug 1790]
COPELAND, Alexander   DECHMAN, James [died 19 July 1829, age 86]
GRANT, George [died 21 Feb 1809, age 61]   GREEN, Alexander
HALLIBURTON, Dr. John [died 11 July 1808]   HOGG, William [died 19 Apr 1811, age 70]
KIDSTON, Richard [died 17 June 1816]   SHAW, William
SMITH, George [died 17 May 1795]   STRACHAN, James
VEITCH, James [died 13 Oct 1811, age 67]

ASSISTING THE TRANSIENT POOR IN NOVA SCOTIA

Nova Scotia followed British practice and placed responsibility for the care of the poor in the hands of each community.[1] In the British Isles a network of civil or ecclesiastical parishes with recognized boundaries had existed for centuries. In such an ancient framework the community was virtually synonymous with the parish.

The settlement of Nova Scotia by any number of people of British origins was barely seventy years old in 1819, and the religious diversity of the colonial population was not congenial to a system of local administration along the line of Anglican parishes. The duty of assisting the poor was therefore placed on each municipal unit, either a township (until 1859) or, failing that, a county. A group known as the Commissioners, or Overseers, of the Poor, administered the aid.

Under a variety of circumstances the township or its poor commissioners were entitled to claim reimbursement from the central provincial government in Halifax for their outlays on behalf of needy persons who were not customary inhabitants of the particular township or county, i.e., transient poor. To ensure the legitimacy of claims for reimbursement, the poor commissioners presented an affidavit taken from the person(s) assisted. In this document the recipient of aid attested to their neediness and the circumstances which led to their being in need of help.

Many of the transient poor were immigrants. They often indicate their birthplaces or state their ages in their affidavits, important information concerning a class of people whose social status and economic condition rarely permitted them to be found as testators of wills or conveyors of real estate. These were the poor whose circumstances had more or less suddenly become a good deal worse than they had been. The colonial poor left very little first-hand documentary evidence of their sufferings.[2] This collection represents a rare exception to that regrettable silence in the record.

The resulting body of documents is replete with human drama: shipwrecked immigrants, families in search of members, people taken ill while en route to a destination far distant from where they wound up, old soldiers fallen on hard times, and much more.

Being able to sign one's name does not necessarily establish that one was literate to any extent. On the other hand, having to make one's mark (X) is a much stronger indicator of illiteracy. Just under seventy percent of the people giving affidavits marked rather than signed their names. A little over one quarter signed, more or less legibly. The remainder seem to have done neither and are marked (?), or their details were given in by third parties.

As a sample of the woes besetting transient folk, the records held in the Nova Scotia Archives and Records Management files supply as good and representative snapshot as any other documents of that time and place. This selection concerning Scots people is part of a larger manuscript which I have compiled on the subject. The cases cited in this small collection are all to be found in NSARM, RG 5, Series 'P'. At the end of each entry the volume and document numbers are given.

---

[1] *Nova Scotia Statutes*, 3 Geo 3rd , cap.7 [1763], "An Act to Enable the Inhabitants of the Several Townships within the Province to Maintain their Poor."

[2] Judith Fingard, "The Winter's Tale: the Seasonal Contours of Pre-Industrial Poverty in British North America, 1815 - 1860," *Canadian Historical Papers*. (Canadian Historical Association, 1974), p. 73.

BENNETT, Anne, Pictou Township, 26 May 1847 (X)
Born in Caithness-shire, Scotland, wife of John Bennett, born in Portsmouth, England. They married about three years ago and lived at Dartmouth, Cole Harbour, and Windsor. Five months ago her husband left for Canada [i.e., Québec and Ontario] to seek work, but has sent no word. She came to Pictou to get help from her husband's relatives. She bore a child a few days previously, but it died.[1] (Vol. 84 #2)

BOYD, John, Pictou Township, 9 June 1847 (signs)
Born in 'the Brig of Johnstone near the City of Glasgow, Scotland' [i.e., burgh of Johnstone, not far from Paisley]. He came to Nova Scotia seven years before. He is ruptured and seeks his passage home to his relations. (Vol. 84 #2)

BRISBANE, Jean, Pictou Township, 6 Jan 1843 (X)
Born in Paisley High Church, Renfrewshire, Scotland, age 29. Came in the barque *Eagle*, Captain Morton, from Greenock to Pictou last September with three children. Her husband, Robert Brisbane, is in London. She now has a fourth child age three weeks. (Vol. 82 #99)

Hugh **BLACK** from Paisley, also came in the *Eagle* with his wife and five children. (signs his name, 15 Feb 1843). List of paupers from High Church Paisley sent to Halifax by 14 Mar 1843: Jean Brisbane 29, William 7, Robert 6, Margaret 3, infant 2 mos.; Mrs. Black 34; her children: Angus 12, Margaret 10, James 6, Hugh 3, William 10 months. (Vol. 82 #99)

BROWN, Robert, mariner, Pictou Township, 19 Oct 1840 (signs)
Born in the Parish of Lochwalt, Gallowshire, Scotland [i.e., Gallowayshire], age 18. He came to Pictou last May in the ship *Isabella*, from Glasgow, Alexander **THOMSON**, master. He wants to take the ship *Albert* home. Given £5 passage money. (Vol. 81 #65C)

CAMPBELL, William, Pictou Township, 2 July 1860 (X)
Born in Greenock, Scotland, sailor, age 25. He was six years in Nova Scotia. (Vol. 88 #54)

DYER, Ann, widow of Anthony, Albion Mines, 15 Feb 1842 (X)
Born in Ayrshire, Scotland, age 45. She and her husband emigrated to NS five years ago. He was a labourer at Albion Mines. He left over two years ago and has not been heard from. He had been a seafarer before they emigrated. Dyer had four children: Margaret, 13; Barbara, 8; Agnes, 6; and William, 4. (Vol. 81 #114)

FRASER, Margaret, Pictou Township,19 June 1847 (signs)
Born in Ross-shire, Scotland. She arrived twelve years ago with her husband, Alexander, who was killed accidentally three years ago.[2] (Vol. 84 #2)

GEDDIES, Ann, Egerton Township, 5 Dec 1844 (X)
Born in the town of Inverness, Scotland, age 60. She was the widow of John Geddies who died in Scotland over twenty years before. She emigrated to Nova Scotia with her only daughter eight years ago, and has lived three years near Albion Mines. (Vol. 82 #55)

---

[1] Samuel **BENNETT**, age 3 weeks, buried St. James, Pictou.

[2] Alexander **FRASER** died of a fall (Inquest held 14 Jan 1845, Egerton Township, Pictou County).

GIBBS, Joseph, Windsor, 1 Mar 1841 (X)
Born in Aberdeenshire, Scotland, age 64.[1] He joined the 92nd Regiment of Foot (Gordon Highlanders) and served with the Duke of York in Holland, and in the Royal Navy '74' *Poictiers*, Captain **BERESFORD**. He had been discharged at Halifax. (Vol. 81 #81)

GOLLAN, Catharine, Pictou Township, 18 Sep 1856 (X)
Born in Scotland. She came out to Pictou last year with her husband William Gollan who went to Canada the following month. She and her children wish to join him there. (Vol. 87 #13)

GRANT, James, labourer, Pictou Township, 15 Aug 1840 (signs)   Born in Calder Parish, Nairnshire, Scotland, age 41. He came here six years ago. He married Janet fifteen years ago. They have six children: Ann, David, Alexander, Robert Shaw, Jean, and Isabella McCulloch. The eldest, Ann, is deranged, while David is partially so. Grant wants to be sent to Gore District, Upper Canada. He was given £10 to go as far as Québec.   (Vol. 81 #65A)

GUNN, Catherine, Pictou Township, 26 Aug 1853 (X)
Born in the Isle of Skye, Scotland, age 34. She came to Prince Edward Island thirteen years since, and to Pictou two years ago. She married in PE in 1842 to Donald Gunn, labourer, by whom she has five children. Gunn left them two weeks ago. (Vol. 85 #119)

GUNN, Christian, Egerton Township, 21 Apr 1842 (X)
Born in Sutherlandshire, Scotland, age 25. She came to Pictou in Sep 1841. Her father lives in Upper Canada and she has relations in Nova Scotia. (Vol. 82 #99)

HALLIDAY, James, yeoman, Pictou Township, 17 Aug 1840 (signs)
Born in Ersdelmoor Parish,[2] Dumfries-shire, Scotland, age 66. His son Andrew is about 30. The two of them have lived in Pictou since 1828. He has asthma and the son 'is an Ideot and a cripple.' (Vol. 81 #65B)

Halliday appears again, 31 Dec 1841, says that his son Andrew is 32 years old. (Vol. 81 #92)

HUNTER, Flora, Pictou Township, 18 Feb 1852 (X)
Born in the Parish of Lochbroom, Ross-shire, Scotland, age 72.[3] She married the late James Hunter on 4 Feb 1818 and had by him six children, of whom three survive. Only one, Mary, age 30, lives with her.   (Vol. 85 #78)

HYMEN, Euphemia, Albion Mines, 31 Jan 1853 (X)
Born in Argyllshire, Scotland. She came to Pictou in May 1847 with her husband Archibald (died March 1852) and one child. Archibald had worked in the mines. Euphemia had 'children'.   (Vol. 85 #105)

---

[1] **GIBBS** was buried 18 Mar 1845 at Christ Church, Windsor, at a reputed age of 75.

[2] Eskdalemuir Parish intended.

[3] If Flora was 72 in 1852, she would have been 38 when she married in 1818. If she had six children in individual births, her stated age in 1852 would appear to be a bit exaggerated

LAWSON, John, Egerton Township, 3 Jan 1856 (X)
Born in Scotland, age 26. Five years ago he went to Philadelphia and in Dec 1854 he came to Albion Mines, Nova Scotia. He became ill.   (Vol. 87 #5)

LONGWILL, John, Egerton Township, 15 June 1842 (signs)
Born in Scotland. He was a joiner who came to St. Mary's, Nova Scotia, in 1840 with his family. On 3 June he journeyed to Egerton en route to Halifax to seek work. Two of his children cannot proceed. (Vol. 82 #99)

LOVEY, William, Egerton Township, 25 Oct 1843 (signs)
Born at Fort George, Inverness-shire, Scotland, age 32. He went to Merigomish, Nova Scotia, in 1838 and later that year married Catherine **MORRISON**. They have three sons: John, Donald, and Peter. (Vol. 82 #99)

McCORCADALE, Catherine, Western Division, Maxwellton, Pictou County, 5 July 1856 (X)
Born in the Parish of Bolesque,[1] Inverness-shire, Scotland, age 85 to 87. She was the wife of James McCorcadale, who emigrated forty-nine years ago. She had been married sixteen years when her husband left Nova Scotia. (Vol. 87 #36)

McCOUSH, Christy, Pictou Township, 25 Oct 1841 (X)
Born in the Isle of Coll, Argyleshire, Scotland, wife of Donald. She came to Cape Breton in Oct 1840 with an infant child. Two weeks ago her husband was sentenced to six months in gaol. (Vol. 81 #92)

McDONALD, Angus, St. Croix, 3 Apr 1857 (X)
Born in Inverness-shire, Scotland, age 29. He came to Canada, then to Nova Scotia,[2] where he worked on the railroad until he lost his arm while blasting a rock. He has a wife and two children. (Vol. 87 #98)

McDONALD, Duncan, Egerton Township, 2 Aug 1842 (signs)
A blacksmith from Inverness-shire, Scotland. He came to Pictou in August 1841. He has dropsy. He came to Egerton in May 1842.   (Vol. 82 #99)

McDONALD, Margaret, Pictou Township, 22 Sep 1841 (X)
Born in Ayr Parish, Scotland. She came to Pictou on 1 Aug with her husband William and their infant son, now ten months old. Three weeks after their arrival, William died of typhus fever. (Vol. 81 #92)

MacGILVRAY, Jane, Malignant Cove, 21 Jan 1858 (X)
Born in Scotland. She came out thirty-two years ago with her brother Ronald and lived with him until last 19 December. He was her only relative in Nova Scotia.   (Vol. 87 #90)

---

[1] Properly Boleskine Parish.

[2] Until 1867 Nova Scotia was not part of 'Canada', a term then applicable to the future provinces of Ontario and Québec.

McINTOSH, James, Pictou Township, 1 Jan 1845 (X)
On behalf of Catherine **McKAY**, 'an old woman . . . living with the deponent' and very old, lame, infirm and helpless. She was born in Scotland and does not understand English.(Vol. 82 #24)

McISAAC, Mary, Judique, 1 Feb 1856 (?)
Born in the Isle of Canna in the Hebrides, Scotland. She emigrated in the ship *Middleton* from Liverpool early last summer with her husband and six children. They were forty days on their way to Saint John, New Brunswick. Two days from land her eldest child, a daughter age 15, died. She was left with four daughters, the youngest ten months old, and her husband in the hospital. She came to Cape Breton on 14 Nov 1855.   (Vol. 86 #51)

McKAY, Catherine, Pictou Township, 26 May 1845 (X)
Born in Sutherlandshire, Scotland. She came to Nova Scotia in 1813 and lived at Rogers Hill for three years at Hugh **CAMPBELL**'s house. Has worked for others since.   (Vol. 83 #8)

McKAY, John, New Lairg, Egerton Township, Pictou County, 16 Jan 1846 (X)
Born in the Parish of Rogart, Sutherlandshire, Scotland, age 21.   (Vol. 83 #63)

McKAY, Rachel, Pictou Township, 12 Jan 1847 (X)
Born in the Isle of Muck, Scotland. She emigrated fifteen months ago, but two months ago became sick.   (Vol. 83 #185)

McKELLAR, Archibald, Pictou Township. 1 Feb 1843 (signs)
Born in Argyllshire, Scotland. He arrived in Newfoundland last May but found no work, so he went to Prince Edward Island. Last September he came to Pictou.   (Vol. 82 #99)

McKENZIE, Alexander, Pictou Township, 31 Mar 1843 (X)
Born in Sutherlandshire, Scotland. He emigrated in the spring of 1840 in the brig *Demon* with his wife and five small children.   (Vol. 82 #99)

McKENZIE, Ann, Pictou Township, 30 Dec 1856 (X)
Born in Inverness, Scotland. Emigrated when young.   (Vol. 87 #17)

McKENZIE, Elizabeth, Pictou Township, 12 Jan 1852 (X)
Born in Scotland, wife of Malcolm McKenzie, a mariner. They have two sons, three daughters, all but the youngest born in Scotland. The youngest was born in Nova Scotia. Malcolm left for Eastport, Maine, in Nov 1850, then to Saint John, New Brunswick, and then sailed for Britain. She has heard that he is now back in Saint John.   (Vol. 85 #66)

McLEAN, Norman, Egerton Township, 21 Apr 1851 (X)
Born in Scotland, age 15. He has been a seaman for the past year and a half. (Vol. 85 #54)

McLEOD, Donald, Pictou Township, 30 Jan 1857 (X)
Born in Scotland. He came to Pictou with his wife and five children last year.   (Vol. 87 #30)

McLEOD, Nancy, Pictou Township, 5 Nov 1855 (X)
Born at Loch Broom, Ross-shire, Scotland, age 60.   (Vol. 86 #72)

McLEOD, Nancy, Pictou Township, 13 Feb 1857 (X)
Born in Inverness-shire, Scotland. She emigrated to Pictou thirty years before. (Vol. 87 #85)

McMILLAN, John, Pictou Township, 15 Dec 1845 (X)
Born in Inverness-shire, Scotland. He came out seven years ago to join his father in the back settlement of Knoydart. Four or five months ago he went to Pictou to work in the shipyard. He has typhus.   (Vol. 83 #191)

McNIEL, Alexander, St. Andrews, Sydney County,[1] 20 Feb 1854 (X)
Born in the Isle of Skye, Scotland, age ca. 99. Discharged from the Royal Navy in 1811 after several years service, and then emigrated to Nova Scotia.   (Vol. 86 #12)

McPHERSON, Isabella, Pictou Township, 1 Nov 1841 (X)
Born in Loth Parish, Sutherlandshire, Scotland. In August she emigrated to Pictou with her husband, James McPherson, six children, and her mother, in the ship *Lady Jane Grey* from Cromarty. Three weeks ago her mother, husband, and eldest child died of typhus fever. The two older children can help themselves, but she and the three youngest ones are destitute. (Vol. 81 #92)

McQUARRIE, Archibald, near Judique, 14 Jan 1857 (signs)
Born in Scotland. He left Glasgow on 4 July 1855 for Montréal. He was on the Great Lakes, then came to Cape Breton in Dec 1855 and has been taken ill.   (Vol. 87 #25)

MARWICK, Hugh, Pictou Township, 10 Dec 1860 (X)
Born in the Orkney Islands, Scotland, shoemaker, age 60. He emigrated fifteen years ago. (Vol. 88 #61)

MATHESON, Hugh, Pictou Township, 30 Aug 1842 (signs)
Born in Sutherlandshire, Scotland. He and his family of five are en route to Upper Canada [Ontario].   (Vol. 82 #99)

MATHESON, William, Pictou Township, 8 July 1844 (X)
Born in Sutherlandshire, Scotland. He emigrated two years ago with his wife and five children. He fell ill about four months since.   (Vol. 82 #31)

MORISON, Philip, New Glasgow, 30 July 1846 (signs)
Born in Renfrewshire, Scotland, blacksmith, age 22. He came to Cape Breton about four years ago. On 13 July he landed at Egerton Township. He fractured his leg.   (Vol. 83 #193)

REDPATH, Elizabeth, Pictou Township, 3 July 1850 (X)
Born in Dingwall, Ross-shire, Scotland, age 53. She emigrated to Nova Scotia in 1833, and was sent to Halifax.   (Vol. 87 #85)
She appears again in Pictou Township, 2 Jan 1858. This time she states arriving in Nova Scotia on 14 June 1850, and has a broken arm.   (Vol. 85 #39)

---

[1] By Act of the Legislature (Statute 26 Victoria, Cap. XXXVII) Sydney County was renamed Antigonish County, 1863.

ROBERTSON, Maria, Albion Mines, Egerton Township, 31 Jan 1853 (X)
Born in Lanarkshire, Scotland, she came to Pictou on May 1848 with her husband John and a young child. John worked at the Mines until his death in March 1851. She has 'children'. (Vol. 85 #105)

ROBERTSON, Robert, Egerton Township, 16 Feb 1842 (signs)
Born in the Parish of Logwraith,[2] Perthshire, Scotland, age 62. Emigrated to Halifax in 1819 and worked there thirteen years as a day labourer. In 1833 he moved to Egerton and worked as a day labourer.   (Vol. 81 #114)

ROBINSON, Augusta, Digby Township, 13 Oct 1857 (X)
Born in Ross-shire, Scotland. Her parents took her to Halifax about twenty years ago. She lived there with them until April 1853 when she married George Robinson and moved to St. Louis, Missouri. On 9 Mar 1857 she left for Halifax to visit her parents. Her husband was then en route to California. She was a passenger in the sailboat *Ceres* on 12 March near Hamilton, Upper Canada [Ontario], when a bridge broke down, killing many. When she reached Halifax, she could not find her parents, who were said to be in Digby. She came by stage and boat to Digby, only to find that her parents were not there.   (Vol. 87 #99)

ROSS, John, Pictou Township, 21 June 1855 (signs)
Born in the Parish of Nigg, Ross-shire, Scotland, labourer, age 71.   (Vol. 86 #72)

SMITH, Mary, Albion Mines, Egerton Township, 15 Feb 1842 (X)
Born at Rosemuth, Ross-shire, Scotland, age 72. Forty-five years ago she married John Smith from Kilmarnock. They came with their family to Albion Mines thirteen years ago. John worked nine years in the colliery until he and their only son were killed in an explosion at the coal works. (Vol. 81 #114)

STEWART, Christy, Pictou Township, 23 Sep 1843 (X)
Born in Sutherlandshire, Scotland.   She emigrated to Pictou eight years ago.   (Vol. 82 #99)

URQUHART, Gregor, Pictou Township, 7 Dec 1846 (signs)
Born at Glen Urquhart, Inverness-shire, Scotland. Emigrated eleven years ago. (Vol. 83 #190)

WHITE, Nancy, Pictou Township, 1 May 1852 (X)
Born at Lairg, Sutherlandshire, Scotland, age 75. She married in 1824 at Pictou, John White, a labourer, who died in 1827.   (Vol. 85 #98)
She appears again on 7 May 1853. (Vol. 85 #118)

Not an affidavit from the distressed, but information provided by the Poor Commissioners to verify assistance that they had given the recipients, and for which they wished to be reimbursed:

Petition of distressed Scots settlers in the south side of St. George's Channel, four miles from the sea, in Cape Breton Island, 26 Jan 1833. They ask for provisions, as their crops have become mildewed. Five of the eighteen petitioners signed: Neill and Norman **McPHAIL**, Duncan **NICHOLSON**, Alexander and Robert **SCHERLAND** [Sutherland?]. The thirteen others made their marks: Archibald, Hugh, Malcolm and Robert **McDONALD**, widow Ann **McGIGEON**, Angus and Duncan **McKENZIE**, Hugh **McPHAIL**, Neill **McPHERSON**, Angus, Donald and Roderick **MORISON**, and Alexander **STEWARD**.   (Vol. 80 #67)

---

[2] This is Logierait.

PASSENGERS IN THE BRIG *HARMONY*, BARRA TO CAPE BRETON, 1821

A major gap in records for those researching immigration history in the Maritime Provinces before 1850 is the small number of passenger lists that have survived, always assuming that such lists were prepared in the first place. Had the vessels landed in an American port, there would be a fair chance that at least those arriving after 1820 were recorded. Moreover, Scots reaching the United States may have become naturalized citizens, thereby creating a paper trail. Scots settling in British North America were, and remained, British subjects.

One of the many examples where we have the year and the name of the vessel, but no contemporary roster of those on board is the brig *Harmony*. Colin S. MacDonald, writing in the 1930s, tells his readers that a vessel named the *Harmony* brought 350 Scots from the Isle of Barra to Cape Breton Island in 1821.[3] His statement appears to be borne out, at least in the broader sense, by the Customs Return of Immigrants at Sydney for 1821, which reports that 276 Scots were landed at that Cape Breton town.[4]

Careful study of a range of contemporary records reveals that neighbours in Scotland tended to settle near one another in the new homeland. Some clan affiliation can be noticed, but separation along lines of religion and place of origin in Scotland played a greater role. Stewartdale attracted people from the Western Isles, the Mabou area had many Scots from Lochaber, and Grand River, Richmond County, Nova Scotia, drew immigrants from Ross-shire. The islands of Lewis and Tiree were heavily represented among those who settled at Little Narrows in Cape Breton. Boisdale and the facing side of Boularderie Island became the new home of settlers from the isles of Barra, Benbecula and South Uist, all strongly Roman Catholic islands.

Thanks to his prolonged research through documents and interviews with seniors, Rev. A. J. MacMillan prepared accounts of many families of the south-western part of Cape Breton County.[5] His work was used to corroborate, debunk or augment my findings from land records and so forth. One result of the process has been preparation of the list which follows, which is offered as a partial reconstitution of the passenger list of the brig *Harmony* on her voyage of 1821.

Since many of the names are in their Gaelic form, some suggested anglicized versions of these follows the putative partial passenger list. The geographic names BARRAIGH (Barra), BEINN NAME FADHLA (Benbecula), UIBHIST A DEAS (South Uist) are given in their English forms. There are nearly one hundred passengers identified, in some cases because oral tradition within the families names the ship that brought the ancestors to North America. The others are suggested as passengers in that voyage for a variety of reasons, such as land petition information or because other records bracket the date of emigration as 1821, and because of the tendency of Highland Scots to settle among people they already knew from back home, and who shared the same religion, Gaelic dialect and cultural traits. Yet, inclusion here must be regarded as speculative, rather than as proven.

---

[3] Colin S. MacDonald, "Early Highland Emigration to Nova Scotia and Prince Edward Island from 1770 - 1853," *Collections of the Nova Scotia Historical Society*, Vol. XXIII, pp. 41- 48.

[4] Colonial Office 217/152, p. 413.

[5] A. J. MacMillan, *To the Hill of Boisdale* (Sydney: privately published, 1986).

1. Niall **BEATON** of Boisdale area, South Uist
2. Catherine **MacINTYRE**, his wife
3-9. Their children: Alaisdair, Domhnull, Seumas, Iain, Caitriona, Mairead, one other.

10. Domhnull **CURRIE**, of Bruernish, Isle of Barra, born ca. 1789
11. Caitriona **MacPHERSON**, his wife
12-14. Their children: Mor, Seumas, Domhnull

15. Eoghann **GILLIS** of Bruernish, Isle of Barra
16. Ciorsdan **MacMULLIN**, his wife

17. Murchadh **GILLIS** of Kyles [of Barra, on the west side of Eriskay]
18. Catherine **MacDONALD**, his wife
19. Their daughter, Seonaid

20. Ruairidh **JOHNSTON** of Isle of Barra
21. Sarah **SHAW**, his wife, formerly widow **MacVICAR**
22-25. Their children: Iain, b. 1803, Mairaid, Flora, Ruairidh, b. 1813

26. Domhnull **MacINTYRE** of Boisdale area, South Uist, b. 1748
27. Iain **MacINTYRE**, his son, b. 1783
28. Caitriona **WALKER**, Iain's wife
29-31. Their children: Aonghas, b. 1808, Seonaid, Fannie, b. 1821
32. Alasdair **MacINTYRE**, his son, b. 1789 [son of #26]
33. Ciorsden **MacINNIS**, Alasdair's wife
34-37. Their children: Domhnull, Mairi, Tormad Mor, Griogair
38. Aonghas **MacINTYRE**, his son, b. 1799 [son of #26]

39. Angus **MacINTYRE** of the Western Isles, b. ca. 1781
40. Mary **MacAULAY**, his wife
41-47. Their children: Maryann, Catherine, Effie, Neil,
    Hector, b. 1815, Angus, b. 1817, John, b. 1821

48. Ruairidh, son of Iain Og **MacKINNON** and Margaret **MacNEIL** of Barra
49. Gilleasbuig **MacKINNON**, his brother
50. Marion **MacDONALD**, Gilleasbuig's wife
51-54. Their children: Mairi, b. 1816, Eachann, Aonghas, Anna
55. Murchadh **MacKINNON**, Ruairidh's brother
56. Mairi **MacNEIL**, Murchadh's wife
57-58. Their children: Eachann, Alasdair
59. Mairi **MacKINNON**, Ruairidh's sister
60. Anna **MacKINNON**, her sister
61. Mor **MacKINNON**, her sister
62. Caitriona **MacKINNON**, her sister
63. Eachenn Beag **MacKINNON**, her brother
64. Mairi **MacNEIL**, Eachenn's wife

65. Niall **MacKINNON** of Allasdale, Isle of Barra
66. Mairi **MacPHEE**, his wife
67-71. Their children: Caitriona, Raonaid, Gilleasbuig, Domhnull, Alasdair

72. Coinneach **MacLEAN** of Frobost, South Uist
73. Pegi **STEELE**, his wife
74-75. Their sons: Domhnull, b. 1820, Torlach, b. 1821

76. Ruairidh **MacMULLIN** of Bruernish, Isle of Barra, b. 1795
77. Caitriona **MacNEIL**, his wife

78. Iain **MacPHERSON** of Isle of Barra
79. Margaret, his wife
80. Aonghus **MacPHERSON**, his brother
81. Mor **MacINTYRE**, wife of Aonghus
82-83. Their children: Donald, Sarah

84. Iain **NICHOLSON** of Cliad [Cleat], Isle of Barra
85. Anna **MacNEIL**, his wife
86-91. Their children: Iain, b. 1802, Flora, Uilleam, Mairi, Pol, Ciorsdan

92. Niall **NICHOLSON** of Cliad [Cleat], Isle of Barra
93. Mairi, his wife
94-98. Their children: Mairi, Caitriona, Ciordan, Iain, Mor

99. Alasdair **STEELE** of South Uist

ENGLISH NAME EQUIVALENTS

Alasdair = Alexander, Alastair
Aonghas = Angus
Caitríona = Catherine, Kate
Ciorsdan = Christi(a)na, Christie, Kirsten
Coinneach = Kenneth
Domhnull = Donald, Daniel
Donnchadh = Duncan, Donough
Dughall = Dougal(d)
Eachann = Hector
Eoghann = Hugh, Ewen
Gilleasbuig = Archibald
Griogair = Gregory, Gregor
Iain = John, Ian
Máiréad = Margaret

Máiri = Mary
Mór = Sarah, Marion, Morag
Murchadh = Murdock, Morgan
Niall = Neal, Neil
Pegí = Peggy
Pol = Paul
Raonaid = Rachel
Ruairídh = Roderick, Rory
Seonaid - Janet, Joan
Séumas = James, Hamish
Torlach = Charles, Terrence
Tormad = Norman
Uilleam = William

One reason for what seem like peculiar spellings is the fact that the Irish and Scots Gaels used an alphabet of eighteen letters (no letters j, k, q, v, w, x, y or z):

A B C D E F G H I L M N O P R S T U

There are differences in spelling between Irish and Scots Gaelic names, but generally you can recognize one in the other, e.g., Domhnull/Domhnall, Máiréad/Maígréad, Séumas/Séamus, or Ruairídh/Ruaidhrí. A few, such as Torlach/Toirdealbhach require more care. By putting *mac* (son of) before male names, you discover surname meanings, e.g., MacNeall = son of Neal, or MacEachann = son of Hector.

THE *WILLIAM TELL*, 1817

In the summer of 1817 a party of newly-landed Scots petitioned the government for relief and assistance.[1] Thirty-four people signed the document, all but one of whom had traveled in the same (unnamed) vessel. The 94 people in the party had come to Pictou that day – 31 July – apparently in poor circumstances. Martell lists no arrivals in Pictou that year, remarking merely that "although no specific records were found for Pictou in 1817, it is known that immigrants were arriving there."[2]

With some interpretation, greater detail can be teased out of the documentation. A contemporary report states that two vessels, the *Hope* and the *William Tell* landed Scots passengers at Sydney, Cape Breton, on 23 and 25 July, respectively.[3] The *Hope*, of Greenock, George Normand, master, carried 161 passengers. The *William Tell*, also of Greenock, John Boan, master, brought 221 people, giving a total number embarked from Greenock of 382 souls.[4]

According to Campey, 302 people were landed at Sydney from those two ships.[5] What of the remaining eighty people? If there had been a shipwreck or an epidemic among the passengers, some notice would survive. An article written in the 1930s says that in 1817 the *William Tell* "came to [the Gut of] Canso, N.S., with settlers from the Isle of Barra."[6] The petitioners themselves mentioned that most passengers in the ship had remained in Cape Breton.[7]

That some of the people at Pictou had originated in the Isle of Barra is supported by the petition for a land grant submitted in 1818 by Murdoch **GILLIS** from the Isle of Barra, in which he describes himself as having arrived in the province the previous year. The same story is told by Roderick **GILLIS** in a petition of 1818. Moreover, he provides a corroborating detail when his petition says that he arrived in 1817 with his wife and six children, exactly the family configuration of the man of that name who signed the petition in July 1817.[8]

It is reasonably certain, then, that the *William Tell* and the *Hope* set out with 382 Scots aboard, and that 302 of them were discharged at Sydney, Cape Breton, between 23 and 25 July 1817. As to how the remaining 80 grew to 122 by the time the *William Tell* reached Pictou, there is the business of the agent, Fraser, and the unkept promises made to the Barra folk he had brought to Cape Breton. Given the immediate dispute that arose, it is likely that some of those disembarked at Sydney, re-embarked and continued on to Pictou in hopes of a better reception.

------

[1] NSARM, RG 5, "GP", Vol. 7, No. 7, dated 31 July 1817.

[2] J. S. Martell, *Immigration to and Emigration from Nova Scotia, 1815 - 1838* (Halifax: Public Archives of Nova Scotia, 1942), p. 45.

[3] NSARM, RG 1, Vol. 329, doc. 109.

[4] D. C. Harvey, "Scottish Immigration to Cape Breton," *Dalhousie Review*, Vol. XXI (1941), pp. 315-6.

[5] Lucille H. Campey, *After the Hector; The Scottish Pioneers of Nova Scotia and Cape Breton 1773 - 1852* (Toronto: Natural Heritage Books, 2004), p. 103.

[6] Colin S. MacDonald, "Early Highland Emigration to Nova Scotia and Prince Edward Island from 1770 - 1853," *Collections of the Nova Scotia Historical Society*, Vol. 23 (1936), p. 45.

[7] See note 1.

[8] NSARM, RG 20, "A", petition of Murdoch Gillis, 1818; another of Roderick Gillis, 1818.

Thanks to the presence of Donald **FERGUSON** and his wife in the *William Tell* at Pictou, we learn that some of the additional passengers through the Gut of Canso may have been, like the Fergusons, among those "who came in the *Latonia* [sic] of Dundee . . . cast away at Cape North in Cape Breton on the 19th. Many narrowly escaped with their lives . . ."[9] At all events, the ocean journey of the passengers in the *William Tell* ended at Pictou late in July 1817.

We can see the configuration of several of these families by finding them in the census taken at Pictou in October 1817. Such families are indicated by an asterisk [*] in front of their names. The numerical sequence shown within square parentheses [ ] was: men over 50, men aged 16 to 50, boys, women, girls, total.

CAMERON, Alexander
***CAMPBELL**, John [0,1,0,0,0=1]
***CAMPBELL**, William, wife, 5 children [1,0,3,1,2=7]
***CRERAR**, Peter, wife, 2 children [0,1,1,1,1=4]
***FALCONER**, Alexander, wife, 4 children [**FALKNER**, 0,1,2,1,2=6]
FRASER, Alexander, wife
***FRASER**, Paul, wife, 1 child [1,0,1,1,0=3]
GILLES, Murdoch, daughter
GILLES, Roderick, wife, 6 children
IRVINE, John
***LINDSAY**, David, wife, 2 children [**LINSEY**, 0,1,1,1,2=5; third child born July-Oct 1817?]
McDONALD, John, wife
McINTYRE, John and Patrick
McKENZY, Kenneth
McLAREN, James
***McNAB**, John, wife, 4 children [1,1,1,1,3=7]
McNABB, Alexander
McNEAL, James, wife, 1 child
McPHERSON, Donald
McPHERSON, John [0,1,0,0,0=1]
MUNRO, Alexander
MUNRO, Hector, daughter
NASH, John, 4 children
PEAT, John, wife, 2 children [**PEET**, 0,1,0,0,0=1]
RICHARDSON, Jonathan [**RICKERSON**, 0,1,0,0,0=1]
STEWART, James, wife, 1 child
STEWART, John
STEWART, Matmilla, 7 children [Widow, 0,1,3,1,3=8]
STEWART, Niel, wife, 1 child
STEWART, Peter, wife, 1 child [0,1,0,1,2=4]
URQUHART, Donald, wife
WEIR, Adam
***FERGUSON**, Donald, wife [1,0,0,1,0=2; joined from the *Latona*]

---

[9] See page 166, note 1. The vessel was the *Latona*, Capt. Craig, which left Dundee for Québec on or about 15 April 1817 - David Dobson, *Ships from Scotland to America 1628 - 1828*, Vol. I (Baltimore: Genealogical Publishing Co., Inc., 1998), p. 72.

SCOTS MARRIED, CATHOLIC CHURCH, HALIFAX, NS, 1803 - 1842

The significance of the region as a way station on the migration route is underlined in this group of thirty-five marriages. Two died at cities on the eastern seaboard of the United States: Thomas **CASSIDY** at Boston, and Alexander **TAYLOR** at New York. Only for eleven has a local record of death or burial been noted. In nine other cases the couple had one to eight children baptised in Halifax before they vanish from local records, suggesting removal to another community outside the local area. It is probable that William **McBETH** of the 8th Regiment was posted elsewhere and could have wound up back in Scotland. Thirteen other couples were married at Halifax and then are gone, presumably migrating to the United States or "upper" Canada. All of this means that this is far from merely a parish record.

17 Sep 1803: Michael, s/o John and Anne (**MORAN**) **MARA**, Kilbarron, Co. Tipperary, Ireland/ Anne, d/o Duncan and Elizabeth **CAMERON**, Fortingall, Perthshire, Scotland.

15 Oct 1805: Neal, s/o Roderick and Catherine (**McNEAL**) **WRIGHT**, Inverness, Scotland/ Mary, d/o James and Mary (**MURPHY**) **MADDOX**, Placentia, NL.

20 May 1810: Capt. George, s/o John and Margaret (**MILLER**) **BROWN**, Huntly, Scotland/ Catherine, d/o Thomas and Catherine (**SHORTIS**) **TOBIN**, Halifax.

1 Feb 1810: James, s/o Robert and Mary (**CARDO**) **STANNERS**, Linlithgow, Scotland/ Elizabeth, d/o Thomas and Elizabeth (**CULLEN**) **LEDWICK**, Placentia, NL.

19 Feb 1810: James[1], s/o Thomas and Mary (**WALSH**) **O'NEIL**, County Kilkenny, Ireland/ Eleanor, d/o Alexander and Euphemia **STUART**, Banff, Scotland.

12 June 1810: Henry, s/o Robert and Anne **GREEN**, Peebles, Scotland/ Mary, d/o Jeremiah and Eleanor (**KEEFE**) **CONNORS**, Midleton, County Cork, Ireland.

10 Aug 1814: Capt. James, s/o Richard and Mary Anne (**DOYLE**) **KELLY**, Co. Wexford, Ireland/ Ann, d/o Ahab and Elizabeth (**MacCALLUM**) **MacFARLANE**, Glasgow, Scotland.

27 May 1818: James[2], s/o Capt. Martin and Mary Ann (**BATCHELOR**) **MEAGHER**, Jeddore, NS/ Anne, d/o Duncan and Margaret (**FRASER**) **McQUEEN**, [Ardclach], Scotland.

9 Dec 1818: John, s/o Angus and Ann **McDONALD**, Scotland/ Catherine[3], d/o Donald and Mary (**SCOTT**) **McDONALD**, Scotland.

6 May 1820: Lawrence, s/o John and Mary (**CASEY**) **GRIFFIN**, County Tipperary, Ireland/ Mary, d/o John and Jennet (**BEVERAGE**) **COOKE**, Fifeshire, Scotland.

21 Aug 1820: Robert[4], s/o Edward and Bridget (**KEHOE**) **BARRON**, Borris, Co. Carlow, Ireland/ Sarah, d/o John and Isabella (**CALDER**) **GRANT**, Scotland.

2 Nov 1820: James, s/o James and Catherine (**BURKE**) **LAWLER**, County Leix, Ireland/ Mary Anne, d/o George and Mary (**MacNAMARA**) **SCOTT**, Scotland.

---

[1] James **O'NEIL** died 23 Oct 1816, age 30, at Halifax.

[2] James **MEAGHER** died 18 Jan 1830, age 37. His widow, Anne, died 21 Dec 1878, age 84.

[3] Catherine **McDONALD** was buried, 11 Feb 1831, age 35, in the Catholic Cemetery, Halifax.

[4] Robert **BARRON** was buried at Holy Cross Cemetery, Halifax, 3 Mar 1862, age 68. Sarah, his wife, died 24 Aug 1822, having had one son.

3 May 1822: Thomas, s/o George and Linette (**ESTES**) **STEWART**, Edinburgh, Scotland/
    Clisea, d/o George and Mary (**CROTTY**) **RAY**, Halifax.
1 Nov 1825: Owen[5], s/o Laurence and Margaret (**HOWLIN**) **O'NEIL**, Tintern, Co. Wexford, Ireland/
    Mary, d/o Alexander and Jane (**MacQUINE**) **CUMMINS**, Scotland.
6 Nov 1825: John, s/o David and Christiana (**DAVISON**) **BYRNES**, Kircaldy, Scotland/
    Charlotte, d/o Nathan and Mary (**MURPHY**) **HATFIELD**, Dartmouth, NS.
7 Jan 1827: James, s/o Walter and Eleanor (**PHELAN**) **DUNN**, County Kilkenny, Ireland/
    Nancy, d/o Angus and Mary **McDONALD**, Scotland.
8 Jan 1829: Peter **GRANT**[6], Banffshire, Scotland; widower of Hannah **GAY**/
    Isabella **CROSBY**, Isle of Coll, Scotland; widow of John **SCOTT**.
2 Mar 1829: George **DOWLING**[7], City of Cork, Ireland; widower of Sophia **COLE**/
    Ellen, d/o John and Ellen (**TURNBULL**) **RICHARDSON**, Edinburgh, Scotland.
7 May 1830: James[8], s/o Duncan and Jane (**DAWSON**) **GRANT**, Scotland/
    Rebecca, d/o Philip and Anne (**HARRISON**) **RILEY**, Lunenburg, NS.
16 June 1830: John, s/o Christopher and Mary (**MARTIN**) **JONES**, County Mayo, Ireland/
    Ann, d/o William and Jane (**STEWART**) **ARCHIBALD**, Scotland; widow of James **TORRENS**.
14 Sep 1830: John **CORMACK**, Scotland, widower of Bridget **COSTLEY**/
    Mary **PIERSON**, widow of James **WALKER**, Halifax.
19 Feb 1833: Patrick, s/o Patrick and Mary (**MOLONY**) **WALSH**, Cashel, Co. Tipperary, Ireland/
    Margaret, d/o John and Rosana (**MORRISON**) **RICHARDSON**, Dumfries, Scotland.
10 Apr 1834: Samuel Charles, s/o Charles and Rosana (**BALENTINE**) **ADAMS**, Stranrowr,
    Scotland/ Mariannne, d/o John and Mary (**CUDDY**) **SPENCE**, County Wexford, Ireland.
7 May 1834: Thomas[9], s/o Thomas and Ann (**POWER**) **CASSIDY**, Halifax; widower of Martha
    ROAST/ Isabella, d/o Neil **McMULLEN**, Edinburgh, Scotland; widow of William **ROBERTS**.
8 Jan 1835: James[10], s/o James and Judith (**CARROLL**) **TOBIN**, Roscrea, Co. Tipperary, Ireland/
    Mary, d/o Alexander and Elizabeth (**CAMPBELL**) **McDOUGAL**, Argyllshire, Scotland.
10 Feb 1835: James **DOYLE**, Borris Parish, County Carlow, Ireland/
    Jane, d/o John and Eliza **FRASER**, Crow End, Inverness-shire, Scotland.
8 Nov 1835: Alexander Herbert[11], s/o Robert and Eliza (**BREBNER**) **TAYLOR**, Aberdeen, Scotland/
    Catherine Johanna, d/o Timothy and Margaret (**LONDRIGAN**) **HEFFERNAN**, Halifax.

---

[5] Owen **O'NEIL**, labourer, was buried at Holy Cross Cemetery, Halifax, 5 Feb 1866, age 76.

[6] Peter **GRANT** died 8 Dec 1870, age 82, at Halifax. Isabella, his wife, died 29 Nov 1843, age 47.

[7] George **DOWLING**, mariner, died 17 Dec 1866, age 78, at Halifax. Ellen, his wife, died 26 Aug 1844, age 37. They had five children.

[8] James **GRANT**, carpenter, age 60, was buried at Holy Cross Cemetery, Halifax,18 Dec 1853.

[9] Thomas **CASSIDY** died 4 May 1840 at Boston, age 32.

[10] James **TOBIN**, county jailer, died 22 May 1850, age 50. Mary, his wife, was buried 7 Nov 1845, age 50, at Holy Cross Cemetery, Halifax. Their only child died in infancy.

[11] Alexander H. **TAYLOR** died 24 Oct 1852, age 30. He and his wife had two children born in Halifax by 1842, after which they removed to New York City.

27 Nov 1835: Lawrence[12], s/o James and Mary (**WHELAN**) **HICKEY**, County Kilkenny, Ireland/ Jennett, d/o James and Isabelle (**CRUICKSHANK**) **LAWSON**, Aberdeen, Scotland.

3 June 1836: Thomas, s/o Robert and Ellen (**KILPATRICK**) **CRO[C]KET**, Dumfries, Scotland/ Ellen, d/o James and Joanna (**EVOY**) **SAUNDERS**, Halifax.

17 Jan 1838: Charles[13], s/o Malcolm and Janet (**McDONALD**) **LAMONT**, Aberdeenshire, Scotland/ Mary, d/o Peter and Margaret (**TAILOR**) **GRANT**, Halifax.

17 Nov 1838: Angus, s/o John and Christiana **CAMPBELL**, Inverness-shire, Scotland/ Margaret, d/o Peter and Margaret (**TAILOR**) **GRANT**, Halifax.

10 May 1839: Thomas **DYMOKE**, County Kerry, Ireland, formerly in the 81st Regt./ Christiana **McDONALD**, Scotland, widow of John **KILEY**.

31 July 1841: William (8th Regt.), s/o Charles and Mary (**CAMERON**) **McBETH**, Stirlingshire, Scotland/ Mary Jean, d/o Joseph and Ann (**LYNOX**) **JULIO**, Halifax.

3 Oct 1841: Thomas, s/o John and Catherine (**SINCLAIR**) **MORRIS**, Campbeltown West, Scotland/ Mary, d/o Thomas and Mary (**FOISEY?**) **KEEFFE**, County Waterford, Ireland.

1 June 1842: William, s/o James and Ann (**FOLLES**) **JAMIESON**, Lochinnock [Ayrshire], Scotland/ Marian, d/o late Samuel and Ellen (**SULLIVAN**) **LAWRENCE**, Halifax.

(35 marriages)

PRINCE EDWARD ISLAND DEATHS

DUNCAN, Andrew, 69, farmer, native of Perthhead, Fifeshire, Scotland, died 10 Apr 1830, buried 12 Apr 1830 (Charlotte Parish, Prince Edward Island, Burial Register).

From the *Polly* Cemetery, Belfast, PE, so-called because it was the burial place of many Scots who crossed to Prince Edward Island in the *Polly* out of Greenock via the Isle of Skye, and landed at Orwell Bay, PE, on 7 August 1803. Three gravestones of natives of the Isle of Skye:

NICHOLSON, Alexander, died 26 Sep 1820, age 40, native of the Isle of Skye.

NICHOLSON, Charles, died 20 May 1864, age 68. His wife Mary who died 23 May 1880, age 80.

NICHOLSON, Donald, died in April 1883, age 96, native of the Isle of Skye.

Wood Islands Pioneer Cemetery has the stones of several natives of the Isle of Colonsay, Argyllshire:

BELL, Archibald, died 12 Aug 1835, age 61.
McMILLAN, James, d. 11 Feb 1861, age 78; his wife Ann **MUNN**, died 10 Mar 1870, age 82; they emigrated to Prince Edward Island in 1806.
McNIEL, Grace, died 3 Jan 1833, age 71, wife of Malcolm **McMILLAN**.
MUNN, Angus, died 27 July 1837, age 63.
MUNN, John, died 1833 at Pictou, NS, age 31; emigrated to Prince Edward Island in 1812.
SMITH, Donald, died 19 Mar 1875, age 78; emigrated to Prince Edward Island in 1820.

---

[12] Lawrence **HICKEY**, coachman, died 15 June 1856, age 44. Jennett, his widow, died 12 Feb 1898, age 80. They had seven children born before 1850.

[13] Charles **LAMONT** died at Dartmouth, NS, 12 Oct 1875, age 78. Mary, his widow, died in 1903.

INDEX OF SHIPS

INDEX OF SURNAMES

The Thistle, Badge of a Proud People